Antisemitism on the Rise

Contemporary Holocaust Studies

SERIES EDITORS

Ari Kohen
Gerald J. Steinacher

Antisemitism on the Rise
The 1930s and Today

EDITED BY ARI KOHEN AND GERALD J. STEINACHER

University of Nebraska Press
LINCOLN

© 2021 by the Board of Regents of the University of Nebraska

All rights reserved

Publication of this important and timely volume was assisted by a donation from Bruce F. Pauley, professor emeritus of history at the University of Central Florida, and his wife, Marianne Pauley.

Library of Congress Cataloging-in-Publication Data
Names: Kohen, Ari, 1977–, editor. | Steinacher, Gerald, editor.
Title: Antisemitism on the rise: the 1930s and today / edited by Ari Kohen and Gerald J. Steinacher.
Description: Lincoln: University of Nebraska Press, [2021] | Series: Contemporary Holocaust studies | Includes bibliographical references and index.
Identifiers: LCCN 2020057443
ISBN 9781496226044 (paperback)
ISBN 9781496228468 (epub)
ISBN 9781496228475 (pdf)
Subjects: LCSH: Antisemitism—History—20th century. | Antisemitism—History—21st century. | Antisemitism—Study and teaching.
Classification: LCC DS145.A6335 2021 | DDC 305.892/4—dc23
LC record available at https://lccn.loc.gov/2020057443

Set in Minion Pro by Mikala R. Kolander.

Contents

List of Illustrations vii
Introduction 1
ARI KOHEN AND GERALD J. STEINACHER

Part 1. History of Antisemitism

1. Underestimating German Antisemitism: The Case of Carl Schmitt, the Frankfurt School, and Weimar Jewish Elites 23
   JOSEPH W. BENDERSKY

2. Antisemitism and Totalitarian Movements: Thinking Again about Hannah Arendt 46
   JEAN CAHAN

3. Nazi Antisemitism as Ideology and Genocidal Practice: The Case of Alfred Rosenberg 75
   JÜRGEN MATTHÄUS

4. "Semites" on Display: David Gordon Lyon and the Jewish Other at Harvard University, 1889–1926 99
   TIMOTHY TURNQUIST

5. Use and Abuse of the Bible: German Christian Antisemitism in the 1930s and 1940s 124
   LEONARD GREENSPOON

6. The Forgotten Jewish Atlantis: Poznań and the Legacy of Antisemitism 151
   ŁUKASZ W. NIPARKO

Part 2. Contemporary Antisemitism

7. Antisemitism and Its Transnational Inhibitions:
   1930s Europe and Now — 183
   R. AMY ELMAN

8. BDS, Antisemitism, and Israeli Identity — 206
   SHLOMO ABRAMOVICH

9. The Role of Antisemitism in Holocaust Education in
   the Jewish and Secular School Classroom — 225
   SCOTT B. LITTKY

   Contributors — 243
   Index — 247

Illustrations

1. Close-up photo of Alfred Rosenberg,
   Paris, November 1940 — 79
2. Alfred Rosenberg and Adolf Hitler confer at military
   headquarters, November 1941 — 82
3. The Semitic Museum of Harvard ("Bible Museum") — 106
4. Artistic performance and installation "Atlantis" in Poznań — 153
5. Artistic performance and installation "Atlantis" in Poznań — 154
6. The antisemitic fresco in the Church of the Most Precious
   Blood of Jesus — 156
7. The New Synagogue in Poznań on September 5, 1907,
   and today — 169

Antisemitism on the Rise

Introduction

ARI KOHEN AND GERALD J. STEINACHER

People all across the United States went to sleep on the night of August 11, 2017, with the sense that something about their country had been fundamentally altered. Earlier in the evening a conglomeration of far-right white supremacists groups, alongside members of the so-called alt-right, marched through the campus of the University of Virginia in Charlottesville carrying torches and chanting neo-Nazi slogans. It was a watershed moment, even for a country whose most politically conscious citizens felt radically divided from one another by the 2016 election of Donald Trump to the presidency on a campaign characterized by racist and antisemitic dog whistles. This feeling, of living in a divided and much-changed America, existed even before the murder of Heather Heyer by a white supremacist who drove his car into a crowd of counterprotesters the next day. Indeed, in announcing his campaign for the 2020 Democratic presidential nomination, former vice president Joe Biden released a video in which he referred to the 2017 Unite the Right rally in Charlottesville as "a defining moment" for the nation.[1]

The torchlit march was the unannounced opening of this rally, scheduled for August 12, whose organizers intended, broadly, to unify the white nationalist movement and, specifically, to protest the planned removal of the statute of Confederate general Robert E. Lee from Charlottesville's Lee Park (now Emancipation Park).[2] The Unite the Right rally was the culmination of a series of white nationalist events in Charlottesville, organized by white nationalist Richard Spencer (May 13, 2017) and the Ku Klux Klan (July 8, 2017), that focused on the planned removal of the Lee statue and, in the words of former KKK grand wizard David Duke, on the promise of a Trump presidency to "take our country back."[3] But while the earlier events drew dozens of white supremacists, the August rally was intended to bring together many hundreds of members of disparate groups from across the country—including the Klan; the National Policy Institute; Identity Evropa; neo-Nazi groups such as Vanguard America, Traditionalist Workers Party, and the National Socialist Movement; neo-Confederate groups such as Identity Dixie and League of the South; and others—that all held a common belief in white supremacy.

Given the makeup of the rally's participants, it is interesting to look back from the distance of a few years and to wonder why anyone was surprised by what took place. What made the August 11 march such a watershed moment? Everyone knew that the people who descended on Charlottesville weren't history buffs who cared deeply about Confederate monuments as symbols of American history. They were members of fringe groups who focused on white identity and who trafficked in fantasies about a restoration of the primacy of white Christians in America. Racial resentment and white grievance were expected from the speakers at the August 12 rally. What was unexpected, on the evening of August 11, was the unmistakable feeling of looking through a window into 1930s Weimar Germany, where everyday citizens, not simply the well-known racists, were comfortable marching through the streets chanting about their hatred of minority groups. Here, on the campus designed by Thomas Jefferson, were young men, well-dressed in khaki pants and white button-down shirts, marching and chanting messages of hatred. The mask had fallen off and the bigotry that had been covered by what suddenly looked like the thinnest veneer of respectability was on display for anyone who cared to look. The violence that followed immediately seemed predictable and obvious.

The expectations, prior to that torchlit march, were that the participants who traveled to Charlottesville were racists, and that their support for Confederate monuments was linked to their white identitarian beliefs. As such, their chanting of "White lives matter!" as they marched made sense to the people who watched on social media in real time as the march unfolded. But then the marchers began to chant the Nazi slogans "Blood and Soil!" and "Jews will not replace us!" The connection between racism and antisemitism was so surprising and seemingly bizarre that, in the initial media rundowns of the march, reporters published accounts in which they reported that the marchers chanted "You will not replace us!"[4] Of course, as the Anti-Defamation League points out, this amounts to a distinction without a difference, as the slogan—whether it specifically mentions "Jews" or simply references replacement theory—"reflects the primary white supremacist worldview that unless immediate action is taken, the white race is doomed to extinction by an alleged 'rising tide of color' purportedly controlled and manipulated by Jews."[5]

Replacement theory, the conspiracy that provides structural support for a good deal of the white supremacist activism we see today, can be traced back to antisemitic conspiracy theorizing in France in the late 1800s that imagined a Jewish plot to bring about the downfall of white, Christian Europe through miscegenation. The best-known version is Édouard Drumont's 1886 *La France Juive*, an immensely popular two-volume work that presaged not only Nazi antisemitic literature but also the contemporary work of Renaud Camus, *Le Grand Remplacement*, in which today's Muslim immigrants stand in for the Jews of Drumont's France. It was the same concept that motivated Robert Bowers to bring multiple weapons into the Tree of Life—Or L'Simcha Congregation in Pittsburgh, Pennsylvania, on October 27, 2018 and murder eleven Jewish worshippers, the deadliest attack on Jews in American history. In the weeks before the mass shooting, Bowers, a white supremacist who had been active on the fringe social media website *Gab*, "complained that President Donald Trump was surrounded by too many Jewish people and blamed Jews for helping migrant caravans in Central America."[6] In a post that linked to a Hebrew Immigrant Aid Society program called National Refugee Shabbat, he wrote, "Why hello there HIAS! You like to bring in hostile invaders to dwell among us?" Another post read, "Open you Eyes! It's the filthy EVIL Jews Bringing the Filthy EVIL Muslims into the Country!!" Just a couple of hours before his murderous shooting spree, Bowers posted, "HIAS likes to bring invaders in that kill our people. I can't sit by and watch my people get slaughtered. Screw your optics, I'm going in."⁷

But perhaps the most alarming aspect is not simply that white supremacist terrorism is on the rise; it's that replacement theory has been mainstreamed over the past few years so that people like Bowers hear their own beliefs spoken by those who reside at the pinnacle of power and influence. After another mass shooting committed by a white supremacist in El Paso, Texas, in 2019, the *New York Times* published an interactive analysis of the similarities in language used in the murderer's manifesto and by the biggest stars in mainstream conservative media, including Sean Hannity, Tucker Carlson, Laura Ingraham, and Rush Limbaugh. In particular, the *Times* outlined the way that words such as "invasion" and "replacement" appear over and over in the murderer's manifesto and in popular television news programming. The authors also point out that "the portrayal of immigration as a menace has returned with force, a shift brought on not just by radio and TV hosts, but by Republican leaders in Congress and the president himself. This year Mr. Trump has used the terms 'invasion' or 'invaded' seven times on Twitter to describe the situation at the border, at one point referring to the approach of the migrants as 'the attempted Invasion of Illegals.'"⁸ And, indeed, the claims about HIAS and a migrant caravan of asylum-seekers from Central America made by the Pittsburgh synagogue murderer are directly connected to mainstream right-wing rhetoric. Most notably, in the weeks prior to the shooting, President Trump suggested that "criminals and unknown Middle Easterners are mixed in" with the group of asylum seekers, and, just days afterward, Trump further spread the baseless conspiracy theory that Jewish billionaire and philanthropist George Soros might be funding the migrant caravan.⁹ That theory was not a new one and it directly informed the actions of Cesar Sayoc, who mailed pipe bombs to Soros and prominent critics of Trump just weeks before Bowers murdered the worshippers in Pittsburgh. The Soros theory was active online in the spring and summer of 2018 but caught fire in early October in the run-up to the midterm election. It began on October 14 with a single antisemitic Twitter user with several thousand followers, but in just a few days the conspiracy had migrated to Facebook and Reddit and had reached millions of people. On October 17, a Republican congressman—Matt Gaetz of Florida—posted about the Soros conspiracy on Twitter and his post was amplified by Ann Coulter and then by Donald Trump Jr. "On Twitter alone, at least 43,000 accounts with a combined 127 million followers carried some message linking Soros to the caravan" on October 16 and 17.[10] The Soros conspiracy theory almost perfectly echoes the old canard about the Rothschild family operating at the head of an international Jewish conspiracy. Indeed, in July 2019, the White House invited conservative and right-wing journalists for a social media summit. Among them was the creator of an unabashedly antisemitic cartoon depicting Soros as an instrument of the Rothschilds pulling the strings of "puppets" in the forms of then–national security adviser and retired general H. R. McMaster and former CIA director and retired general David Petraeus.[11] The image of the Jewish puppet master pulling the strings is an old and well-known antisemitic cliché, but the straightforward connection of Soros to the Rothschilds, the presumed Jewish conspirators of centuries past, leaves no doubt about the intent of the image.

Nor, unfortunately, was the mass shooting in Pittsburgh an isolated incident. Six months later, in April 2019, another man armed with an assault-style rifle murdered one worshipper and wounded three others at the Chabad Lubavitch Synagogue in Poway, California. The attacker, an avowed white supremacist, wrote in an open letter that he was fighting back against the Jews because they were plotting a genocide of the white European race. In these dangerous antisemitic fantasies Jews are always conspiring to harm gentiles and bring evil to the world; thus, any action to draw attention to their nefarious plots and put a stop them is justified. This sort of belief stands at the heart of antisemitism throughout the centuries and across the globe. While antisemitism is not easy to define and often seems to have, for many, a certain "I know it when I see it" quality, the Anti-Defamation League summarizes it as "belief or behavior hostile toward Jews just because they are Jewish. It may take the form of religious teachings that proclaim the inferior-ity of Jews, for instance, or political efforts to isolate, oppress, or otherwise injure them. It may also include prejudiced or stereotyped views about Jews."[12] In studying incidents of antisemitism we can learn very little, if anything, about Jews, but we learn a lot about the hate fantasies and negative stereotypes that gentiles have about Jews. Antisemitism operates by using fictional allegations, often centered around complicated conspiracy theories, which is why fighting it with factual arguments is so often difficult. Doris Bergen notes that "prejudices are habits of thought; they are not reasoned responses to objective realities."[13] While we do not have sufficient space here to detail the full historical scope of these prejudices, what follows is some basic historical information that will offer background and context for the chapters in this volume.

In 70 CE the Romans destroyed the Temple in Jerusalem, which had been the religious and political center of Judaism for centuries. This meant the end of the Jewish uprising and the dispersion of the survivors all over the Roman Empire. This was the beginning of the Diaspora, or Jews living as a religious minority without a state of their own. Around that time a small sect among Jews formed its first communities. They believed in Jesus of Nazareth as the long-expected prophetic Messiah. These Judeo-Christians were initially a small group, but quickly grew in numbers because they were also committed to proselytizing among the gentiles.

In 380 CE Christianity became the state religion of the Roman Empire. While non-Christians were persecuted and killed, the Jews remained the only religious minority tolerated (if only barely) in the Christian world. St. Augustine, an influential theologian of the early church, laid the basis for a widely adopted practice. He argued that Jews should be despised and kept in misery, but not killed. They should not be killed, he reasoned, because there is hope for their ultimate conversion when they accept Jesus as the Messiah. Jews were segregated in ghettos within or adjacent to Christian cities and towns, and were banned from many professions and from owning land. The Middle Ages saw the creation of allegations against Jews, some of which are still present in our societies. Church leaders accused the Jews of being in the service of Satan and conspiring against Christians. Because Jews were barred from most professions in Christian societies, where an emerging merchant class was in need of a ready supply of capital to borrow, and because Christians were religiously prohibited from lending money to other Christians at interest, moneylending was one of the few professions open to Jews. This is why many Jewish families, including the Rothschilds and the Lehmans, would become prominent in the banking and financial sectors; not surprisingly, this occupation also made them many enemies.[14] Jews were often despised as "bloodsuckers" by gentiles who owed them money and were accused of slyly taking advantage of the naivety or the bad luck of honest Christians. Shakespeare's depiction of Shylock, the Jewish moneylender in *The Merchant of Venice*, is the most famous example of these views. Jews, a minority that constituted less than one percent of the total population of Western Europe, became the scapegoats for all societal and even personal ills—anything that could not be easily explained and was therefore particularly frightening. Jews were accused of causing the plague, poisoning wells, and kidnapping Christian children (especially boys) to slaughter them in religious rituals and bake with or drink their blood. Massacres known as pogroms often followed these unfounded and horrible allegations against the nearest Jewish population.[15]

As the Enlightenment came to dominate European thought in the eighteenth century, Jews were eventually afforded citizenship rights and allowed to leave their ghettos (sooner in some regions and much later in some countries including Russia and Romania, which resisted the enfranchisement of Jews into the twentieth century). Even with this progress, however, religious antisemitism not only remained but was joined by a secular version of antisemitism. Under pseudoscientific theories of race, Jews now were seen not merely as adherents of a different religion, but as people of a separate race. As a consequence, conversion or assimilation was not an option to solve "the Jewish question." The term "antisemitism" was eventually coined in 1870 by the German journalist Wilhelm Marr (1819–1904) as a "scientific" term for the secular hatred of Jews. To this day, antisemitism contains a potent mix of religious, racist, and political charges and beliefs.[16] Antisemitism traveled to the Americas with European emigration, bringing many of the centuries-old stereotypes and accusations, such as the "blood libel," common in the old world. One famous case is that of Leo Frank, who was lynched in 1915 in Georgia for allegedly murdering Mary Phagan, a thirteen-year-old Christian girl. Frank was kidnapped from prison and murdered by a group of armed men who were infuriated by the governor's decision to commute Frank's death sentence to life imprisonment. The consensus of researchers today is that Frank was wrongfully convicted.

Of particular impact are conspiracy theories claiming that Jewry is plotting to take over the world and dominate Christians. One of the most widely distributed lies centers around the *Protocols of the Elders of Zion*, an antisemitic forgery put together by the Russian secret police and first printed in 1905. It purports to recount the minutes of a series of meetings of anonymous Jewish leaders and is set around the first Zionist Congress in Basel, Switzerland, in 1897. These Jewish leaders were allegedly plotting to bring Christians under their rule worldwide by undermining Christian societies with the ideas of socialism and liberalism. The forgers did not invest much time in constructing the *Protocols*, as they mostly plagiarized from a number of French and German books, and just switched the main characters. Despite being repeatedly exposed as a complete fabrication, the document was quickly translated into all major world languages and became a classic of antisemitic propaganda. In the United States, it was none other than automobile pioneer Henry Ford who published the "Protocols" as a serial in his newspaper, the *Dearborn Independent*, starting in 1920. Under the title "The International Jew: The World's Problem," the columns accused Jews of controlling the media and the financial system in order to enslave Americans.[17] Hitler admired Ford and the Nazi government awarded him the Grand Cross of the German Eagle, the highest honor for a non-German. Throughout the interwar period, Ford, an American hero and titan of industry, was one of the most significant forces for antisemitism in the United States.

Theodor Herzl of Vienna, one of the fathers of modern political Zionism, hoped that a Jewish state might end antisemitism. Sadly, he was wrong. The foundation of the state of Israel in 1948 merely changed certain aspects of antisemitism. In recent years, critiques of Israel with more or less antisemitic undertones have occurred frequently on both the political (far) right and the political (far) left. This "Toxifying Israel" is a phenomenon that has become more recognizable and more pronounced over time.[18] At the heart of these issues is the conflict in the Near East. Recounted briefly, the idea of Jewish statehood never completely vanished during the Diaspora. Herzl saw the foundation of a (new) Jewish state as an answer to European nationalism when he wrote his influential book *Der Judenstaat* in 1896. Political Zionism eventually led to renewed Jewish immigration to Jerusalem and Palestine, which was first controlled by the Ottoman Empire and then, after 1917, by Britain. After World War II and the Holocaust, Jewish organizations strengthened their efforts to transform the Jewish settlements in Palestine ("Yishuv") into an independent state by diplomatic means, but also by guerilla fighting against the British army and Arab nationalists. In 1947 the United Nations decided on a partition plan for a Jewish state and an Arab state in Palestine, and in 1948 Israel formally declared its statehood. The small nation was immediately attacked by its Arab neighbors but prevailed. The internationally guaranteed 1949 armistice line established the division between Israeli territory (including West Jerusalem) and the West Bank of the Jordan River and the Gaza Strip. These borders remained unchanged until 1967, when Israel defeated a military coalition of Egypt, Jordan, and Syria. As a result, Israeli forces permanently occupied East Jerusalem, the West Bank, Gaza, and the Golan Heights. The status of these territories remains disputed and the status of the mostly Palestinian Arab population of the West Bank and Gaza remains uncertain even after the landmark but unfinished Oslo Peace Process of the 1990s.

Since the days of the grassroots Palestinian uprising in the late 1980s, known as the Intifadah, European and American leftists have often sympathized with the Palestinians and supported their struggle for liberation. In recent years, the best-known and most effective leftist group aligned in opposition to Israel is the Boycott, Divestment, and Sanctions movement (BDS), which criticizes Israel for its treatment of Palestinians and its government-endorsed program of settlement expansion in the West Bank. Of course, not every critique of Israel is automatically antisemitic. Every government can and should be criticized if democratic standards are transgressed or if human rights violations occur. But many of Israel's supporters contend that the critiques and the demands made by BDS seem to go far beyond ordinary political opposition by tacitly or explicitly questioning the legitimacy of Israel's very existence. World-renowned scholar Deborah Lipstadt argues that "one of the stated goals of the BDS movement is establishing a right of return for Palestinians throughout the world, which in practical terms would result in Jews being in the minority in Israel, and its end as a Jewish state."[19] On some university campuses, left-wing groups have been very active and have fostered hostile environments for some, just as right-wing groups have done for others. Verbal assault and interruptions of Israeli or pro-Israeli speakers on campuses are very common, which (among other things) shows the lack of civil discourse on campus and the increase of divisiveness.[20] Groups such as Students for Justice in Palestine have caused major controversies on campuses including those of the University of Michigan, New York University, the University of California—Los Angeles, San Francisco State University, the University of Vermont, and others.[21]

Antisemitism in Islamic countries is very common, and at times openly encouraged and sponsored by the political leadership. Scholar Alvin Rosenfeld summarized this very well when he wrote: "As disturbing as these developments are, they are surpassed by a far more militant rhetoric of antisemitic denunciation, vilification, and incitement emanating from many Muslim-majority countries. . . . Aggressive anti-Jewish sentiments are pervasive today in the Arab world, Iran, and Turkey. They are also to be found within Europe's growing Muslim communities."[22]

In her 2019 book about antisemitism, Lipstadt writes, "As horrific as the Holocaust was, it is firmly in the past. When I write about it, I am writing about what was. Though I remain horrified by what happened, it is history. Contemporary antisemitism is not. It is about the present. It is what many people are doing, saying and facing *now*. That gave this subject an immediacy that no historical act possesses."[23] Given the events of 2018–2019, Lipstadt's concerns seem both prescient and extremely pressing. Still, many, especially in the United States, were taken completely by surprise not only by the rise of antisemitism but also by its deadly character. Prominent opinion columnist Bari Weiss wrote, "I had always thought it wasn't possible for this kind of cancer to metastasize in the United States, for three fundamental reasons. One is the special nature of America. The United States, with its promise of free speech and religion, with its insistence that all people are created equal, with its tolerance for difference, with its emphasis on shared ideas rather than shared bloodline, has been, even with all of its ugly flaws, a New Jerusalem for the Jewish people."[24] Weiss, of course, was wrong to think of America as somehow special or exempt from the moral rot of antisemitism, but she represents the majority of American Jews, among Americans more generally, who have found themselves stunned and uncertain of how to respond to the rising tide of antisemitism.[25]

The immediacy of this problem is what motivated us to choose antisemitism as the topic of the 2019 Sommerhauser Symposium on Holocaust Education, a biennial workshop that began in 2015 under the auspices of the Harris Center for Judaic Studies at the University of Nebraska—Lincoln. According to the Anti-Defamation League the number of antisemitic incidents surged by sixty percent in 2017.[26] This was the biggest single-year increase in reported anti-Jewish hate since the ADL started tracking such data almost forty years ago. Our own campus has also seen its fair share of antisemitic incidents. These have included antisemitic internet activities, graffiti, and statements by individual students who self-identify as white nationalists or white supremacists. Jewish students, a microscopic minority, have written letters to the editor of the university's student newspaper to express that they don't feel safe on their campus anymore. It is this environment that creates the sense of immediacy that Deborah Lipstadt speaks about. And it is this environment that calls for the Sommerhauser Symposium. The conference proceedings published here can help us try to make sense of the rapid rise in antisemitism in the United States and abroad. By looking into the past, into the 1920s and 1930s, we might, despite all the differences between then and now, see some common elements and some parallels. The 1920s and 1930s also saw a rapid spread of nativism, xenophobia, nationalism, and antisemitism. Why did it happen then and why is it happening now? The rise of antisemitism today is by no means limited to the United States; after all, antisemitism was and is an international cancer. What can we learn when comparing American antisemitism to antisemitism in Europe? How can we better understand the underlying ideas and ideologies that seem to transcend time and place? How can we best fight them? And, once we have some answers, how do we best communicate them to those outside of academia?

This last question—how best to communicate what we have learned through all our research to those outside of academia—is the question that makes the Sommerhauser Symposium different from other initiatives. How can we best educate about and fight this old hatred and the conspiracies that demonize Jews? What are the best teaching resources and teaching methods that individuals and institutions can deploy? And, perhaps most importantly, symposia like this one will sensitize universities and the wider public to the need for and utility of such a dialogue.

We started the Contemporary Holocaust Studies series, published with the University of Nebraska Press, in 2017. The first volume, which focuses on the phenomenon of Holocaust rescue and those who effected it, is titled *Unlikely Heroes: The Place of Holocaust Rescuers in Research and Teaching* and came out in May 2019. This book follows the format of the series and is centered around a two-part conversation about antisemitism. The first section looks into the 1920s and 1930s in Europe and the United States and the rise of antisemitism after World War I. The second section analyzes several contemporary forms of antisemitism across Europe and the Near East. We conclude with a look into methods and strategies to best educate students and the wider public about this crucial topic. As we wrote in the introduction to our first volume, our aim in this series is to bring together the work of university professors, high school educators, and local and national experts. High school teachers and those who train them tend to focus on pedagogy, while academics are always looking to engage with new research. This explains why the contributions in the various sections of this volume are written in different styles and structures; these differences exist by design and, in our minds, represent a strength of the project undertaken in this book series. The questions at the end of each chapter are also closely tied to the nature of this project. They help to foster discussion and the exchange of knowledge and opinions.

The aim of this collection is not to provide an all-encompassing work about antisemitism. The topic, as every expert can attest, is far too large to cover in a single volume, and doing so is not our goal. We have collected here some important examples on the topic of antisemitism to illustrate new research findings and teaching techniques in order to show the issues at stake. We begin with some new research on antisemitism at two distinct historical moments: the interwar period and today. First, Joseph W. Bendersky considers the failure of the Weimar Republic's Jewish intellectual elites to understand the nature of German antisemitism in the 1920s and 1930s. He focuses on Franz Neumann and Otto Kirchheimer, both prominent members of the well-known Frankfurt School, who were based originally in the Institute for Social Research at the University of Frankfurt and then exiled to the United States after the Nazi takeover. As Bendersky points out, the Frankfurt School has long been criticized for its late and inaccurate analyses of antisemitism. Looking through the lens of Marxism, for these German Jewish scholars, racism and antisemitism were merely a sideshow for the essential class struggle. Ultimately, their academic expertise did not help Kirchheimer and Neumann to better grasp the extent of German antisemitism. Quite the contrary—they stuck to an idealistic and one-sided view of German mentality and culture, and downplayed the potential for violent antisemitism. As Bendersky states, "many assimilated Jewish liberals and leftists shared Neumann's and Kirchheimer's comforting and reassuring view of their fellow Germans, attesting that their country was the 'least antisemitic of all.'"

In the next chapter, Jean Cahan analyses the views of the influential German American political philosopher Hannah Arendt on the origins of antisemitism and totalitarianism. While Arendt's concept of totalitarianism as a political religion was innovative and powerful, her interpretation of the origins of antisemitism remains controversial. Cahan contends that Arendt focused a great deal of her attention on individual biographies and socioeconomic factors influencing anti-Jewish hatred since the eighteenth century, while largely ignoring its centuries-old Christian and Islamic roots. Arendt believed that modern antisemitism arose from the Christian lower class's disdain for powerful Jewish bankers; she pointed to the Austrian case, noting that Jewish bankers—namely the Rothschilds—were in control of the Austrian railroads, and therefore antisemitic Austrian politicians pushed for nationalization. The empirical facts about the Austro-Hungarian railway market, however, do not support such claims. Cahan thus argues that Arendt falls too easily into the trap of generalizations, without much (or any) empirical evidence backing her claims. The Austrian politician Georg von Schönerer, who was part of a new generation of politicians running on platforms of fanatical ethnic nationalism and antisemitism, occupies a prominent place in Arendt's analyses. According to Arendt, the alleged arrogance of Jews as the chosen people drew the ire of pan-German ethnic nationalists such as Schönerer (who was himself obsessed with the Rothschilds). Not all Jews were bankers, of course, and not all bankers were Jewish, and Cahan argues that at times Arendt appears to have internalized some of the antisemitic interpretations of modern European history. Such interpretations show that even a critical spirit like Arendt's was not entirely immune to antisemitic stereotypes.

Alfred Rosenberg was one of the very few top Nazi leaders who put his personal thoughts on paper. A few years ago his diaries were rediscovered and published. Jürgen Matthäus provides some crucial insight into Rosenberg's unique blend of obsession and opportunism regarding the Nazis' "Jewish question." From a young age, Rosenberg held deeply antisemitic views, which he expressed in far-right-wing publications; those writings influenced Hitler's views on Jews and Soviet communism, particularly during the early years of the Nazi Party. His 1930 book, *The Myth of the Twentieth Century*, quickly became a kind of bible for Nazi believers, second only to Hitler's 1925 *Mein Kampf*. With the invasion of the Soviet Union, the Nazis committed to a full-scale genocide of European Jewry, and Rosenberg, originally from Estonia, was put in charge of the occupied territories of the East, where most European Jews lived. His "Ostland" was expected to be the territory of the "biological eradication of all of Jewry in Europe," as he openly stated.[27] For his crimes, Rosenberg was executed at Nuremberg in 1946, but his hateful teachings did not disappear with him—on the contrary, his writings have achieved a kind of renaissance on the websites of today's extreme right.

In his chapter, "'Semites' on Display: David Gordon Lyon and the Jewish Other at Harvard University, 1889–1926," Timothy Turnquist looks at the rising antisemitism in American academia after World War I. David Gordon Lyon was an American Assyriologist at Harvard (1882–1922) who studied ancient Semitic civilizations in the Middle East. Funded generously by Jacob Schiff, a German Jewish immigrant, Lyon emphasized the civilizing contributions of the Jews, a "Semitic" minority, in mainstream narratives of Western and American greatness. Turnquist's chapter explores Lyon's career as a window into shifting perceptions of Jews at Harvard. Culture wars between liberals and conservatives framed the Jewish *Other* as racially and mentally un-American. Liberals constructed the Jews as foundational to American educational and political institutions and suggested they ought to easily assimilate into the country's social fabric. Conservatives feared an oversaturation of non–Northern European immigrants, and pushed for the adoption of restrictive quotas in immigration and higher education to maintain white Protestant power. In an era of racial and political tension, Lyon's tenure demonstrated an ideologically complex quest for Jewish recognition and American self-definition.

Leonard Greenspoon examines antisemitism in the German Christian context in his chapter, "Use and Abuse of the Bible: German Christian Antisemitism in the 1930s and 1940s." In particular, Greenspoon looks carefully at the ways in which the Bible was used (or, more accurately, abused) to support anti-Judaism. He assesses the ways in which Christians misread or misapplied passages from the Hebrew Bible for their antisemitic ends, and also explores passages from the Christian Bible that specifically criticize and even demonize "the Jews." While Greenspoon's focus here is on the Nazi period, he also compares the abuses of the Bible at that time with two other instances in the nineteenth and twentieth centuries. He also rightly recognizes the small minority of Christians whose encounters with the Bible led them to live, and sometimes die, in opposition to the Nazis.

Finally, to round out the first section, Łukasz W. Niparko assesses almost one thousand years of the history of Poznań Jews. The city of Poznań is the capital of the second largest region in Poland and, in the sixteenth century, was home to the largest Jewish community in the Polish-Lithuanian Commonwealth. It is to Poznań we can trace the beginnings of Polish statehood as well as the relics of one of the oldest Jewish communities inhabiting Poland. The often uneasy coexistence of different ethnic groups and religions ceased altogether due to totalitarian regimes. What is left today is the hidden landscape of Jewish history and culture exemplified by the Poznań synagogue, turned into a swimming pool by the Nazis—a symbol reminiscent of Atlantis, the city that disappeared under the water. In the case of Poznań, what disappeared is the culturally diverse urban space that was sundered by antisemitism, genocide, war, and modern-day nationalism.

In the volume's second section we turn to research on contemporary antisemitism and also how to teach it. The first chapter in this section, from R. Amy Elman, considers the response, or lack thereof, from European Union politicians to the rise of antisemitism. Elman looks specifically at anti-Zionism and Holocaust inversion, along with antisemitism among European Islamic extremists. She details the problems facing European Jewry today, comparing it with the past, and also considers possible avenues for remedy through the human rights infrastructure of the European Union. Elman raises the problem of antisemitism in the guise of social justice, a topic that eludes many of the people who fill out the ranks of the anti-racist, pro–human rights left. Then, Shlomo Abramovich expands on this notion of anti-Zionism as antisemitism, and looks specifically at the ways in which the prominent Boycott, Divestment, and Sanctions movement plays out in discussions about Israeli politics and identity. Abramovich's intent is explicitly not to answer the question of whether or not BDS should be understood as fundamentally antisemitic—there is a growing body of literature on this topic and a great deal of political disagreement—but instead to consider what exactly is gained by Israel when BDS is framed as antisemitic. To do so, Abramovich highlights the changing nature of antisemitism and, specifically, how anti-Zionism has come to be seen as antisemitic because of the redefinition of the concept in light of the politics, in Israel and in the West, surrounding the Israeli-Palestinian conflict.

Finally we explore the challenges of effectively teaching young people about antisemitism. To that end, we turn to colleagues with a great deal of experience in explaining the Holocaust, antisemitism, and other forms of bigotry. Scott Littky, the director of the Institute for Holocaust Education in Omaha, Nebraska, examines the role played by antisemitism in Holocaust education in classrooms. Littky notes that the concept of antisemitism is often misunderstood, provides several examples, and then considers better ways to teach such a crucial topic. In particular, Littky wants to reconsider some of the core texts that are used to teach antisemitism and the Holocaust in both public and Jewish schools.

Taken together, these contributions offer a serious look at some aspects of contemporary research on antisemitism, alongside a focus on bridging the gap between research and teaching on the topic. While we have organized the chapters into two distinct sections, we believe that researchers will find much of interest in the second section of this volume and teachers will feel the same way about the first section. With that in mind, we have called on veteran educators to provide discussion questions throughout in order to make every chapter as useful as possible to teachers and researchers alike. These questions aim to deepen the understanding of the material presented and are specifically intended for students in middle school, high school, and college classes.

We are extremely grateful to each one of the scholars and educators who came together for the thought-provoking discussions throughout the Sommerhauser Symposium in April 2019. We also must extend a special and heartfelt thanks to the Sommerhauser family, without whose generous support these biennial symposia would never have been organized and would not be possible. The editors also want to thank the Harris Center for Judaic Studies, the Forsythe Family Program for Human Rights and Humanitarian Affairs, and the departments of history and political science at the University of Nebraska—Lincoln for the financial support they have given to this initiative, as well as to the editorial staff at University of Nebraska Press for their enthusiasm about this project. Finally, the editors are extremely grateful to our colleague and friend Jean Cahan for her support, guidance, and assistance throughout the process of setting up both this symposium and this book series. Last, but not least, special thanks to our colleagues from the Institute for Holocaust Education in Omaha, Scott Littky, Kael Sagheer, and Jennifer Goodman, for providing questions for further discussion for each chapter.

Notes

1. Ian Schwartz, "Biden Launches 2020 Campaign: 'Everything That Has Made America America Is at Stake,'" *Real Clear Politics*, April 25, 2019, https://www.realclearpolitics.com/video/2019/04/25/biden_launches_2020_campaign_america_is_at_stake.html.

2. Garth Stapley, "'This Is a Huge Victory.' Oakdale White Supremacist Revels after Deadly Virginia Clash," *Modesto Bee*, August 14, 2017, https://www.modbee.com/news/article167213427.html.

3. Libby Nelson, "'Why We Voted for Donald Trump': David Duke Explains the White Supremacist Charlottesville Protests," *Vox*, August 12, 2017, https://www.vox.com/2017/8/12/16138358/charlottesville-protests-david-duke-kkk.

4. In the years since the Unite the Right rally, most accounts agree that the dominant chant referred to "Jews" rather than to the much more unusual "you." But this is complicated by the fact that Identity Evropa adopted the phrase "You will not replace us" as its slogan as early as February 2017 and this phrase was chanted by Identity Evropa founder Nathan Damigo and National Policy Institute leader Richard Spencer at the May 13, 2017, Charlottesville rally.

5. Anti-Defamation League, "White Supremacists Adopt New Slogan: 'You Will Not Replace Us,'" ADL *Blog*, June 9, 2017, https://www.adl.org/blog/white-supremacists-adopt-new-slogan-you-will-not-replace-us.

6. Nicole Chavez, Emanuella Grinberg, and Eliott C. McLaughlin, "Pittsburgh Synagogue Gunman Said He Wanted All Jews to Die, Criminal Complaint Says." CNN, October 31, 2018, https://edition.cnn.com/2018/10/28/us/pittsburgh-synagogue-shooting/index.html.

7. Masha Gessen, "Why the Tree of Life Shooter Was Fixated on the Hebrew Immigrant Aid Society," *New Yorker*, October 27, 2018, https://www.newyorker.com/news

/our-columnists/why-the-tree-of-life-shooter-was-fixated-on-the-hebrew-immigrant-aid-society.

8. Jeremy W. Peters, Michael M. Grynbaum, Keith Collins, Rich Harris, and Rumsey Taylor, "The New Nativists: How the El Paso Killer Echoed the Incendiary Words of Conservative Media Stars," *New York Times*, August 11, 2019, https://www.nytimes.com/interactive/2019/08/11/business/media/el-paso-killer-conservative-media.html.

9. Bess Levin, "Trump: 'A Lot of People Say' George Soros is Funding the Migrant Caravan," *Vanity Fair*, October 31, 2018, https://www.vanityfair.com/news/2018/10/donald-trump-george-soros-caravan.

10. Brad Heath, Matt Wynn, and Jessica Guynn, "How a Lie about George Soros and the Migrant Caravan Multiplied Online," *USA Today*, October 31, 2018, https://www.usatoday.com/in-depth/news/nation/2018/10/31/george-soros-and-migrant-caravan-how-lie-multiplied-online/1824633002/.

11. Amir Tibon, "White House Disinvites Artist Who Drew 'Blatantly Anti-Semitic' Cartoon," *Haaretz*, July 11, 2019, https://www.haaretz.com/us-news/white-house-disinvites-artist-who-drew-blatantly-anti-semitic-cartoon-following-backlash-1.7487669. The White House disinvited the cartoonist at the last minute after heavy criticism from American Jewish groups.

12. Anti-Defamation League, "Anti-Semitism," accessed July 1, 2019, https://www.adl.org/anti-semitism.

13. Doris Bergen, *War and Genocide: A Concise History of the Holocaust* (Lanham MD: Rowman and Littlefield, 2016), 3.

14. *The Lehman Trilogy*, a three-act play about the history of Lehman brothers by Italian dramatist Stefano Massini, premiered in 2015. This German Jewish family immigrated to the United States in the mid-1850s and became one of the most influential and well-known families of bankers and stockbrokers in American history. The play, which depicts Jews and immigrants in general in a very positive light, was translated into a number of languages and performed on stages across Europe and the United States. It had its North American premiere on March 27, 2019.

15. The last massacre against Jews based on false "blood libel" charges occurred in Kielce, Poland, in 1946. Forty-two Jews were murdered.

16. John Efron, Matthias Lehmann, and Steven Weitzmann, *The Jews: A History* (New York: Routledge, 2019).

17. Deborah Lipstadt, *Denying the Holocaust: The Growing Assault on Truth and Memory* (London: Penguin Books, 2016), 41.

18. Deborah Lipstadt, *Antisemitism: Here and Now* (Melbourne: Scribe, 2019), 167.

19. Lipstadt, *Antisemitism*, 171.

20. Lipstadt, *Antisemitism*, 167.

21. Tammi Rossman-Benjamin, "Academic BDS and the Calculus of Hypocrisy," *Inside Higher Ed*, March 20, 2019, https://www.insidehighered.com/views/2019/03/20/scholars-who-support-bds-are-denying-academic-freedom-students-opinion.

22. Alvin H. Rosenfeld, ed., *Resurgent Antisemitism: Global Perspectives* (Bloomington: Indiana University Press, 2013), 5.

23. Lipstadt, *Antisemitism*, ix.

24. Bari Weiss, *How to Fight Anti-Semitism* (New York: Crown, 2019), 19.

25. For a better understanding of the recent upsurge of antisemitism see also *Deciphering the New Antisemitism*, edited by Alvin H. Rosenfeld (Bloomington: University of Indiana Press, 2015).

26. Anti-Defamation League, "Anti-Semitic Incidents Surged Nearly 60% in 2017, According to New ADL Report," February 27, 2018, https://www.adl.org/news/press-releases/anti-semitic-incidents-surged-nearly-60-in-2017-according-to-new-adl-report.

27. Speech by Rosenberg at a press reception, November 18, 1941, printed in Jürgen Matthäus and Frank Bajohr, *The Political Diary of Alfred Rosenberg and the Onset of the Holocaust*, Documenting Life and Destruction: Holocaust Sources in Context (Lanham MD: Rowman & Littlefield in association with the USHMM, 2015), 385–89.

Part 1

History of Antisemitism

1

Underestimating German Antisemitism
The Case of Carl Schmitt, the Frankfurt School, and Weimar Jewish Elites

JOSEPH W. BENDERSKY

In August of 1931 two Social Democratic lawyers, Franz Neumann and Ernst Fraenkel, showed the prominent conservative legal theorist Carl Schmitt around the trade union offices in Berlin. After dinner they talked about contemporary political issues. This engagement was typical of Neumann's relationship with Schmitt during these years. To Neumann, such an invitation no doubt also indicated an assumption of mutual personal and intellectual respect. Their differences were of a purely political and ideological nature—basically socialism versus conservatism. However, when Schmitt noted this event in his private diary, he punctuated it with the comment: "Unheimlich, Juden und Sozialisten" [Uncanny, Jews and Socialists].[1] Neumann probably never became aware of Schmitt's long-concealed antisemitic attitudes. Neumann's underestimation of German antisemitism generally was an illusion he shared with his colleagues in the Frankfurt School as well as with other Weimar Jewish elites who interacted with Schmitt.

Neumann was then emerging as a prominent member of the Frankfurt School, a Weimar movement anchored originally in the Institute for Social Research at the University of Frankfurt, which moved to Columbia University after Hitler's seizure of power. The Frankfurt School significantly reinterpreted Western Marxism to go beyond its crude nineteenth-century economic determinism. Known as *critical theory*, the Frankfurt School's Western Marxism extended the critiques of modernity and capitalism into the spheres of philosophy, psychology, sociology, and modern mass culture. The worldwide influence of critical theory remains today in fields as diverse as philosophy, cultural studies, film studies, and political and legal theory. After World War II, Neumann also served as an influential advisor to the Nuremberg War Crimes Trials and as a leading figure in the development of political science in the nascent Federal Republic of Germany.[2]

A more illustrious leader in the Frankfurt School, Theodor Adorno, remains one of the most studied and respected figures in cultural studies and social theory. His name is essentially synonymous with critical theory. He, like Neumann, greatly misconstrued German antisemitism. As late as 1941, Adorno emphasized that Jewish assimilation and acceptance had reached the point that "in pre-Hitler Berlin it was impossible to distinguish a Gentile high executive from a Jewish one."[3] Yet, to certain members of the German elites, for whom public antisemitism was not *salonfähig*, the distinction was nonetheless still eminently clear. Schmitt's diary entries contain numerous derogatory comments about the physical and behavioral characteristics of Jews. A few months after his trade union visit with Neumann, Schmitt passionately lamented that he "lived in this Jewish city, [where he was] insulted and defamed by Jews."[4]

The Frankfurt School has long been criticized for its belated, inadequate, and inaccurate treatment of antisemitism.[5] And Neumann, with his intellectual association with Schmitt, is often the focal point for this criticism. Another exponent of critical theory who had an even longer and closer personal relationship with Schmitt was Otto Kirchheimer. But even though he virtually neglected antisemitism in his writing, Kirchheimer never suffered the same reproach as Neumann. From my perspective, Kirchheimer's evasion of the issue is just as revealing as Neumann's specific approach to it. They both either could not perceive, or were psychologically and ideologically incapable of accepting, the distressing nature and implications of such antisemitism in their society and especially among the elites with whom they interacted.

As the practitioner of critical theory most committed to economic and legal analyses, Neumann handled antisemitism within the neo-Marxist framework of the development and crisis of corporate monopoly capitalism. Even so, he did not take up the issue until after the outbreak of war. From the Frankfurt School's first preliminary project on antisemitism in 1941 to the second edition, in 1944, of his classic study *Behemoth: The Structure and Practice of National Socialism*, it was Neumann's "personal conviction ... that the German people were the least Anti-Semitic of all."[6] He conceded that there existed a long German intellectual tradition of antisemitism and nineteenth-century antisemitic political currents, but insisted that antisemitism "had failed to strike root in the population."[7] The antisemitism that did exist was largely economically based, with some reinforcement from the association of Jews with disruptive modern cultural currents threatening traditional societal norms and sensibilities. Essentially, from his Marxist worldview, "racism and anti-Semitism [were] substitutes for the class struggle."[8] For the Nazis, the image of the Jew as the pervasive enemy would serve as the integrating factor overriding class differences in favor of a racially based national community (the ideal *Volksgemeinschaft*). This new social structure would preserve "the powerful financial and industrial capitalists," while "satisfying the anti-capitalistic longings of the German people."[9] That antisemitism was a "propaganda device ... shows how weak anti-Semitism actually is as a spontaneous popular movement" even in the Third Reich.[10] Nazi "economic persecution of the Jews was a mere diversion intended to conceal the assault on the middle classes as whole."[11] Neumann interpreted Nazi manifestations of Jewish oppression and even violence, such as Aryanization and Kristallnacht, as attempts to manipulate the masses from above.

In August of 1941, Neumann confidently asserted that "the internal political value of anti-Semitism will, therefore, never allow a complete extermination of the Jews. The foe cannot and must not disappear; he must always be held in readiness to have attributed to him all the evils originating in the socio-political system."[12] At that point, Neumann was obviously unaware that the Final Solution was underway in eastern Europe and Russia. Nonetheless, when he learned of the exterminations, Neumann still insisted that the real targets were not Jews. They were, he asserted, only "guinea pigs."[13] Antisemitism and the "exterminations of the Jews [are] only the means to the attainment of the ultimate objective, namely the destruction of free institutions, beliefs, and groups."[14] Moreover, he continued to exclude inherent or latent antisemitism from his interpretation of the broader German population's involvement in the exterminations. Instead he presented their involvement, as well as that of the German army and civil service, as an attempt by the Nazis to ensure a "collective guilt" that would prevent these societal sectors from abandoning the criminal regime.[15] As late as his last publication, in 1954, Neumann attributed only a "relatively minor" role to antisemitism.[16]

Perhaps the most important explanations for the stubborn adherence of Neumann and his Frankfurt School colleagues to this version of German antisemitism was their rigorous commitment to Marxist ideology. Critics have also argued, however, that this rigid Marxist mentality interacted with a variety of other factors. The Frankfurt School was too theoretical. It lacked empirical data, and was too susceptible to Freudian theories of mass psychology in seeking to comprehend complex sociopolitical phenomena.[17] Ehrhard Bahr, in his probing analysis of the Frankfurt School's study of antisemitism, added another dynamic at work: the German origins of Critical Theory. Frankfurt School thinkers were so convinced of the success of Jewish integration and assimilation in Weimar society that they truly believed that, with the exception of certain atavistic currents and groups, "discrimination had largely disappeared."[18] Thus, even in the face of the success of Nazism, they continued to downplay the centrality of antisemitism within the broader scope of German society and particularly within Nazi ideological visions for Europe's future that would culminate in mass murder. Although Bahr did not elaborate on this contention, the case of Neumann and Kirchheimer substantiates it and requires further exploration.

Retrospective on the German Jewish Illusion

The illusion of almost complete German Jewish acceptance was poignantly portrayed in the unpublished memoir of John Herz, a distinguished émigré political scientist at The City College of New York. During the Nazi seizure of power, Herz was the assistant to the renowned legal theorist Han Kelsen at the University of Cologne, one of Schmitt's most formidable intellectual rivals. Although a critic of Marxist ideology and politics, Herz would later establish close personal and intellectual relationships with members of the Frankfurt School, particularly Kirchheimer, while working together in the Office of Strategic Services (OSS) during World War II. After serving as an advisor to the prosecutors at the Nuremberg Trials, a disillusioned Herz became a vocal critic of what he perceived as the failure of the United States to adequately pursue the denazification of Germany. After the Nazi experience, the cultured Germans he had previously confidently believed to be so accepting of Jews he now pessimistically regarded as requiring control, punishment, and denazification—-a process he felt they could not undertake themselves, but had to submit to from the democratic victors.

Hertz's earlier *Weltanschauung* of "bliss [and] protection" began at birth. Born into the most advanced culture—Germany—of the center of civilization itself—Europe—he grew up "as a Jew in an environment in which discrimination of a religious or racial nature seemed to vanish."[19] As a royal Prussian judge, his father had risen to the height of social status, confirming the apparently irreversible process of assimilation and equality. Herz recalled his father's clearly Prussian characteristics. The entire extended family exhibited deeply optimistic "liberal and enlightened attitudes" within a mixture of Christian and secularized German culture.[20] They celebrated not Chanukah, but Christmas (displaying a tree without a crib). Modernized relatives were baptized for social or professional reasons, pursuing what "Heinrich Heine had called 'the entrance ticket to European civilization.'"[21] There were so many mixed marriages in Germany that, had it not been for Hitler, Jewish identity would probably have disappeared in a few generations.

Even in his old age Herz felt the "special irreplaceable aura" of the Lower Rhine of his youth, of the Cologne Cathedral and baroque churches.[22] And even though German Jews were inextricably linked, as creators and promoters, with various modernist trends of Weimar culture, their devotion to and sponsorship of traditional German culture remained an intimate part of their assimilation and identity. Their cultural values were truly that of the German-Jewish synthesis. Theirs was the humanism of the liberal bourgeoisie. Their "patronage of art and artists," modern and traditional, was a "moral obligation," an expression of gratitude for their acceptance into this traditional culture.[23] Herz's youthful intellectual and cultural affinities were for German classicism and romanticism, and also included admiration for Bach's music and Hölderin's poetry and philosophy. His artistic heritage ranged from Dürer to German expressionism. Herz even found Oswald Spengler's *The Decline of the West* an inspiring insight into the cultural crisis of the early twentieth century. And, despite all that Germany had done to him during the Nazi era, Herz introduced each chapter of his memoir with quotes from Goethe, Rilke, and other German cultural icons.

Contrary to Nazi canards that Jews were anti-German international capitalists or subversive communists, most German Jews were socially progressive moderate democrats devoted to a republican form of government. Most shared the exuberance, and some even the sense of cultural superiority, of German nationalism. Herz's father tried to enlist immediately upon the outbreak of war in 1914; his uncle and cousin proudly displayed their iron crosses on their field-grey uniforms. The young Herz enthusiastically pinned flags on a map designating German battlefield advances. As a university student he retained a strong emotional attachment to "Germany" as a people and nation to which he belonged. It was this German identity, though somewhat tempered by his Jewishness, that led him to reject the Marxism of some of his peers and the Zionism of others. Thus the intensification of the extreme German *völkisch* racial nationalism of late Weimar produced an identity crisis in Herz that he described in his memoir as a sense of "renewed emotional confusion."[24] Nonetheless, his "yearning for belonging" to that nation remained strong.[25]

Among his schoolmates and family Herz experienced little antisemitism, if any. Educated assimilated Jews appeared to be accepted into the broader culture. In fact, educated, non-observant German Jews themselves sometimes held antisemitic attitudes of superiority towards the *Ostjuden*, and ridiculed their retention of traditional customs in the ghettos of large cities. Otherwise, Herz acquired stereotypical images of Jews, not from personal experience, but from negative depictions in nineteenth-century German novels. He identified with the "idealistic" Christian German characters, chastising himself for having certain inherited "inferior Jewish traits."[26]

The question of whether residual Jewish traits inhibited full acceptance and completion of the German Jewish synthesis later surfaced in the Frankfurt School's "Research Project on Anti-Semitism." One of the institution's leading figures, Max Horkheimer, warned against ignoring the "so-called character traits of Jews and the genesis of the traits."[27] Dismissing racial interpretations, he subsequently ascribed these "shades of behavior and gesture" to the historical development of Jews.[28] The "Jewish mentality," he wrote, manifested "the tendency to resort to rational argument rather than to force; the inclination toward abstract thinking, the transformation of *quaestiones facti* into *quaestiones juris*; distrust of any tendency to exalt an existing entity to the rank of the Absolute (skepticism); readiness to confess his fear where others are bound to conceal their weakness."

This sense of Jewish mental traits can likewise be found in Karl Loewenstein, a Jewish émigré professor at Amherst College and founder of the vigorous anti-fascist movement in the United States known as "militant democracy." In 1947 Loewenstein had unsuccessfully attempted to have Schmitt tried as a war criminal at Nuremberg. Loewenstein shared Herz's frustration with the denazification process.[29] Nonetheless, as late as 1972 Loewenstein averred that the "behaviorist nonsense" emerging within political science in the United States was due to the fact that the majority of its adherents were a "plethora of Jews." As he wrote to Herz, such social science was "a flashback to their former Talmudic training. . . . The subtle distinctions, the use of mathematical or pseudo-mathematical formulae, the graphs, etc. require a specific turn of mind that seems to me altogether Talmudic."[30]

This uneasy undercurrent of Herz's Jewish self-consciousness notwithstanding, the German Jews of his pre-Nazi social milieu enjoyed the optimistic psychological security, as well the ultimately naïve complacency, of what he called *Geborgenheit*. It is a "blissful" feeling of being born into a harmonious world of security and meaning, a sense of place and belonging where one is sheltered and protected.[31] "Foolishly, over-optimistic," he lamented, "we believed in an inevitable and continually progressing process of assimilation; we simply felt to be Germans, members of a culture into which we were born."[32] This blinded them, he regretted, to the changing attitudes "right before our very eyes" of those increasingly attracted to rightist political extremism. Accordingly, they downplayed clear manifestations of dangerous racial antisemitism, such as the assassination of the German Jewish intellectual, industrialist, and prominent political leader Walter Rathenau. So deeply rooted were these traditional and emotional attachments that, even after the sufferings of Nazi oppression, they were never "able to abandon completely a sense of connectedness with the country of our origin."

Herz's notion of cultural *Geborgenheit* might aptly be applied to the Frankfurt School, despite its Marxist orientation. Herz, having acclimated to American culture, did not succumb to the strong urge to return to postwar Germany, but Frankfurt School intellectuals always remained alienated from their New World refuge. Its most prominent members, Adorno and Horkheimer, returned early; Neumann and Kirchheimer were about to return before their untimely deaths. In fact, the fundamental intellectual framework of the Frankfurt School indicated that its practitioners were indeed products of the peculiarly German cultural process of *Bildung*.

Such deeply rooted, inescapable personal affinity with their German cultural heritage also affected their approach to antisemitism. As Peter Hayes noted, even though Neumann became more and more aware of the reality of antisemitism in the Third Reich, "he could not bring himself to treat persecution as the product of [a Nazi] obsession, rather than of opportunism."[33] Neumann's son, Michael, confirmed this inference, recalling that at home his father often emphasized the limited nature of German antisemitism. However, while Hayes attributed Neumann's stance on antisemitism to his Marxism, Michael Neumann ascribed it to his "personal experience and background."[34]

Carl Schmitt and Jews

An important part of the experience that helped to form and confirm the perspectives that Kirchheimer and Neumann held on Germans and Jews came from their relationships with members of the German elite such as Schmitt. Their association with Schmitt presents an illuminating, yet disturbing, case study. Schmitt was one of the most renowned and widely read political and legal theorists of the Weimar Republic. His prolific oeuvre included insightful works on constitutional theory, dictatorship, presidential emergency powers, and political theology. Although he was a Catholic conservative whose work was subjected to scathing assaults in several quarters, Schmitt's ideas were recognized as brilliant and often invoked by both the left and the right. This was particularly true of the basic political realism in his friend-enemy theory and his critique of liberalism, as well as his incisive analysis of the deficiencies of the contemporary practice of parliamentary democracy in Weimar.[35]

Between 1930 and 1933, Schmitt was the constitutional advisor to the coterie around President Paul von Hindenburg, who, during the years of the Great Depression, parliamentary paralysis, and extreme radicalization, governed the country through presidential decrees. Although Hindenburg is often accused of undermining Weimar democracy and paving the way for Hitler's dictatorship, archival evidence makes it abundantly clear that Schmitt's political advice was always intended to keep Hindenburg's strategy and actions, including his emergency decrees, within the legality of the Weimar constitution and his legitimacy in the eyes of the German people. Schmitt's biographer, Reinhard Mehring, has corroborated that "Schmitt rejected handing over power to Hitler" and supported Hindenburg's presidential system as an instrument to prevent a Nazi seizure of power.[36]

For various personal, professional, and political reasons, Schmitt collaborated with the Third Reich between 1933 and 1936. While his relationship with the new regime was always tenuous, he was now perceived as the Nazi *Kronjurist*. By lending his intellectual prestige to the Third Reich he helped legitimize Hitler's dictatorship. As his opponents within the Nazi regime increasingly attacked him for his prior anti-Nazi activity, the non-racial character of his political theory, and his associations with Jews, Schmitt made ever more reprehensible capitualations to Nazi racial ideology. For the first time he also inserted antisemitic remarks in his publications and public stances. Unconvinced of his loyalty, the Nazis purged him from party offices in 1936 for ideological deviance and opportunism, though he retained his professorship at the University of Berlin. With his reputation tainted forever, he would become persona non grata in postwar Germany.

Although Schmitt has remained overshadowed by his Nazi past, the 1980s witnessed the beginnings of an international Schmitt renaissance that continues to the present. His works have been translated into numerous languages and studied not only in Europe but also in the United States, Latin America, Japan, and China. The subject of over four hundred books and two thousand articles, Schmitt has been both criticized as a dangerous mind and recognized as offering incisive perspectives on various crises of the tumultuous twenty-first century.[37]

The 1991 publication of *Glossarium* (Schmitt's private notes from 1947 to 1951) significantly complicated the burgeoning field of Schmitt studies by undermining the interpretative consensus that his antisemitism had been essentially sham opportunism. The antisemitism in his notations stunned even his faithful defenders. Although his remarks were dispersed over years (absent for many of these and lacking cohesion), they were vehemently antisemitic. He portrayed himself as the victim of the "terror of Nazis and Jews," as the returning émigrés were, in his mind, seeking revenge on Germany and him under the hypocritical guise of justice and humanitarianism. He exclaimed, "better Adolf Hitler's enmity than the friendship of these returning emigres and humanitarians."[38] Elsewhere he composed a short antisemitic poem about these "Isra-Eliten."[39] The subsequent publication of Schmitt's pre–World War I diaries and those of 1930–1934 clearly established a continuity in his antisemitism, which was often expressed crudely and viciously.

Nevertheless, the diaries reveal that Schmitt was a peculiar kind of antisemite. His references to Jews reflected all the inconsistent complexities and contradictions that characterized his changing relationships with Jews throughout his life. His entries about Jews were similar to the prejudiced and caustic remarks he made about Prussians, militarists, Marxists, Catholics, and the materialistic bourgeoisie generally. His antisemitic attitudes were not ideological in nature; he scornfully dismissed racial theories as unfounded speculation. The diaries also confirm that, before the Nazi years, his acclaimed political and legal theories were entirely devoid of antisemitism.[40] His Jewish publishers, and intellectuals such as Kirchheimer and Neumann, found his ideas insightful and groundbreaking. Still, he displayed the biases of his social background and the bigoted nineteenth-century Catholic milieu of his upbringing. He distinguished respectable from detestable Jews. He expressed *Angst* at Jewish power and influence, particularly regarding the role of Jews as accelerators of cultural modernization.[41]

And yet Schmitt's closest personal relationships were with Fritz and Georg Eisler. It would be difficult to find a more intimate personal and intellectual bond between two heterosexual males than that of the youthful Schmitt and his Jewish companion Fritz. They studied and traveled together, shared a common cultural pessimism about the detrimental aspects of modernization, and coauthored a parody of German intellectuals and the *gebildete* bourgeoisie. Schmitt was emotionally shattered and distraught when Eisler fell on the battlefield at the start of World War I. Thereafter, Schmitt established an equally close friendship with Georg and the Eisler family in Hamburg, noting in his diary "I began to respect the Jews."[42] Schmitt dedicated his classic 1928 study *Constitutional Theory* to the fallen Fritz.

But while living in Berlin after 1930, in the heart of a modernized "Weimar culture" of which Jews were a significant part, Schmitt's antisemitism intensified. He not only blamed Jews for destroying German culture but felt that Jews were personally attacking him, as well as his theories and students. He reacted with private emotional outbursts, which, though dispersed over a period of years, reveal his deep sentiments: "The eternal, ineradicable cruelty of the Jews against all Christians, all human decency" and "Jews exploit everything."[43] He expressed fear of Jewish "danger and cunning" and of Jews' "triumph." He resorted to the medieval trope of "ritual murder" to criticize Jewish behavior in academia and politics. The Jewish mode of thinking, he asserted, originated in the synagogue; it was "purely logical, purely juristic, purely scholarly." The latter, in retrospect, sounds eerily familiar to the comments of Horkheimer and Loewenstein. Schmitt disparaged certain *Ostjuden*, as well as the "impudence of the assimilated."

As indicated by his fondness for the Eislers, and his relationship with Kirchheimer for most of this period, Schmitt's sentiments regarding Jews remained complex, nuanced, and contradictory. And none of them involved any consistent or systematic analysis of the "Jewish Question." Indeed, he had similar rages and *"Angst* about" the politics of the Social Democrats, Catholic Center Party, and naïve Prussian elites.[44] Simultaneously, he respected the ideas and friendship of Ludwig Feuchtwanger, his longtime Jewish publisher. He also held in high regard certain fellow Jewish jurists such as Albert Hensel, Gerhard Leibholz, and Karl Loewenstein. He coauthored his famous paper on presidential emergency powers with Erwin Jacobi, with whom he cochaired the legal defense of the presidential system before the supreme court in 1932. To Schmitt, the young philosopher Leo Strauss was "ein feiner Jude," whose scholarship he praised, and with whom he relished intellectual discussions. Schmitt strongly recommended Strauss for a Rockefeller Fellowship.[45] In the early stages of the Third Reich, Schmitt would vouch for the loyalty of Hensel and Jacobi. But in July of 1935, when his own faithfulness to National Socialism, like his past associations with Jews, was coming under increasing condemnation within the Nazi party, Schmitt never responded to Feuchtwanger's heartrending plea to intercede on his behalf. As a German citizen and world war veteran with a presidential citation, Feuchtwanger sought an exemption from the loss of his publishing house due to a policy decision by the Nazi Chamber of Culture.[46]

During the April 1933 Nazi anti-Jewish boycott, Schmitt and his wife had become seriously concerned for the wellbeing of the Eisler family. Although a woman of known antisemitic prejudice, his wife traveled to Hamburg to comfort the Eislers, as Schmitt did by phone. Schmitt later helped the Eislers emigrate.[47] Paradoxically, it was during that same time that Schmitt was gradually drawn into the Nazi orbit. As directed by Vice-Chancellor Franz von Papen, Schmitt helped compose the Law for the Coordination of the States with the Reich. That law undermined the autonomy of state governments and their ability to counteract Hitler's consolidation of power. And, though he had strong reservations about the Nazis, Schmitt reluctantly joined the National Socialist Party on May 1, 1933. Such was the complexity of German gentile and Jewish associations and sentiments.

Schmitt, Kirchheimer, and Neumann

Kirchheimer had been Schmitt's student since the 1920s and wrote his dissertation under Schmitt at the University of Bonn in 1928. Kirchheimer's 1930 essay "Weimar—and What Then?" was a theoretical and political admixture of Marxist and Schmittian thought.[48] Between 1930 and 1933 Kirchheimer was an active leftist in Berlin, where he maintained a close personal and intellectual association with Schmitt. Schmitt was "very fond" of Kirchheimer, whom he considered quite intelligent and personally likeable. Kirchheimer often visited Schmitt's home, and Schmitt knew Kirchheimer's family. Despite Schmitt's disdain for Marxism and Kirchheimer's radical socialist political agenda, the intellectual respect was sincere and mutual. Schmitt praised Kirchheimer's work in a recommendation for a Rockefeller fellowship. Although in his diary entries Schmitt lashed out at others as "Jews" for years, he never identified Kirchheimer as a Jew, nor was critical of him. Schmitt became alarmed when his wife "spoke stupidly about the Jews" in Kirchheimer's presence.[49]

That good relationship changed quickly and drastically in mid-1932, when President Hindenburg declared a state of emergency and deposed the Social Democratic state government in Prussia that Kirchheimer supported. Schmitt was engaged to defend the state of emergency before the supreme court. Kirchheimer published a critical analysis of Schmitt's *Legality and Legitimacy*, which had provided theoretical justifications for the presidential authority to intervene in Prussia. Clearly irritated by a conversation with Kirchheimer on the subject, Schmitt felt Kirchheimer's ideological and political blinders made any discussion useless. And then, for the first time, Schmitt noted in his diary about Kirchheimer: "Scheusslich, dieser Jude" [Horrible, this Jew].[50]

Neumann had also attended Schmitt's Berlin seminars between 1930 and 1932. He submitted some of his manuscripts to Schmitt for critique.[51] And it is no longer in dispute that Neumann, like Kirchheimer, integrated Schmittian concepts into his own Marxist analyses.[52] In response to Schmitt's *Legality and Legitimacy*, Neumann wrote to his mentor, "It will be my task in the future to substantiate your opinion from an economic and sociological point of view."[53] By fall of 1932, Schmitt's association with the Hindenburg government, and the political situation created by the Prussian crisis, had also strained their relationship, but had not severed it. Neumann maintained his personal and professional respect for Schmitt.[54] Privately, though, Schmitt had strong reservations about Neumann's "revolutionary attitude."[55] Nonetheless, when Kirchheimer and Neumann emigrated in 1933, they listed Schmitt as a primary mentor in law and political science. Neumann noted Schmitt's support for his application for a position at the Technische Hochschule in Berlin in fall 1932.[56]

However, Kirchheimer and Neumann soon eschewed any identification with Schmitt, as their mentor increasingly took on the aura and offices of the Nazi *Kronjurist*. Under the patronage of top Nazis Hans Frank and Hermann Göring, Schmitt became editor of the leading law journal and head of the Association of National Socialist German Jurists. And in August 1934 he published his infamous article "The Führer Protects the Law," justifying Hitler's bloody purge of the SA leadership.

Thereafter, Kirchheimer made only a few brief and critical references to Schmitt in his publications.[57] But, though clearly embittered by Schmitt's betrayal, Kirchheimer never fully escaped from Schmitt's thinking. As Herz observed in his personal intellectual discussions with Kirchheimer, "next to Marx there remained, though in decreasing measure, the influence of his teacher, Carl Schmitt."[58] Arnold Price recalled that, in discussions with OSS Frankfurt School colleagues, Kirchheimer occasionally defended

Schmitt's pre-Nazi ideas. Whether or not Kirchheimer was conscious of this enduring intellectual legacy, it was obvious to others. As late as 1957 another Frankfurt School intellectual, Arkadij Gurland, thoroughly disagreed with the manuscript of Kirchheimer's magnum opus, *Political Justice*, because "the root of the evil is your genuinely Schmittian construct."[59] Years after its publication, Loewenstein concurred, criticizing the book's "Marxian fixation" and "the influence of the miserable Carl Schmitt."[60]

In contrast, Neumann began, in late 1933, an assault on Schmitt as someone whose constitutional interpretations brought "into contempt liberty, Parliament, and so-called Western democracy."[61] Neumann's critique of Schmitt culminated in *Behemoth*, in which he condemned his former mentor as a theorist of "brute force" who sought to undermine liberal democracy and the rule of law. Neumann attributed Schmitt's Nazi collaboration to opportunism—his "conformist instincts."[62] While there was nothing distinctive in viewing Schmitt as an opportunist, another aspect of the Kirchheimer-Neumann approach to Schmitt and the Third Reich is noteworthy. Other émigrés attacked the antisemitism gradually emerging in Schmitt's Nazi works, especially the peak it reached in 1936, when he organized a conference on "Purging the Jewish Spirit from German Law."[63] Yet neither Kirchheimer nor Neumann ever addressed Schmitt and the "Jewish Question," not even to label it hypocritical opportunism, as other émigrés had done.

This silence continued into the postwar era. Neumann died in 1954 before Schmitt again became a controversial subject. But Kirchheimer reestablished contact with Schmitt's former circles as early as 1947, including Ernst Friesenhahn, who later served on the Constitutional Court of the Federal Republic. Kirchheimer also visited Schmitt as early as 1949, and they corresponded intermittently until 1961.[64] Among the most revealing sources from this period is the Kirchheimer-Friesenhahn correspondence between 1948 and 1965. Detailed and confiding, these letters contain frequent critical discussions of Schmitt's work lambasting his flawed character. Completely absent is any reference or hint regarding Schmitt's antisemitism or Jews.[65]

Conclusion

Kirchheimer's and Neumann's "personal experience and background" did not put them in a better position to grasp the extent of German antisemitism than did subsequent scholars. Instead, their experiences reinforced their "illusions" about Jews and Germans. But this assessment of their perceptions should be tempered, as Hayes has suggested, by what they could have known.[66] Before the revelations of Schmitt's antisemitism in the 1990s there was no reason to suspect him of such prejudice. His theories were not racially based. He offered no public hints of antisemitism, whereas much of the German right was vehement and vocal in its political antisemitism. Many of his close associates, students, and most intimate friends were Jews. He had dedicated his most important work to his beloved Jewish friend who died in World War I; he wrote a work praising the Jewish constitutionalist Hugo Preuss. Schmitt invited Kirchheimer and Neumann to his home; they took long walks together discussing intellectual and political matters. He tried to advance Kirchheimer's academic career. That Schmitt had crossed the Jewish-German cultural divide more than most members of the German elite was recognized by Jews and non-Jews alike. It was for this reason that Jewish émigrés and Nazis agreed that his post-1933 antisemitism was sheer opportunism. But Kirchheimer and Neumann did not know that they were excluded from the intimate conversations Schmitt had within his trusted conservative circles, which contained overt antisemites.[67] It would have been difficult for these young Jewish scholars and activists to imagine the vicious antisemitic rants that appear in Schmitt's diaries, or his true sentiments hidden behind his outward façade of cordiality and intellectual respectability.

One might argue that Schmitt's case is too unique and limited. Drawing implications for broader German-Jewish relations would certainly require a more extensive evidentiary basis. But documenting non-overt antisemitism, as with any study of prejudice, is difficult. Thus, most works on the subject have focused on segments of the German population that openly expressed antisemitism, and on the ideology and politics of groups from the traditional right to the National Socialists.⁶⁸ Or they studied public opinion during the Third Reich.⁶⁹ Here the Schmitt documents offer something that other studies do not. They provide rare explicit evidence, though it is often contradictory, of the innermost thoughts, feelings, and attitudes toward Jews of a prominent German who had been intimately connected personally and intellectually with Jews. Schmitt was often greatly admired by them as an exception to what existed in other conservative intellectual circles.

There are further indications that such a duplicitous distinction between public relationships and private prejudice was not unusual among elites who went through the German university system with Kirchheimer and Neumann. The young legal scholar Ulrich Scheuner, for example, was associated with two of Schmitt's staunchest Weimar opponents, Heinrich Triepel and Rudolf Smend. Scheuner displayed no inklings of antisemitism; he would later significantly influence the development of law in the Federal Republic. Nonetheless, in 1934 he had privately defended the Nazi "measures against non-Aryan" professors. One had to understand, he wrote, "the inordinate strength exercised by Jewish forces in the bureaucracy in the last ten years."⁷⁰

Many assimilated Jewish liberals and leftists shared Neumann's and Kirchheimer's comforting and reassuring view of their fellow Germans, attesting that their country was the "least anti-Semitic of all."⁷¹ And Germany certainly was not a land of "eliminationist anti-Semites" as some would later contend.⁷² Indeed, as even the Schmitt case demonstrates, German-Jewish relations and perceptions were complex, nuanced, and incongruous. Nonetheless, there existed much more antisemitism among their friends, colleagues, and neighbors than German Jews recognized or were willing to concede. The amount of progress Jews had made in Germany, together with the limited nature of overt antisemitism, created a false sense of the degree of acceptance. They failed to realize how many of those with whom they interacted personally, professionally, and sometimes intimately still perceived them as different from "real Germans" and equal citizens. German Jews likewise never sufficiently grasped that many of their fellow Germans did not regard their societal advancement as beneficial or desirable. Their professional and economic achievements often bred resentment on the part of those who were not as successful or faced their competition. Though German Jews might have felt a deep affinity for traditional German culture, to some others such Jewish cultural engagement appeared an unwarranted and undesirable alien intrusion into "their" culture. On the other hand, many conservative-minded Germans considered Jewish affiliation with modernizing intellectual or cultural trends not only non-German but dangerous and subversive.

Antisemitism in the Third Reich did not need to be contrived or manipulated by the Nazis from above. Neither was antisemitism merely an issue cynically exploited by the Nazis who had other fundamental ideological and political goals in whose pursuit the Jews were only a useful pawn. However, the confident assumption among Jews that antisemitism had to be artificially incited against the basic tendencies of most of the German population was also "self-illusionary." The sincere perception of limited antisemitism conveniently fitted into the social and political mental frameworks held dear by many Jews in Germany. That view suited both the liberal notions of enlightenment and human progress and the neo-Marxist view that the true driving forces of antisemitism were corporate monopoly capitalism and fanatical Nazis. Jews were quite confident that most of their fellow Germans had to be immune to such appeals. After all, members of the Frankfurt School were themselves products of that cherished German culture. It was a sense of intellectual, often emotional, identity so deeply engrained that, even after they suffered as Jews, they were never able to extricate themselves from their inherent Germanness. Moreover, their fellow Germans were the very ones that thinkers such as Kirchheimer and Neumann had sought to save or redeem.

Questions for Further Discussion

1. Was antisemitism uniquely German, or was it widespread among other European societies?

2. Do you know any famous people of Jewish background from central Europe? You surely know about Albert Einstein, but can you name others?

3. Why did the patriotic German Jewish population strongly believe in the promises of national unity? How were German nationalism and German antisemitism connected?

4. How could have the Jews of elite German society been more in touch with the realities of antisemitism?

5. Does complete assimilation (giving up Jewish religious and cultural identity) always protect against antisemitism? What happened in the German case?

6. Is the belief held by some that a Jew should always be worried about antisemitism a valid viewpoint, and does this chapter prove or disprove that belief?

Notes

1. Carl Schmitt, *Carl Schmitt Tagebücher 1930–1934*, ed. Wolfgang Schuller and G. Giesler (Berlin: Akademie Verlag, 2010), 129–30.

2. The standard work on this subject is still Martin Jay, *The Dialectical Imagination: A History of the Frankfurt School and the Institute for Social Research, 1923–1950* (Boston: Little Brown, 1973). For a more skeptical perspective see Zoltan Tar, *The Frankfurt School: The Critical Theories of Max Horkheimer and Theodor W. Adorno* (New York: Wiley, 1977).

3. Theodor Adorno, "Re: Questionnaire on Anti-Semitism," n.d., 3, in "Anti-Semitism—Spearhead of Nazism," questionnaire, box 2, Carl J. Friedrich Papers, Harvard University Archives (HUGFP) 17.24, Harvard University.

4. Schmitt, *Tagebücher 1930–1934*, 159–60.

5. Ehrhard Bahr, "The Anti-Semitism Studies of the Frankfurt School: The Failure of Critical Theory," *German Studies Review* 1, no. 2 (May 1978): 125–38; Martin Jay, "The Jews and the Frankfurt School: Critical Theory's Analysis of Anti-Semitism" in "Germans and Jews," special issue, *New German Critique*, no. 19 (Winter 1980): 137–49. See also Joseph W. Bendersky, "Dissension in Face of the Holocaust: The 1941 American Debate over Antisemitism," *Holocaust and Genocide Studies* 24, no. 1 (Spring 2010): 85–116.

6. "Research Project on Anti-Semitism," *Studies in Philosophy and Social Science* IX (1941): 124–43; Franz Neumann, *Behemoth: The Structure and Practice of National Socialism, 1933–1944* (New York: Oxford University Press, 1944), 121.

7. Neumann, *Behemoth*, 110.

8. Franz Neumann, "Re: Anti-Semitism—Spearhead of Nazism," August 25, 1941, 9–10, Friedrich Papers.

9. Neumann, "Re: Anti-Semitism," 2, 6; Neumann, *Behemoth*, 116–19; Adorno, "Re-Questionnaire," 5.

10. Neumann, "Re: Anti-Semitism," 2, 6.

11. Neumann, *Behemoth*, 116.

12. Neumann, *Behemoth*, 125.

13. Neumann, *Behemoth*, 108–29; Jay "Jews and the Frankfurt School," 140.

14. Neumann, *Behemoth*, 550–51.

15. Neumann, *Behemoth*, 108–29, 552.

16. Jay, "Jews and the Frankfurt School," 140.

17. Bahr, "Frankfurt School," 125–26, 135–37.

18. Bahr, "Frankfurt School," 136.

19. John Herz, "On Human Survival: How a World-View Emerged," unpublished manuscript, box 2, folder 22, John H. Herz Papers, German and Jewish Intellectual Émigré Collection, M. E. Grenander Department of Special Collections and Archives, State University of New York at Albany Library.

20. Herz, "On Human Survival," 33–37.

21. Herz, "On Human Survival," 35.

22. Herz, "On Human Survival," 182.

23. Herz, "On Human Survival," 33, 166.

24. Herz, "On Human Survival," 103.

25. Herz, "On Human Survival," 48, 62–64, 103, 182. On the enthusiastic Jewish support for the German war effort that belied the catastrophic "stab-in-the-back" myth see the recent study by Tim Grady, *A Deadly Legacy: German Jews and the Great War* (New Haven: Yale University Press). German Jews went beyond mere patriotic duty in advancing the cause of German annexations in the East, with some Jews arguing for German superiority as a justification for such expansionism.

26. Herz, "On Human Survival," 43–44.

27. "Research Project on Anti-Semitism," 124–25.

28. Max Horkheimer, "Re: Anti-Semitism—Spearhead of Nazism," August 28, 1941, 3, Friedrich Papers.

29. Joseph W. Bendersky, "Carl Schmitt's Path to Nuremberg: A Sixty-Year Reassessment," *Telos* 139 (Summer 2007): 6–34.

30. Karl Loewenstein to John H. Herz, February 5, 1972, box 3, folder 73, Herz Papers.

31. Herz, "On Human Survival," 15, 25.

32. Herz, "On Human Survival," 78.

33. Peter Hayes, introduction to *Behemoth: The Structure and Practice of National Socialism, 1933–1944 by Franz Neumann* (Chicago: Ivan R. Dee, 2009), xiv.

34. See Michael Neumann's response to Jonathan Bush, "Raul Hilberg (1926–2007) In Memoriam," *Jewish Quarterly Review* 100, no. 4 (Fall 2010): 664, 671–72, 685.

35. For an extensive examination of Schmitt's life based upon Schmitt's personal papers see Reinhard Mehring, *Carl Schmitt: A Biography*, trans. Daniel Steuer (Malden MA: Polity, 2014).

36. Mehring, *Carl Schmitt*, 271. See also Joseph W. Bendersky, "Ausnahmezustand, Staatsnotstandsplan, and Ermächtigungsgesetz," in *From Weimar to Hitler: Studies in the Dissolution of the Weimar Republic and the Establishment of the Third Reich, 1932–1934*, ed. Larry E. Jones and Hermann Beck (New York: Berghahn, 2018), 52–78.

37. The most complete list of worldwide publications on Schmitt is Alain de Benoist, *Carl Schmitt: International Bibliographie der Primär-und Sekundärliteratur* (Graz: Ares Verlag, 2010).

38. Carl Schmitt, *Glossarium: Aufzeichnungen der Jahre 1947–1951* (Berlin: Duncker & Humblot, 1991), 81, 232

39. Schmitt, *Glossarium*, 252, 255, 264, 297.

40. The efforts by Raphael Gross to discredit all of Schmitt's political and legal theory as inherently antisemitic has not withstood the assessment of scholars around the world, including those of Jewish heritage, who, while greatly disturbed by the revelations of his antisemitism, acknowledge the continuing significance of his numerous intellectual contributions. See Raphael Gross, *Carl Schmitt and the Jews: The "Jewish Question," the Holocaust, and German Legal Theory*, trans. Joel Golb (Madison: University of Wisconsin Press, 2007).

41. Carl Schmitt, *Carl Schmitt Tagebücher: Oktober 1912 bis Februar 1915*, ed. E. Hüsmert (Berlin: Akademie Verlag, 2003), 314–15.

42. Schmitt, *Tagebücher: Oktober 1912 bis Februar 1915*, 99, 200, 220–23, 226, 282, 304.

43. Schmitt, *Tagebücher 1930–1934*, 9, 109, 172, 184, 243, 255, 271, 344, 402, 408–9, 424, 427.

44. Schmitt, *Tagebücher 1930–1934*, 94, 269.

45. Schmitt, *Tagebücher 1930–1934*, 149, 159, 171, 195, 200.

46. Ludwig Feuchtwanger to Carl Schmitt, July 23, 1935, in Carl Schmitt and Ludwig Feuchtwanger, *Briefwechsel, 1918–1935*, ed. Rolf Rieβ (Berlin: Duncker & Humblot, 2007), 397–98.

47. Schmitt, *Tagebücher 1930–1934*, 274–77.

48. John Herz and Erich Hula, "Introduction to Otto Kirchheimer," in *Politics, Law, and Social Change: Selected Essays of Otto Kirchheimer*, eds. Frederic S. Burin and Kurt L. Shell (New York: Columbia University Press, 1969). See also William E. Scheuerman, *Between the Norm and the Exception: The Frankfurt School and the Rule of Law* (Cambridge MA: MIT Press, 1994), and *The Rule of Law under Siege: Selected Essays of Franz L. Neumann and Otto Kirchheimer*, ed. William E. Scheuerman (Berkeley: University of California Press, 1996).

49. Schmitt, *Tagebücher 1930–1934*, 53, 60, 62, 64, 70, 97, 116, 128, 136–37, 146, 149, 157, 159, 164, 181, 206–7, 210, 355.

50. Schmitt, *Tagebücher 1930–1934*, 231.

51. Franz Neumann to Carl Schmitt, November 12, 1930, April 21, 1932, Carl Schmitt Nachlass, Nordrhein-Westfälischen Hauptstaatsarchiv, Düsseldorf, RW 265-10356-10357.

52. See Scheuerman, *Between the Norm and the Exception*.

53. Franz Neumann to Carl Schmitt, September 7, 1932, Schmitt Nachlass, RW 265–10358/1–3.

54. Franz Neumann to Carl Schmitt, December 12, 1932, Schmitt Nachlass, RW 265–10359/1–3.

55. Schmitt, *Tagebücher 1930–1934*, 220.

56. Franz Neumann letter of July 22, 1933, and Otto Kirchheimer curriculum vitae, February 4, 1941, "Emergency Committee in Aid of Displaced Foreign Scholars," boxes 18 and 25, Manuscripts and Archival Collections, New York Public Library.

57. Otto Kirchheimer, "State Structure and Law in the Third Reich"; and "Criminal Law in National Socialist Germany," in Scheuerman, *The Rule of Law under Siege*, 142–43, 173. Otto Kirchheimer, "In Quest of Sovereignty," in Burin and Shell, *Politics, Law, and Social Change*, 191.

58. Herz, "On Human Survival," 159.

59. Arkadij Gurland to Otto Kirchheimer, October 11, 1957, box 1, Otto Kirchheimer Papers, German and Jewish Intellectual Émigré Collection, State University of New York at Albany Library, Series 1, Personal Correspondence, 1927–1965.

60. Karl Loewenstein to John H. Herz, August 11, 1969, Herz Papers, box 3, folder 73.

61. Franz Neumann, "The Decay of German Democracy," in Scheuerman, *The Rule of Law under Siege*, 40.

62. Neumann, *Behemoth*, 43, 45, 49, 65–66, 71, 74, 98, 125, 152–54, 163, 448, 453, 469, 480–83, 492–93, 516, 523.

63. See the attacks on Schmitt by Waldemar Gurian and Otto Knab in *Deutsche Briefe: Ein Blatt der Katholischen Emigration*, ed. Heinz Hürten, 2 vols. (Mainz: Matthias-Grunwald Verlag, 1969). On Schmitt's struggles with Nazi rivals and his compromises culminating in the Jewish Conference see Joseph W. Bendersky, *Carl Schmitt: Theorist for the Reich* (Princeton: Princeton University Press, 1983), 223–31, 240–42; and Mehring, *Carl Schmitt*, 359–60, 378–80.

64. Carl Schmitt-Otto Kirchheimer Correspondence, Schmitt Nachlass, RW 265-7593-7605, 20483.

65. Otto Kirchheimer-Ernst Friesenhahn Correspondence, box 1, Kirchheimer Papers, Series 1, Personal Correspondence, 1927–1965.

66. Hayes, introduction to *Behemoth*, xv.

67. See Siegfried Lokatis, "Wilhelm Stapel und Carl Schmitt—Ein Briefwechsel," *Schmittiana: Beiträge zu Leben und Werk Carl Schmitts*, ed. Piet Tommissen, Band V (1996); Carl Schmitt-Hugo Fischer Correspondence, Schmitt Nachlass, RW 265-3564-3624.

68. For the most recent significant research of this kind see Larry E. Jones, "Conservative Antisemitism in the Weimar Republic: A Case Study of the German Nationalist People's Party"; Brian E. Crim, "Weimar's 'Burning Question': Situational Antisemitism and the German Combat Leagues, 1918–1933;" and Ulrike Ehret, "Antisemitism and the Jewish Question in the Political Worldview of the Catholic Right," in *The German Right in the Weimar Republic: Studies in the History of German Conservatism, Nationalism, and Antisemitism*, ed. Larry E. Jones (New York: Berghahn, 2014), 79–108, 194–243.

69. See, for example, David Bankier, ed., *Probing the Depths of German Antisemitism: German Society and the Persecution of the Jews, 1933–1941* (New York: Berghahn, 2000), and *The Germans and the Final Solution: Public Opinion under Nazism* (Oxford: Blackwell, 1992).

70. Ulrich Scheuner to Carl J. Friedrich, February 28, 1934, box 37, Friedrich Papers (HUGFP) 17.6.

71. Neumann, Behemoth, 121.

72. For a critical discussion of this interpretation see Robert R. Schandley, ed., *Unwilling Germans: The Goldhagen Debate*, trans. Jeremiah Riemer (Minneapolis: University of Minnesota Press, 1998).

2

Antisemitism and Totalitarian Movements
Thinking Again about Hannah Arendt

JEAN CAHAN

A volume of essays surveying and reassessing much of Hannah Arendt's work was published in the year 2000 in the Cambridge Companion series.[1] The essays are, of course, at the highest level of scholarship and subtlety. But one additional theme might have deserved its own chapter: antisemitism as an element in totalitarian movements. Although antisemitism is touched upon in several of the essays in the volume, it does not receive any extended treatment. Two other sets of essays, by Richard J. Bernstein and George Kateb, deal more extensively with Arendt's analysis of antisemitism and its connection to totalitarianism, but they share a major shortcoming that I would like to address.[2] Especially in a forum dedicated to studying methods of teaching about the Holocaust, it is appropriate to reassess the methodological as well as substantive issues raised by Arendt's analysis of antisemitism and its place in her renowned work on totalitarian movements. A related matter is the concept of a political religion as a means of explaining totalitarian movements. I shall briefly examine Arendt's views on this as it relates to her analysis of antisemitism.

The paper follows the theme of antisemitism mainly in Arendt's groundbreaking work *The Origins of Totalitarianism* (1951), though I shall occasionally refer to other writings. It is my contention that Arendt not only used sources that were themselves antisemitic, as has been noted, but that her own analysis perpetuated certain antisemitic tropes. This is astonishing in the work of a philosopher known for highlighting the problematic legal and political status of refugees and the stateless, and for promoting a cosmopolitan worldview, universal human rights, and the unity of humanity. In the current climate of resurging antisemitism her analysis of antisemitism is, to say the least, not helpful.

Arendt's Account of Antisemitism

It has been remarked that the reader's first impression of the *Origins* is its strangeness. I think this bewildering quality arises from Arendt's unacknowledged use of two different methods for writing about her subject. In all three volumes, though she devotes the majority of the description and analysis to economic, social and political *systems*, she tends also to put a great deal of weight on the role of certain *individuals* whom she regards as emblematic of the phenomenon she is discussing. In volume one it is Proust and Dreyfus; in volume two it is Cecil Rhodes, Lord Cromer, and later Georg von Schönerer; and in volume three it is Hitler and Stalin. This leads her to the border of psychological rather than political interpretation, and to large claims based on single biographies. The generally problematic nature of her method has been noted by the distinguished political theorist Seyla Benhabib, who wrote that "it is too systematically ambitious and overinterpreted to be a strictly historical account; it is too anecdotal, narrative, and ideographic to be considered social science; and although it has the vivacity and the stylistic flair of a work of political journalism, it is too philosophical to be accessible to a broad public."[3]

The view of Western European antisemitism put forward by Arendt in volume one of *The Origins of Totalitarianism* is mainly an economic and social one.[4] Barely noticing millennia of antisemitic traditions and tropes—religious, economic or cultural—and dismissing the Eastern European framework, she begins her broadly chronological account of modern antisemitism with the claim that there were significant shifts in the socioeconomic position of Western European Jews after the eighteenth century, which helped to establish a distinctively modern antisemitism that had the potential to become an element of later totalitarianisms. Prior to the French Revolution (1789), a small number of court Jews performed useful financial and commercial functions for various monarchic rulers and received special privileges in return.

The vast majority of Jews lived at a considerably lower economic level and enjoyed few protections, if any; they neither possessed nor sought to acquire any form of political responsibility or social hope. After the Revolution a broader class of Jewish financiers emerged that was useful to the state. Intellectuals, and educated Jews more generally, also now became socially somewhat more acceptable and in communication with, if not exactly integrated into, the ruling classes. Rahel Varnhagen, Moses Mendelssohn, Marcel Proust, and Benjamin Disraeli are all examples here. This trend, in Arendt's account, came to a bitter end with the Dreyfus Affair, a disruption of the first order.

Let us listen to Arendt's language in describing this purported pattern of development: "Thus a perfect harmony of interests was established between the powerful Jews and the state."[5] "Many of these bankers [who were both needed and exploited by the class of small shopkeepers] were Jews and, even more important, the general figure of the banker *bore definite Jewish traits* for historical reasons."[6] Arendt does not say what these distinctive traits might be, but the Rothschilds were a prime example. In Arendt's view, this explains the resentment toward Jews that led many lower and lower middle-class workers, shopkeepers and artisans to adhere to conservative and antisemitic political parties.

Although it should be obvious that not all European bankers were Jewish, at times Arendt seems to suppose that they were. She states, for example, that Jewish bankers—namely the Rothschilds—controlled the Austrian railroads, and that therefore certain members of the Austrian Parliament were understandably in favor of seeking a policy of nationalization.[7] But this is simply not an accurate description of the situation. First, while in the particular case of the *Nordbahn* there was an extended debate within the cabinet and parliament as to private versus public ownership, it was not a debate about private *Jewish* ownership. Other Austrian railroads had long been in the hands of the state; there was, therefore, a precedent for public ownership that had nothing to do with removing Jewish shareholders. Second, it was only after construction of the Nordbahn was well underway, and costs far exceeded the planned budget, that the Rothschilds stepped in with a very large cash infusion. Subsequently, the Nordbahn line between Vienna and the eastern province of Galicia (with the capital of Lviv/Lemberg) became quite profitable for the shareholders (of various ethnicities). Certain ministers' doubts about a state takeover of the line centered on the costs to the state of such a takeover and how that would affect spending on foreign policy objectives, including military expenditures. These doubts were not the result of what Arendt presumes to be the Jewish stranglehold on state finances.[8]

The issue of ownership of the Nordbahn did become an occasion for antisemitic incitement on the part of right-wing extremists, who nonetheless remained a very small minority. But it is difficult to understand how, given the facts of the matter, Arendt could write the following about Georg von Schönerer, a vehement antisemite and leader of the (Austrian) German Liberal Party:

> His main advantage was that he could base his antisemitic propaganda on *demonstrable facts*: as a member of the Austrian Reichsrat he had fought for nationalization of the Austrian railroads, *the major part of which had been in the hands of the Rothschilds since 1836* due to a state license which expired in 1886. . . . The close connection between the Rothschilds and the financial interests of the monarchy became very obvious when the government tried to extend the license under conditions which were patently to the disadvantage of the state as well as the public. Schönerer's agitation in this matter became the actual beginning of an articulate antisemitic movement in Austria.[9]

As noted above, the government was actually quite divided on the question of the future of the Nordbahn line, and renewing the private license did not disadvantage the state. Nor was it any kind of giveaway; it was the result of hard negotiations in which the Rothschilds themselves were not altogether satisfied.[10] Again, contrary to Arendt's claim about "demonstrable facts," the history of share ownership in the Austrian railroads was a great deal more complicated than she allowed. Although for an initial stretch of railroad from Vienna to Bochnia, Galicia, the Rothschilds owned the larger part of shares (the building concession for what was to be called the *Kaiser Ferdinand Nordbahn* was acquired by the

Rothschilds in 1835), they soon sold those shares to the Nordbahn company, in which other investors, including members of the public, also participated. The imperial government launched a public investment program in 1841.[11] Further, while the Rothschilds were major shareholders in the Nordbahn, this was not the case in the many other Austrian railroad branches or networks such as the Southern Railway, which went to the region of Trieste. By 1854 (not 1886, as Arendt would have us believe) seventy percent of railways in Austria were state-owned. Arendt also neglects to mention (though, or because, her main source was a biography of von Schönerer published in 1935) that von Schönerer's father, Matthias von Schönerer, was a major participant in the development of the Southern Railway.[12] A Greek financier, Georgios Sinas, also had a large role.

There are many pages in this vein. Arendt's biographer, Elisabeth Young-Bruehl, later described Arendt's disapproval of the French Rothschilds' philanthropic efforts in the 1930s and of their unwillingness to rock the boat, which she saw as the result of their "parvenu" rather than "pariah" status; perhaps this was in the back of Arendt's mind as she wrote about the Rothschilds in *Origins*.[13] Nonetheless it is surprising that none of the major scholars of Arendt's work have commented on these claims, which seem uncomfortably close to longstanding antisemitic complaints about Jews as being exceptionally devoted to money and ensconced in mysterious cabals relating to finance and power. As we will see in volume two of *Origins*, Arendt seems to have adopted some of the very antisemitic "interpretations" of modern history—by various analysts on both the right and the left—that she is seeking to understand. A much more detailed and nuanced analysis of the socioeconomic classes existing in all the European empires—French, German, Russian, and Austrian—and their relations to Jews and to antisemitism would be required to support any such claims about Jewish financiers, state power, and the emergence of modern antisemitism.

Shulamit Volkov's work contains much better grounded analyses of the rise of German and Austrian antisemitic political parties, and their appeal (or lack of it) to German artisans and lower-class workers more generally. Volkov argues that *political* antisemitism (as opposed to socioeconomic antisemitism), in which antisemitic attitudes and rhetoric were instrumentalized for wider political purposes, arose in the revolutionary period around 1848—much earlier than the late 1880s, when Arendt's schema would have it appear. Second and third waves arose between 1875 and 1882 and then in the 1890s. But political antisemitism, according to Volkov, was an erratic phenomenon, not strictly correlated with economic depression, imperialism, or the collapse of the nation-state, which were all vital factors for Arendt. It was also limited: the political parties that utilized antisemitic "codes" did not attain more than about 2.3 percent of the popular vote even at their height. Artisans and shopkeepers were not uniformly antisemitic in the second half of the nineteenth century.[14]

For Volkov, the antisemitism of the pre–World War I era was primarily a cultural phenomenon. Antisemitic texts and tropes provided one unifying theme in worldviews that were actually conglomerations of many other views: generally anti-modern attitudes; hostility to liberalism, capitalism, democracy, and socialism; a longing for imperial greatness as well as extreme nationalism; nostalgia for bygone eras of (imagined?) greater community (*Gemeinschaft*); fascination with war. In addition, there were the massive disruptions of the economic depression of 1873 and the strains of the wars of German unification.[15] All of these elements worked to create a crisis of identity. Antisemitic, anti-Jewish language and slogans functioned as a code or keyword for this entire constellation of beliefs, attitudes, and resentments, which were often pulled together by a given political spokesperson or party. But the fortunes of these parties were very uneven.

Volkov also maintains that this constellation collapsed around 1918. The antisemitisms of the Weimar Republic and the Nazi era were not the same, despite some initial and superficial similarities. Here Volkov touches upon the vexed question of continuity in both German history and Jewish history. While Volkov might seem to be aligning herself with what she sees as Arendt's own emphasis on a radical break between traditional and modern antisemitism, I don't think Arendt was unambiguous in drawing such a

Trennungsstrich. Arendt insisted, especially in volume three of *Origins*, on the novelty of nineteenth-century political antisemitism and the phenomenon of totalitarianism, but unlike Volkov she also saw a continuity between the modern political antisemitism of the nineteenth century and the antisemitism of the Hitler and Stalin periods. The significance of Schönerer, for Arendt, lay in his influence on Hitler. That was surely the point of devoting the first volume of *Origins* to the antisemitic element of totalitarianism. Though we might note here that Arendt did not carry out a comparable analysis of antisemitism as an element of ideological Bolshevism—either because she had no time, or because it simply wasn't there in a comparable way until long after the 1917 revolution.

Although much has been made in the scholarly literature of Arendt's use of the term *element* to replace any notion of cause, and a related metaphor of crystallization rather than development or evolution, Arendt held to a certain amount of chronological continuity between the political antisemitism of the nineteenth century and the post–World War I contexts and also affirmed a good measure of spatial or geographical similarity: "To a certain extent, what happened in France in the eighties and nineties happened thirty and forty years later in all European nation-states. Despite chronological distances, the Weimar and Austrian Republics had much in common historically with the Third Republic [in France], and certain political and social patterns in the Germany and Austria of the twenties and thirties seemed almost consciously to follow the model of France's *fin-de-siecle*."[16] This is certainly convenient from a scholarly point of view, as, if true, it would save one a lot of academically specialized spadework. But as the small example of Rothschild railroad ownership shows, each national case has to be investigated much more exactly than Arendt cared to.

I turn now to the heart of her analysis, volume two of *Origins*, on nineteenth-century imperialism and Arendt's understanding of how it related to both the antisemitism and totalitarianism of the twentieth century. A remaining major theme arising in volume one of *Origins* is that of political responsibility and the Jews' lack of it. But I defer that discussion to a later section.

Imperialism and Racism

According to Arendt, the main contribution of nineteenth-century European imperialism to the advent of twentieth-century totalitarianism was twofold: racism and bureaucracy. Racism developed primarily in South Africa, and bureaucracy in Algeria and Egypt. But both became important elements of totalitarianism in Germany and Russia.

At the most general level Arendt held to a broadly Marxist-Leninist analysis of imperialism. In this view imperialism was the process of export of surplus financial capital from Europe to Africa and other parts of the world. Export of money was eventually accompanied by the export of government and military power. In this way "the position of financiers in general and Jewish financiers in particular was consolidated."[17] The imperialist era was one in which "businessmen became politicians."[18]

Along with the export of capital and government power went the removal of "human debris" from the arena of Europe. It would take us too far afield to examine Arendt's idiosyncratic conceptualization of mobs, masses and superfluous people. On the one hand it is a conception that revealed a great deal of empathy for, and insight into the political conditions of, people displaced by the economic crises and wars that took place in Europe between 1866 and 1933. On the other hand it is a largely undifferentiated conception, extremely vague as to the time periods, geographic locations, and ethnicities involved. It also carries a slightly contemptuous tone—what one might describe today as elitist. Be that as it may, Arendt held that European human debris fled to Africa, Canada, and Australia in order to find a solution to the now-permanent "evil" of superfluity.[19] Thus an alliance was formed between surplus people and surplus capital.[20]

Southern Africa drew all kinds of displaced and superfluous persons, adventurers, and even middle-class professionals because of its richness in gold and diamonds. Once there, these "lost" Europeans discovered that the actual hard work of mining gold or diamonds could be shifted to indigenous people. In this way began a practical, experiential division between whites and blacks that was soon followed by an ideology justifying the increasingly exploitative and cruel state of affairs. "Racism is the main ideological weapon of imperialist [expansionist] politics."[21] Racists of all kinds, especially those of southern Africa, rejected, usually consciously, any assumption of the unity of humanity or the fundamental equality and relatedness of all human beings. Their ideology laid out in considerable detail the exclusion of certain peoples and races from humanity, and the necessary superiority of certain races and people over others. While Arendt devoted many pages to race-thinking within Europe (mainly in France and Germany), she saw the manifestations of racism in Africa as perhaps the most important source of later totalitarian thinking in this regard.

In general, she holds, whites in southern Africa came to believe in and openly claim an essential superiority over blacks. The main example of this is to be found among the Boers, but holds true of all the whites: they assumed the nonexistence of any fundamental commonality with blacks—that is, they denied the underlying unity of humanity. This point, Arendt believed, marked the first time in history when Christianity ceased to function as a "curb on the dangerous perversions of human self-consciousness."[22] An interesting point when one considers some of the later weaknesses of Christian churches under the Nazi regime.

According to Arendt, the Boers, adhering to the Dutch Reformed Church, were the most egregious example of this process. "Like the Jews, they saw themselves as a chosen people, with the essential difference that they were not chosen for the divine salvation of mankind, but lazy domination over another species." They stood apart from Christian missionaries of all other denominations. In their distorted version of Christianity, they themselves were to be worshipped as divinities. According to this interpretation "miserable white men [recent descendants of European debris] were [to be worshipped] by unfortunate black men."[23]

Arendt provides no evidence that Boers actually held these beliefs, or that these views on race relations derived from the theology of the Dutch Reformed Church. She merely makes another of her typical summary statements: the Boers changed passages of the Old Testament "which did not yet transcend the limits of old Israelite religion" in such a way that their own (Boer) views became a superstition that "one could not even say amounted to a heresy."[24] I take this to mean that the Boers translated some particularistic, nationalistic, early passages in the Hebrew Bible, before Judaism became a religion containing universalistic ideas, in such a way as to support the parochial, nationalistic view they had of their own importance.

As was her wont, Arendt passed over a complicated social as well as religious history, in this case of colonization.[25] There were significant social and cultural differences between various groups of settlers—for example, between settlers in the western and eastern parts of southern Africa, and between Lutheran and Calvinist settlers. These differences led at times to varying moral outlooks on matters of daily importance as well as race. Moreover, the example of the ancient Israelites was interpreted in a multiplicity of ways, not only in regard to chosenness. There was a profound sense of being in the natural wilderness and dependent on forces beyond their control, or divine providence, as the Jews believed themselves to have been. Boer settlers were constantly aware of the unpredictability of their enterprise, especially during the Great Trek. Nonetheless Arendt was doubtless correct in pointing to Afrikaner biological racism: the distinction between "black blood" and "Christian blood" that can be found in diaries, traveler accounts, and sermons (though she herself did not rely on such sources). But the fateful consequences of this particular racism played out mainly in Africa itself. Arendt does not explain why this form of racism, as opposed to earlier forms of racism on the part of Europeans in the Americas, should have been the main forerunner of Nazi racism. Nor do Herbert Spencer or social Darwinism make any appearance in her analysis.

Despite the substantial shortcomings of Arendt's historical and theological analysis of the Boers, it is of interest for our topic because Arendt goes on to relate the Boer sense of chosenness to two other matters: the role of Jews in the development of South Africa, and the role of Boer racism in the ultimate emergence of Nazi ideology via the so-called European pan-movements.

As in volume one on the question of Austrian railroad ownership, so here in volume two, in the case of the South African diamond and gold rushes, Arendt highlights the role played by Jewish financiers and fails to note the presence of financiers from other ethnicities and religious backgrounds. "This gold rush [at Witwatersrand] was financed, organized and connected with the ordinary European economy through accumulated superfluous wealth and with the help of Jewish financiers. From the very beginning 'a hundred or so Jewish merchants who have gathered like eagles over their prey' actually acted as middlemen through whom European capital was invested in the gold and diamond industries."[26]

"Financiers were mostly Jews but they were only representatives, not owners, of the superfluous capital."[27] While this lack of ownership meant that Jews were not the ones who "introduced violence into [capitalist or financial] speculation," it also meant that the Jews remained in some sense detached from ultimate reality; they had a "phantom-like existence" in South Africa, and by implication in the European field as well. Their existence was tinged with "futility" and irresponsibility, to use one of Arendt's favorite words.[28] In fact, Jewish financiers were in the company of Lutheran, Dutch, German, and Swedish financiers, among others, as common sense would predict.[29] In some cases Jews were owners of capital and were involved in joint investment projects with non-Jews, the Wernher-Beit Company being a prominent example.

As if the reference to Jewish financiers' vulture-like qualities were not enough, Arendt carries on with her description in more pejorative terms. The Jewish managers or non-owners of investment capital in South Africa were part of "the mob," the human debris that Arendt saw everywhere.[30] The mob were not the masses. They "belonged to a class formed in the 1870s and 1880s in all European capitals where they had come to try their luck in the international stock-market gamble." The older, more assimilated and refined Jewish families of European capitals were "too weak to stop the unscrupulousness of the newcomers."[31] The new Jewish financiers, some of whom participated in South African enterprises, "had become as superfluous in legitimate Jewish banking as the wealth they represented had become superfluous in legitimate industrial enterprise." In South Africa they were the middlemen between "capital and the mob" and "soon became more conspicuous than anybody else."[32] Faintly aware that she might be perpetuating a harmful negative stereotype, Arendt adds, "The fact of their Jewish origin added an undefinable symbolic flavor to their role of financiers. To this must be added their actual international connections, which naturally stimulated the general popular delusions about Jewish political power all over the world."[33] However, as we have seen, Arendt herself did nothing to correct this delusion. Indeed she fueled it with her focus on Jewish financiers as opposed to others, and her claims about their mob origins and unscrupulousness.

Arendt seems—without apparent self-consciousness—to have simply imported or concocted a superficial analysis of South African history and Jewish economic activity in South Africa. Possibly the influence of Marxism-Leninism and its suspicion of Jews and Judaism came through her husband Heinrich Bluecher and his reading of Rosa Luxemburg; he was a committed communist. It is known that Arendt discussed her book in great detail with him.[34] Margaret Canovan, a leading authority on Arendt's political philosophy, argues that the question of Arendt's relation to Marxism is not all that important.[35] Far more important than the socioeconomic analysis of imperialism, for Canovan, is Arendt's great political insight that imperialism was the idea of expansion for expansion's sake, and power for power's sake. This was imperialism's contribution to totalitarian movements: the notion that power, expansion of territory, and expansion of domination over others, are intrinsic goods and ends in themselves. I think this is right. But if we are to be serious in understanding antisemitism as an element of modern political movements, then surely it will not do to simply pass over in silence Arendt's own errors in regard to the nature and role of antisemitism in these wider political processes. I cannot accept Canovan brushing past Arendt's tendency to blame the victim, that is, to assign the causes of antisemitism to Jews themselves, with their "undefinable symbolic flavor."

Arendt goes on to argue that the Boer notion of chosenness, their belief in the inherent superiority of their race and nation, as well as their hostility to all foreigners and especially to Jews (though she does not cite examples of the latter) was emulated—even if not entirely consciously—by the pan-German and pan-Slav movements, significant forerunners of both Nazism and Bolshevism. "Nazism and Bolshevism owe more to Pan-Germanism and to Pan-Slavism than to any other ideology or political movement."[36] While the part of this statement that concerns Bolshevism is simply false, the influence of pan-Germanism on Nazism is more readily demonstrable, and I turn now to a further exploration of that point. But in closing this section I would like to note one of Arendt's more perspicacious comments about South Africa and the Boers. She remarks that the Boers were probably the first to sacrifice all rational motives, and especially the profit motive, to race. She gives the example of the removal of Bantu employees from work on the railroads in South Africa while white workers were hired at more than double the cost. This is an illuminating precursor to the apparently irrational—because perhaps ultimately not economically beneficial—motives of the Nazis in their administration of the concentration and death camps. Also interesting is Arendt's conclusion that Boer beliefs about race were overtaken by the Nazi attempt to "turn the German people into a race."[37] Thus the Boers remained in a sense the model for race-thinking, but became, as it were, outdated. This is consonant with Arendt's view that, by the time the Nazis came to prominence, the socioeconomic importance of the Jews in Europe, so evident in the nineteenth century, had been eroded. While one would have expected that antisemitism—understood by Arendt to be primarily socioeconomic in nature—therefore also declined, this turned out not be the case. Antisemitism, like the Jewish financiers, became detached from reality.

Antisemitism and the Pan-Movements

As Sartre had done before her in his essay "Anti-Semite and Jew," Arendt drew a distinction between "ordinary" ethnic chauvinism or power politics and a new type of ethnicity-based thinking and aim of world conquest. She called the latter *continental imperialism* (in contrast to the overseas imperialism of the late nineteenth century). The goals of a Germanized central Europe or a Russianized eastern and southern Europe were no longer the issue; something mystical, transcendent was at play. Behind a "smokescreen" of talk about national rights of self-determination, the emerging totalitarian movements in Germany and Russia actually pursued new levels of expansionism and "inherited an aura of holiness."[38] They recalled the glories of the Holy Roman Empire of the German Nation and of Holy Russia; the latter name would be chosen for a small extremist pan-Slavic movement. Here Arendt begins to adumbrate what would later become the concept of a political religion, articulated by scholars such as Eric Voegelin, Waldemar Gurian, Hans Maier, and most recently by Emilio Gentile and Michael Ley.[39] Continental imperialism, pan-Germanism, and pan-Slavism were corollaries to what Arendt saw as a new form of nationalism in the late nineteenth century, which she termed "tribal nationalism" and asserted was different from "Western nationalism."[40] Tribal nationalism was "pseudo-mystical nonsense, enriched by arbitrary historical memories." This nonsense was a powerful emotional catalyst and "seemed to transcend . . . the limitations of nationalism."[41] Tribal nationalism claimed that even those born and raised far from the core of the nation possessed the relevant tribal consciousness and should be counted as members. Thus, for example, men of French ancestry born in North Africa should be considered French, whether or not they could speak French or had any knowledge of French culture; the same could be said of Baltic Germans and many other subgroups. In each case what counted were "some mysterious qualities of body or soul." This peculiar identification of national identity with spirit or soul, Arendt argued, would prove very dangerous through its manifestations in the pan-movements.

Arendt's main example of a pan-movement is the pan-Germanism of the Austrian Georg von Schönerer. Again, as we saw earlier in this chapter and in volume one of *The Origins of Totalitarianism*, Arendt returns to von Schönerer's preoccupation with the wealth of the Rothschilds. But now, in the context of the "pseudo-mystical nonsense" of tribal nationalism and of the pan-movements, antisemitism must be seen in a new light, for the Jews' domination of the Austrian railroad system "by itself is not enough to generate antisemitism as the mainstay of a national ideology."[42] Rather, "the clue to the sudden emergence of antisemitism as the center of a whole outlook on life and on the world"—as it would become in the Nazi ideology—"lies in the nature of tribalism."[43] This is no longer the antisemitism of the Dreyfus Affair or earlier episodes of German antisemitism. "The true significance of the pan-movements is that hatred of the Jews was for the first time severed from all actual experience concerning the Jewish people ... and followed only the peculiar logic of an ideology." Though I would argue with Arendt's assertion that this was the first time in history that antisemitism was detached from actual experience of Jews and Judaism, I believe she is pointing to an essential feature of the Nazi form of totalitarianism, one which Gavin Langmuir has also analyzed: namely, its hallucinatory quality or, to put it another way, its religious intensity.[44] Volume three of *Origins* will again pick up this theme of political religion: the masses want to escape from the reality of their essential homelessness and therefore sink into totalitarian ideologies and movements.[45] While von Schönerer and his party, as Arendt notes, obtained a relatively small number of votes and parliamentary seats, their ideas resonated far into the future, into the mind of Hitler.

Arendt attributes the rise of tribal nationalism and its constituent antisemitism to rootlessness on a mass scale, as she does with just about every other feature of modernity. A great deal has been written about this concept in Arendt's work, and its echoes of Heidegger's "thrownness." It would take us too far afield to consider it further here. But whether or not this is a concept that comports well with historical reality, I think Arendt has a correct insight when she says that, while "traditional" nationalism by itself may not have been a means of satisfying religious needs in a secularized world, the new tribal nationalism or the pan-movements did "offer a new religious theory and a new concept of holiness."[46] It was this quality that not only permitted but encouraged extraordinary sacrifice, of oneself but mostly of the other. "This kind of fanaticism does not simply abuse religious language—behind it lies a veritable theology which gave the earlier pan-movements their momentum and retained a considerable influence on the development of modern totalitarian movements." In this theology the people or nation in question is seen as having its own divine origin, not one that can be accounted for through the Biblical conception of a common human origin. Individuals born into such a nation receive whatever dignity they have through the nation, and do not possess it in themselves except indirectly.[47] To deny or give up one's nationality is thus to deny one's intrinsic nature and obligations; it is, in short, to betray.

In a somewhat surprising passage, given what Arendt has had to say about Jews, Arendt underscores a further difference between the pan-movements and what she sees as the Judeo-Christian tradition: not only do they differ in regard to the common origin of humanity, they differ in the political consequences of their metaphysical outlooks. A consequence of the Judeo-Christian tradition is that a commonality and equality of political purpose can be established on the basis of the religious and metaphysical assumption of a common original humanity. But for the pan-movements, because no such equality of origin exists, political rights and purposes also cannot be equal. "Racism denies the common origin of man and repudiates the common purposes of humanity. There is a divine origin of one people and not of others."[48] This line of thought was especially appealing to eastern Europeans, whom Arendt relishes referring to as "the belt of mixed populations" from the Baltic to the Adriatic (the phrase occurs several times not only in *Origins*, but in the book on the Eichmann trial and other essays). These largely deracinated eastern European peoples "felt earlier the terror of the ideal of humanity and the Judeo-Christian faith in the common origin of man. They did not harbor any illusions about the 'noble savage.'"[49] The implication is that eastern European populations were therefore especially susceptible to the enticements of pan-Slavism or even totalitarianism, though she does not explain this further.

Unfortunately, Arendt then goes on to link the thinking behind the pan-movements to "the rootless existence of the Jewish people."[50] Arendt does not question whether the Jewish people were in fact rootless, but points to Jews being perceived as "a perfect example of a people in a tribal sense."[51] This would mean that, though

Jews often had no knowledge of their own original language or culture, being a dispersed people par excellence, they retained a belief in a sort of spiritual unity and organized themselves accordingly. Their capacity for cohesive organization "became the model that the pan-movements were striving to emulate," and constituted "proof of the correctness of racial theories."[52] She then adds, "Although other nationalities in the Dual Monarchy [Austria-Hungary] were but weakly rooted in the soil, and had little sense of the meaning of a common territory, Jews had no home at all but had kept their national identity."[53] This statement is extremely dubious at best. Jewish communities from Worms to Warsaw had been in their respective locations for hundreds of years—often for well over a thousand years. How can one say that European Jews "had no home at all"? This is simply a regurgitation of an empty and pernicious stereotype, though it is true and well-known that the idea of a common past in Biblical Palestine, and the hope for a future there, were also an ideational reality that contributed importantly to Jewish identity.

Arendt's main point in discussing pan-German attitudes to Jews is to underscore the desire to imitate the ineffable sense of Jewish unity, of "Jewishness" as opposed to Judaism: just as "some mysterious inherent psychological or physical quality made them the incarnation of Germanism if not Germany, [the Pan-Germans] knew that the Jewishness of assimilated Jews was exactly the same kind of individual embodiment of Judaism and that the peculiar pride of secularized Jews, who had not given up the claim to chosenness, really meant that they believed they were better."[54] It was therefore logical for both pan-movements to turn hostile to Jews, because the sense of chosenness on the part of both religious and secular Jews "came dangerously close to its racial perversion."[55] It was the Jews, according to Arendt, who had imported fanaticism into Western culture through the idea of chosenness. Their ancient myths enabled "modern mob leaders to drag God into the petty conflicts between peoples.... The hatred of the racists against the Jews sprang from a superstitious apprehension that it might actually be the Jews, and not themselves, whom God had chosen ... [they] feared that the Jews would be the final victors in world history."[56]

There are so many things wrong with this analysis that it is difficult to know where to begin. First, one cannot prove that secularized Jews had a self-conception of being "better" or that they had simply translated religious chosenness into secular life and culture. The category of secularized Jews is vast; whom exactly did she have in mind? (Herself, perhaps.) While many politically engaged persons of Jewish ancestry were indeed preoccupied with redeeming the world, so were many other non-Jewish revolutionaries and reformers. But beyond them were innumerable Jewish-origin scientists, scholars, and professionals. Did they all share this purported sense of superiority? Second, and perhaps more important, is Arendt's misconstruing of the Jewish religious idea of chosenness, a misreading shared by generations of Christian and other antisemites. It is as much or more a sense of *obligation* than of *superiority* or obligation following upon superiority. Third, Arendt's psychological analysis here is speculative; empirical evidence relating to Georg von Schönerer's beliefs seems less to show someone entangled in quasi-religious, transcendent "pseudo-mystical nonsense" than a very pragmatic member of parliament bent on passing specific legislation against Austrian Jews out of simple hatred and prejudice. At other moments, however, he had no interest in parliamentary democracy and sought to overcome or destroy the state as such. In the assessment of one historian, he was either a confused obstructionist or a reluctant and failed revolutionary.[57] Later examples, such as Martha Ludendorff (wife of General Ludendorff, who oversaw the defeat of the German armed forces in World War I), who was a devoted member of the Thule Gesellschaft (forerunner of the Germanen Orden), might have better served Arendt's purpose of describing a mystical sense of Germanness.

Volume two of *Origins of Totalitarianism* closes with continued ruminations on the nature and meaning of rootlessness, statelessness, and the universal human right of membership in a political community. Arendt's analyses of these topics are rightly seen as conceptually innovative and powerful, providing bases for further thought still needed today, and encouraging a cosmopolitan stance that may be timely in an age of resurgent nationalism. But again, interspersed, are comments on the roles of Jews that would leave many Jews as aghast as they were in response to Arendt's later *Eichmann in Jerusalem*.

One of the main consequences of World War I, according to Arendt, was the further spread of ideas of *inequality*, especially in the form of increasing disparagement of equality under moral and political laws. Such disparagement had already been promulgated by imperialist racism and the pan-movements. Now, as a result of widespread migration, homelessness, and statelessness in the aftermath of war, and the reconfiguration of national territories through the many postwar peace treaties, the problem of ethnic minorities presented itself anew on a very large scale. The Jews were a familiar case, being likewise affected by the various minorities treaties of the early 1920s. For this problem Hitler was to find a "solution"; his system of extermination camps became "an eloquent demonstration to the rest of the world how really to 'liquidate' all problems concerning minorities and the stateless."[58] However, Arendt continues, Hitler's solution did not *really* solve the Jewish question. It was solved only after the war, "namely, by means of a colonized and then conquered territory—but this solved neither the problem of the minorities nor the stateless. On the contrary, like virtually every other event in our century, the solution of the Jewish question merely produced a new category of refugees, the Arabs, thereby increasing the number of stateless and rightless by another 700,000. . . . What happened in Palestine was repeated in India."[59]

Margaret Canovan, referring to volume one of *Origins*, has acknowledged that Arendt's analysis of antisemitism "has a subtext which is in some ways even more abrasive than that which Arendt's Jewish critics detected and excoriated later in *Eichmann in Jerusalem*."[60] She accounts for Arendt's "abrasiveness" through Arendt's distinctive ideas on political responsibility and Zionism and "her desire to claim for the Jews equal status as a people among peoples."[61] But through her calm explication of Arendt's views on other topics (e.g., political responsibility), Canovan papers over the ugly "subtext" that she herself spells out: "the predicament of the Jews had largely been their own doing," "they had conducted themselves in certain ways without ever asking themselves what the political implications of their conduct might be," and in this way contributed to the development of racism.[62] Canovan takes no notice of the paragraph in volume three on the question of Palestine, quoted above, or Arendt's statement that, even after the Holocaust, the "Jewish question" remained unsolved until another atrocity was committed against Arabs in the course of the establishment of Israel.

Similarly, Richard Bernstein and George Kateb, distinguished analysts of Arendt's thought, seek to respond to the disturbing text—not subtext—by arguing for what they see as Arendt's intellectual honesty and rigorous conception of political responsibility.[63] Like Canovan, Bernstein points to Arendt's view, expressed in volume one, that Jews "do not wish under any circumstances to discuss their share of responsibility."[64] Arendt constantly emphasized that "it is our responsibility to look after the world and for what is done in our name."[65] For centuries if not millennia, according to Arendt, Jews avoided political action in this sense, and they were therefore completely unable to cope with new forms of antisemitism and the Hitler regime. Jews "avoided all political action for two thousand years. The result was that the political history of the Jewish people became even more dependent on the unforeseen and accidental factors than the history of other nations, so that the Jews stumbled from one role to the other and accepted responsibility for none."[66] For George Kateb,

> Arendt's greatness lies precisely in her honesty. She sweeps aside all that would make her ethnic fellows and herself comfortable. . . . In her judgement, modern antisemitism depends on the character of modern Jews. She never stupidly says that the Jews deserved what they got in the nineteenth and early twentieth centuries. Rather, she is trying to show that given certain patterns of Jewish life, the response of antisemitism was not beyond the realm of normal human meanness. . . . Yet so painful is the subject that an extraordinary effort is required to see the unobscured truth.[67]

But did Arendt discover the "unobscured truth"? It is time to say that, with respect to antisemitism, Arendt's *Origins of Totalitarian-*

ism is not merely abrasive and unrevealing of historical truths; it is a distorted version of history that deliberately repeats old antisemitic themes. It cannot be excused on the ground that "she was less interested in writing history than in presenting a model of the political possibilities and dangers of her time."[68] How can political possibilities and dangers be assessed on the basis of faulty, not to say false, empirical evidence and history? Apart from the very questionable analysis of imperialism in volume two (which, if anything, did not involve surplus capital but capital put at risk, as in the building of the Suez Canal), Arendt persistently engages in what can perhaps best be described as the production of Jewish counterhistory: "Counter histories form a specific genre of history written since antiquity.... Their function is polemical. Their method consists of the systematic exploitation of the adversary's most trusted sources against their grain."[69] While Arendt does not use important Jewish *sources* for her histories (on the contrary, she was drawn to non-Jewish and antisemitic ones, such as J. A. Hobson), like a heat-seeking missile she targets the best-known aspects of Jewish *self-understanding*, and likewise turns them against the grain (in the famous phrase of her admired friend Walter Benjamin). Thus the millennia-long non-emancipation, that is, exclusion of Jews from citizenship or any meaningful possibilities for political action in any part of the world is read as an evasion of political responsibilities; cultural concentration on religious texts, rituals, and ideas—especially in the context of a relative lack of political hope—is seen as a reckless disregard for the workings of the state. In Arendt's interpretation, only the Shabbtai Zvi movement and near-genocidal Zionism could and did count as instances of Jewish political action, because at least they represented real popular action.

Such a view is not an admirable stance in favor of real popular action and political responsibility. It is a form of blaming the victim in a way that scarcely anyone today, except perhaps some on the extreme right, would find acceptable in the case of any other victimized people. The claim that Jews historically evaded political responsibility would echo in—or maybe was an echo of—the idea that millions of European Jews went passively to the gas chambers like sheep to the slaughter. It does not show intellectual courage, but an astounding lack of empathy for those historically constrained to live under authoritarian or terror regimes of various kinds. Despite the attention Arendt gives to police forces under totalitarian regimes, she reveals a mental bracketing of the daily realities of great-power politics at both the individual and group levels. It is of a piece with the later essay on Eichmann.[70]

Objective Enemies

Although volume two already contained numerous allusions to Bolshevism and the Soviet form of totalitarianism, volume three is almost entirely devoted to the similarities and differences between Nazi fascism and the regimes of Lenin and Stalin, especially the latter. Some significant observations regarding antisemitism and Jews are also to be found in this volume, but the element of totalitarianism fades into the background while the concepts of conspiracy, secret societies, police powers of the state, labor and concentration camps, totalitarianism as a new form of domination, and the permanent need in such regimes for "objective enemies" to be exterminated come to the fore. For my purposes, the most relevant remarks relate to the *Protocols of the Elders of Zion*.

In the course of describing what she sees as the fictional worlds of totalitarian leaders and movements, Arendt states that the notion of a Jewish world conspiracy was the most efficacious fiction in the Nazi propaganda repertoire. She traces the origin of this notion to the end of the eighteenth century, "when the intimate connection between Jewish business and the nation-state had become visible."[71] Belief in this connection was fortified by the real "international relationship and interdependence of a Jewish people dispersed all over the world," and the "ambiguous role Jews played in European society since their emancipation."[72] Their role was ambiguous, it seems, because their actual financial usefulness to and influence over the state was declining while they appeared to become more conspicuous. An example of this curious situation, Arendt finds, is to be found in attempted peace negotiations during 1917: "The German government, following a long-established tradition, tried to use its Jews for tentative peace negotiations with the Allies. Instead of addressing itself to the established leaders of

German Jewry, it went to the small and comparatively uninfluential Zionist minority."[73] It did this because, unlike the assimilated bourgeois Jews, the Zionists "still believed in the existence of a Jewish people independent of citizenship," and they would therefore be more likely "to render services which depended upon international connections and an international point of view."[74] The Zionists, however, did not come through: They "did something that no Jewish banker had done before; they set their own conditions.... The old Jewish indifference to political issues was gone." It is difficult to follow Arendt's reasoning here. Her argument seems to be that the Jews had been useful only when they were a visibly non-assimilated group, in her words "aloof" from the rest of society (but connected within their own community); the Zionists were not assimilated, therefore they were the best candidates to lead a peace negotiation. She seems to mean that the Germans believed that, through their (international) connections to other non-assimilated Jews, the Zionists could somehow effectuate a peace negotiation. This argument rests on the fact that a German approach was made to the Zionist Chaim Weizmann, then in London. But it is likely that he was approached not because he was a Zionist with connections to international "Jewry," but because he had good relations with several people in the *British* government, who would be crucial protagonists in any future peace negotiations.[75] In any case, her point is that, despite the loss of their purported historical functions, Jews became increasingly the targets of antisemitic and Nazi propaganda.

The Nazis were especially clever, Arendt thinks, in that they made "the Jewish issue" a matter of personal and national identity, and not merely a matter of opinion. The legal and political need to establish Aryan and non-Jewish identity "gave the masses of atomized, undefinable, unstable and futile individuals a means of self-definition . . . [and] created a kind of spurious stability."[76] In this context the Nazis, who were far from alone in utilizing the infamous *Protocols of the Elders of Zion*, made an important social-psychological discovery: they realized that "the masses were not so frightened by Jewish world rule as they were interested in how it could be done."[77] Arendt believes this was certainly the case for Hitler himself. Therefore, just as Stalin used the fiction of a Trotskyite conspiracy, so Hitler used the fictions of the *Protocols*, not for ideological suasion but to facilitate *organization* within the struggle for power. "Once these propaganda slogans [concerning Jewish or Trotskyite conspiracies] are integrated into a 'living organization,' they cannot be safely eliminated without wrecking the whole structure. The assumption of a Jewish world conspiracy was transformed by totalitarian propaganda from an objective, arguable matter into the chief element of the Nazi reality; the point was that the Nazis *acted* as though the world were dominated by the Jews."[78] Thus there was a fusion of speech and action, or perhaps even a sublimation of speech into practice, against which rational argument and objective evidence was impotent. "Nazism as an ideology had been so fully 'realized' that its content ceased to exist as an independent set of doctrines . . . ; destruction of the reality therefore left nothing behind, least of all the fanaticism of believers."[79] This is an interesting, indeed powerful, analysis of the nature of totalitarian propaganda. But it has the shortcoming that one may infer that it is futile to pursue rational argument and objective evidence, at least in extreme cases. And it seems that Arendt drew exactly that inference when she wrote that if "a patent forgery like the 'Protocols . . .' is believed by so many people that it can become the text of a whole political movement, the task of the historians is no longer to discover a forgery. The fact that it is believed is more important than that it is a forgery."[80] But it was not in fact a *patent* forgery to many people; that was and remains the problem. The *Protocols* is still in wide circulation today, for example in the Arab world. Surely the fact that it is a forgery is relevant and in urgent need of dissemination. The same holds true for many other notions of Jewish conspiracy: that Jews employed at the World Trade Center on September 11, 2001, knew an attack was coming and stayed away; that the Mossad was somehow behind the Iranian Revolution of 1979; that Jewish financiers were the main underwriters of gold and diamond mining in South Africa in the nineteenth century . . . Without relentless fact-checking, that is, without the painstaking historical investigations for which Arendt had limited patience, all kinds of mistaken political conclusions may be drawn and poorly grounded actions taken.

Conclusion: How Should One Think about Jewish Self-Criticism?

Hannah Arendt remains an influential, even revered, figure in modern political thought. Her influence is discernible in not only some of the best writing in contemporary political theory, but also further afield. Her origin in an assimilated German Jewish family who became refugees enhances her authority on the themes of homelessness and human rights as well as on the nature and history of Judaism, about which many Westerners know very little. This same authority to speak "as a Jew" should have made her more sensitive to the effects that her statements about Jewish history could have. Her frequent and inaccurate pointing to the singular and excessive power that Jewish financiers had in European and imperial history mirrored rather than explained the role of antisemitism in the emergence of totalitarian ideologies and movements. How is this phenomenon, on the part of such a gifted thinker, to be explained?

It is tempting to follow scholars such as Margaret Canovan and George Kateb in seeing Arendt's critique as a courageous example of escape from the self-deception, marketing, or propaganda of the group to which one belongs. In Arendt's case it would be a form of intellectual honesty prefigured by such luminaries of Jewish origin as Spinoza and Marx. Indeed, Arendt's writing resurfaces the question of how one should think about the nature of dissent within the Jewish community broadly construed: at least from Spinoza's *Theologico-Political Treatise*, with its eminently reasoned and empirically fortified (within certain limits) critique of Judaism, to Marx's essay "On the Jewish Question," a piece of writing that is shocking in its crudity, Jewish communities have been faced with thoroughgoing intellectual and cultural dissent.

Leading further into to this avenue of exoneration is Arendt's methodological distinction between truths of fact and truths of interpretation, discussed at some length in her essay "Truth and Politics." Here, as in the remarks on the *Protocols of the Elders of Zion* noted above, it is evident that, for Arendt, political action is ultimately more important than pure scholarship and the extensive empirical work that often entails.[81] For Arendt, scholarship is in any case never pure; it is always theory-laden and imbued with interests of some kind. To carry out a critique of the historical and socioeconomic role of Jews may have been, in her view, a form of praiseworthy political action, removing veils of illusion among Jewish communities themselves.

Perhaps a better way to understand Arendt is to place her alongside other German Jewish intellectuals, including those discussed by Joseph Bendersky elsewhere in this volume. As Bendersky shows, many German Jewish intellectuals were so thoroughly immersed in German life and culture that it was literally inconceivable to them that antisemitism (especially in Germany) could pose a substantial threat. While Arendt was not quite so far gone, her attachment to her German identity may have allowed her to incorporate certain common German prejudices—such as those against eastern European Jews mentioned above—into her analyses quite unthinkingly.

In the end, Arendt may be seen as an especially sophisticated example of Jewish self-hatred. Sander Gilman defined self-hatred on the part of a group as "the acceptance of the mirage of themselves generated by their reference group, the group which they see as defining them."[82] This certainly fits Arendt, with her long lingering at the heights of German and Christian philosophy, her reconnection to Heidegger after the war, and her indifference to Judaism as a religion, especially in eastern Europe.

Questions for Further Discussion

1. Some of Arendt's writings have not aged well with modern understandings of race and politics. What can we do today to ensure that the lens we are seeing through and projecting outward to others won't need to be corrected in the future?

2. Arendt purposefully uses the term *element* rather than *cause* throughout her writings. She also talks about Jews "gathered like eagles over their prey." How does her choice in words affect the validity of her work? Do you think her word choice is intentional or unintentional, and why?

3. How do Arendt's generalizations of the roles played by Jews, such as overstating their stake in Austrian railroad ownership and South African diamond financing, play into the stereotypes of Jews at the time? Why do you think none of her peers at the time called her out for these overgeneralizations?

4. Arendt talks about tribal nationalism and how it related to antisemitism in the pan-movements. What current-day parallels of tribal nationalism can you think of and what similarities and differences are there to what Arendt describes?

5. The author talks about Arendt's use of non-Jewish and antisemitic sources when researching for her writings. What do you think Arendt could have or should have done to better prepare herself to write more objectively?

6. Arendt looks at propaganda and its role shaping perception. Do you think Arendt was a victim of any of the propaganda of her time, or that it had an effect on her writings? Why or why not?

Notes

1. Dana Villa, ed., *The Cambridge Companion to Hannah Arendt* (Cambridge: Cambridge University Press, 2000).

2. Richard J. Bernstein, *Hannah Arendt and the Jewish Question* (Cambridge MA: MIT Press, 1996); George Kateb, *Hannah Arendt: Politics, Conscience, Evil* (Totowa NJ: Rowman & Allanheld, 1984).

3. Seyla Benhabib, "Hannah Arendt and the Redemptive Power of Narrative," *Social Research* 57, no. 1 (2012): 173.

4. A summary of Arendt's whole account may be found in Benhabib, "Hannah Arendt," 175–78.

5. Hannah Arendt, *Antisemitism: Part One of The Origins of Totalitarianism* (New York: Harcourt, Brace & World, 1951), 33. Hereafter *Origins*, vol. 1.

6. Arendt, *Origins*, vol. 1, 37. Emphasis mine.

7. Arendt, *Origins*, vol. 143.

8. Compare William A. Jenks, *Austria Under the Iron Ring 1879–1893* (Charlottesville: University Press of Virginia, 1965), 157.

9. Jenks, *Austria Under the Iron Ring*, 157. Emphasis mine.

10. Jenks, *Austria Under the Iron Ring*, chapter 8.

11. Frederick Morton, *The Rothschilds: A Family Portrait* (New York: Atheneum, 1962), 111.

12. *Katalog der Deutschen Nationalbibliothek* (online): http://d-nb.info/qnd/130476838.

13. Elisabeth Young-Bruehl, *Hannah Arendt: For Love of the World* (New Haven: Yale University Press, 1982), 120.

14. Shulamit Volkov, *Antisemitismus als kultureller Code: Zehn Essays*, 2nd ed. (Munchen: Verlag C.H. Beck, 2000), 15, 38.

15. Volkov, *Antisemitismus als kultureller Code*, 20.

16. Arendt, *Origins*, vol. 1, 79.

17. Arendt, *Imperialism: Part Two of The Origins of Totalitarianism* (New York: Harcourt, Brace and World, 1951), 16. Hereafter *Origins*, vol. 2.

18. Arendt, *Origins*, vol. 2, 18.

19. Arendt, *Origins*, vol. 2, 30.

20. Arendt, *Origins*, vol. 2, 35.

21. Arendt, *Origins*, vol. 2, 40.

22. Arendt, *Origins*, vol. 2, 75.

23. Arendt, *Origins*, vol. 2, 77.

24. Arendt, *Origins*, vol. 2, 75.

25. The following comments are based on J. Alton Templin, *Ideology on a Frontier: Theological Foundations of Afrikaner Nationalism, 1652–1910* (Westport CT: Greenwood, 1984).

26. Arendt, *Origins*, vol. 2, 78.

27. Arendt, *Origins*, vol. 2, 80.

28. Arendt, *Origins*, vol. 2, 81.

29. Wikipedia, s.v. "Randlords," accessed July 14, 2020.

30. Arendt, *Origins*, vol. 2, 81.

31. Arendt, *Origins*, vol. 2, 81.

32. Arendt, *Origins*, vol. 2, 82.

33. Arendt, *Origins*, vol. 2, 82.

34. Young-Bruehl, *Hannah Arendt*, 222.

35. Margaret Canovan, *Hannah Arendt: A Reinterpretation of Her Political Thought* (Cambridge: Cambridge University Press, 1992), 30.

36. Arendt, *Origins*, vol. 2, 102.

37. Arendt, *Origins*, vol. 2, 80.

38. Arendt, *Origins*, vol. 2, 106.

39. Compare Jean Cahan, "Can Antisemitism Have a Sacral Quality? Reflections on Wistrich and Others," *Antisemitism Studies* 3 (April 2019): 1.

40. Arendt, *Origins, vol.* 2, 106.

41. Arendt, *Origins*, vol. 2, 106.

42. Arendt, *Origins*, vol. 2, 108.

43. Arendt, *Origins*, vol. 2, 109.

44. Gavin Langmuir, *Toward a Definition of Antisemitism* (Berkeley: University of California Press, 1990).

45. Arendt, *Totalitarianism: Part Three of The Origins of Totalitarianism* (New York: Harcourt, Brace and World, 1951), 112–14. Hereafter *Origins*, vol. 3.

46. Arendt, *Origins*, vol. 2, 113.

47. Arendt, *Origins*, vol. 2, 113.

48. Arendt, *Origins*, vol. 2, 114.
49. Arendt, *Origins*, vol. 2, 115.
50. Arendt, *Origins*, vol. 2, 119.
51. Arendt, *Origins*, vol. 2, 119.
52. Arendt, *Origins*, vol. 2, 119.
53. Arendt, *Origins*, vol. 2, 119.
54. Arendt, *Origins*, vol. 2, 120.
55. Arendt, *Origins*, vol. 2, 122.
56. Arendt, *Origins*, vol. 2, 122.

57. Andrew Gladding Whiteside, *The Socialism of Fools: Georg Ritter von Schönerer and Austrian Pan-Germanism* (Berkeley: University of California Press, 1975); and Whiteside, *Austrian National Socialism before 1918* (New York: Springer-Science and Business Media B.V., 1962), 60–66, 83–85.

58. Whiteside, *The Socialism of Fools*, 169–70.
59. Whiteside, *The Socialism of Fools*, 169–70.
60. Canovan, *Arendt*, 44.
61. Canovan, *Arendt*, 44.
62. Canovan, *Arendt*, 44.
63. Kateb, *Arendt*, 59.
64. Bernstein, *Arendt*, 56.
65. Bernstein, *Arendt*, 57.
66. Arendt, *Origins, vol.* 1, 8.
67. Kateb, *Arendt*, 59.
68. Canovan, *Arendt*, 58.

69. Amos Funkenstein, *Perceptions of Jewish History* (Berkeley: University of California Press, 1993), 36.

70. Compare Elhanan Yakira, *Post-Zionism, Post-Holocaust: Three Essays on Denial, Forgetting, and the Delegitimization of Israel*, trans. Michael Swirsky (Cambridge: Cambridge University Press, 2010), 263.

71. Arendt, *Origins*, vol. 3, 52.
72. Arendt, *Origins*, vol. 3, 52.
73. Arendt, *Origins*, vol. 3, 52–53.
74. Arendt, *Origins*, vol. 3, 53.

75. Jonathan Schneer, *The Balfour Declaration: The Origins of the Arab-Israeli Conflict* (New York: Random House, 2010).

76. Arendt, *Origins, vol.* 3, 54.
77. Arendt, *Origins, vol.* 3, 56.
78. Arendt, *Origins, vol.* 3, 60.
79. Arendt, *Origins, vol.* 3, 63.
80. Arendt, *Origins, vol.* 1, 7.

81. Compare David Luban, "Explaining Dark Times: Hannah Arendt's Theory of Theory," *Social Research* 50, no. 1 (Spring 1983): 215–48.

82. Sander L. Gilman, *Jewish Self-Hatred: Antisemitism and the Hidden Language of the Jews* (Baltimore: Johns Hopkins University Press, 1986), 2.

3

Nazi Antisemitism as Ideology and Genocidal Practice
The Case of Alfred Rosenberg

JÜRGEN MATTHÄUS

This chapter of the book deals with some historical aspects of antisemitism. No part of this history resonates more than the Holocaust as we grapple with today's antisemitism, racism, and other forms of stigmatization. My text provides some glimpses into the ideas and actions of one of the leading propagandists and politicians in the Nazi party, Alfred Rosenberg, who played a crucial yet still under-researched role in bringing about a "final solution of the Jewish question."[1] The case of Alfred Rosenberg raises questions about the interrelation between antisemitic theory and practice, more precisely: what were the factors that made Nazi anti-Jewish policy take the genocidal turn, and how relevant are any of these factors today? I will start with a summary of Rosenberg's life and career and then take a closer look at some decisive events during 1941 as hazy ideas became deadly reality for hundreds of thousands of Jews. I will intersperse my telling of that history with references to broader issues that relate to our topic and its current manifestations as addressed in other contributions to this book.

Rosenberg as Ideologue and Careerist

Alfred Rosenberg (January 12, 1893–October 16, 1946) was the most influential Nazi ideologue and, in the course of his political career, accumulated a number of important party and state functions. Born in Reval (then Russia; now Tallinn, Estonia) to Baltic German parents, he studied architecture before leaving Russia in late 1918 for Germany, where the population was reeling from the disastrous effects of four years of war, a humiliating defeat, and political upheaval. When he arrived in Munich the city was about to outdo Berlin as center of a growing radical right-wing scene. This brings us to the first factor of contemporary relevance: what was evolving at that time was a dynamic and eclectic, but increasingly organized and internationally networked movement of like-minded people, most of whom were men. They shared fantasies of power that centered around an imaginary racial community allegedly threatened by outside enemies, most notably Jews. In the emerging Völkisch movement, with its strong antisemitic and anti-democratic bent, Rosenberg quickly found a home. In early 1919 he became a member of the precursor organization to the Nazi party and started writing for it. He joined the staff of the party's flagship newspaper, *Völkischer Beobachter*, in 1921 and became its editor in 1923.[2]

Rosenberg's standing among party leaders in general and Hitler in particular resulted in large part from his firsthand experience with the Russian revolution of 1917, which he and other right-wingers rationalized as a Jewish attempt at ruling the world. To characterize Rosenberg as the foremost Nazi thinker is correct in that no one else in the party was as focused on ideas, but incorrect in the sense that he never really thought things through on the basis of facts. Instead, he processed information to find confirmation for preconceived notions that he never questioned and tirelessly propagated in ultra-nationalist publications and speeches.[3] In his journalism, antisemitic and racist diatribes featured prominently. His efforts helped spread the notorious forgery the *Protocols of the Elders of Zion* in Germany and denounce the Weimar Republic as an aberration born out of national shame and run by so-called Jewish traitors. His first book, *The Tracks of the Jew throughout the Ages (Die Spur des Juden im Wandel der Zeiten)*, published in 1920, echoed segregationist ideas in vogue among radical German nationalists. It was followed by *Immorality in the Talmud (Unmoral im Talmud*, 1920), *Zionism as an Enemy of the State (Der staatsfeindliche Zionismus*, 1922), and a flood of antisemitic articles in periodicals, among them a journal edited since 1924 by Rosenberg under the programmatic title *Der Weltkampf*. It was meant for an international audience in the hope of attracting "the white race" to the Nazi cause.[4]

The second factor that Rosenberg shares with like-minded activists now is a lack of intellectual originality and a reliance on selective readings of works by others, from the classics to contemporaries. That includes right-wingers abroad, such as the American Theodore Lothrop Stoddard, whose phrase "the menace of the underman," contained in the title of a book he published in 1922, was adapted by Rosenberg into the term *Untermensch*, which in turn alludes to earlier writings by German literary figures.[5] Rosenberg seems to have influenced the formulation of the 1920 Nationalsozialistische Deutsche Arbeiterpartei (NSDAP) party program and its antisemitic clauses, as he later published on the program's relevance and meaning.[6] On November 9, 1923, Rosenberg participated in the Munich Beer Hall Putsch that ended with Hitler's arrest. Charged by the imprisoned party leader with keeping the dysfunctional Nazi movement going, the deeply loyal but uncharismatic Baltic émigré struggled to prevent its disintegration among intense infighting. After Hitler's release, Rosenberg curtailed his ambitions within the party and in 1930 published what would become his magnum opus: *The Myth of the Twentieth Century* (*Der Mythus des 20. Jahrhunderts*). The book sold more than one million copies by 1945 and boosted Rosenberg's standing within the party. With the exception of Hitler, no other leading Nazi had produced or would produce an equally elaborate vision of Germany's destiny. Combining references to a range of philosophers, race theoreticians, and neo-pagan authors, Rosenberg's *Myth* represents a dichotomist worldview built around the concept of racial ideal types. At its core, he positions "us" versus "them," the "Aryan" versus the Jewish or "anti-race" (*Gegen-Rasse*) in an eternal struggle for dominance and survival.[7]

This points at two interrelated factors, also relevant today, that could be labelled the antiestablishment pair: the interpretation of complex social problems in a biologistic, Manichean manner to call for a simple yet radical solution, combined with aggression masked as a defensive, quasi-natural, and supposedly heroic reaction to a threat painted as deadly and imminent. To some readers at the time, the importance of the ideas elaborated in Rosenberg's *Myth* seemed obvious. William Bayles, an American journalist posted in Germany between 1934 and 1940 as correspondent for *Time* and *Life* magazines, wrote in 1940 that the book "caused an intellectual furor among the Jews, scholars and clergy, but unfortunately was practically overlooked by politicians and foreign statesmen."[8] Bayles surmised few Germans outside party circles read the book and claimed it "foretold ten years in advance the Jewish pogrom [of November 1938], the invasion of Poland, the crushing of France, and the manner in which Nationalist Socialist Europe would be governed." Although Bayles was certainly right about the discrepancy between the book's sales success and the small number of Germans, even among the Nazi leadership, who read beyond its cover, it would go too far to see Rosenberg's *Myth* as a policy blueprint. For concepts as nebulous, artificially constructed, and incoherently related as the ones favored by Rosenberg to become reality, a political process and active agency were required.[9]

Once Hitler's party was in power, Rosenberg's burning ambition for higher office collided with that of more skillful competitors. Furthermore, his limited ability to forge tactical alliances and his reputation as an inept organizer damaged his political career. Compared to other members of the top Nazi elite—Göring, Ribbentrop, or Goebbels—until 1941 Rosenberg lacked the executive power and resources that came with a cabinet portfolio. But he received a boost in October 1940 when he was put in charge of the newly founded Einsatzstab Reichsleiter Rosenberg (ERR), a sprawling organization devoted to the systematic robbery of Jewish libraries, archives, art collections, and other assets in the countries overrun by the Wehrmacht. The ERR was not the only Nazi agency involved in the looting of Jewish property, but it quickly became the most successful. Less than four years after its founding, it had shipped almost 1.5 million railcar-loads of looted artwork from all of German-controlled Europe to the Reich.[10]

Rosenberg's Nazi star shone most brightly in early 1941 in the run-up to the German attack on the Soviet Union when Hitler consulted him on the plans for the destruction of the Soviet Union and its systematic exploitation. The Führer's birthday on April 20, 1941, marked Rosenberg's appointment as "plenipotentiary for the central handling of questions relating to eastern Europe"

1. Close-up photo of Alfred Rosenberg, Paris, November 1940. (Credit: United States Holocaust Memorial Museum #75932, courtesy of Robert Kempner.)

(*Beauftragter für die zentrale Bearbeitung der Fragen des osteuropäischen Raumes*), a task promising, as Hitler put it, the arrival of the Rosenberg's "great hour."[11] On July 17, 1941, less than a month after the beginning of Operation Barbarossa, Hitler signed Rosenberg's promotion to Reich Minister for the Occupied Eastern Territories. In this capacity he was the chief administrator of an area stretching from Poland's former eastern border to the Ural mountains in the East, and from the Baltic Sea to the Caspian Sea. As the Wehrmacht advance stalled before Moscow in late 1941, the actual realm of Rosenberg's influence was much reduced, yet still comprised the Baltic states and parts of Belorussia and Ukraine, more than half a million square kilometers altogether and home to roughly thirty million people. Here Rosenberg's Ostministerium held political authority over the region's brutal exploitation for the benefit of the German war effort and its reshaping for the purpose of securing long-term German domination.[12]

The German war of annihilation against the Soviet Union claimed the life of millions of civilians and Soviet prisoners of war. The prime agencies of destruction were the Wehrmacht, with its three million soldiers on the eastern front, and Himmler's SS and police units deployed to ensure the rapid "pacification" of the occupied territory. From the first days of the campaign, Jews were among the prime victims of German violence.[13] The establishment of Rosenberg's civil administration starting in late July 1941 coincided with mass executions. While critical of the waste of manpower caused by the deliberate neglect that led to the death of two million Soviet POWs in Wehrmacht camps in the first year of the campaign, Rosenberg did nothing to avert, undermine, or delay the mass murder of Jews and other groups stigmatized as "unwanted."[14] Instead, as we will see, he encouraged his representatives to explore possibilities for more radical measures on an even larger scale. In dealing with these outgroups, all options, as one would say today, were on the table. There was no inevitability to any later events, but the arc of Nazi policy was clearly bent towards extremist violence. Within that mindset, Jews were special in that they were seen as the driving force behind all other enemies, especially Communists and Stalin's regime. Jews were thus what Nazi propaganda called "enemy number one."[15]

The growing intensity of the military campaign, the surge in partisan warfare caused by brutal German measures, and the regime's determination to supply the troops and the home front at the expense of the local population made Rosenberg's civil administrators join forces with the police and Wehrmacht for the so-called "pacification" of the region. That meant more terror in the form of depopulated regions, burnt villages, and civilians killed or deported for forced labor until the German retreat from Soviet territory. At the end of the war Rosenberg was arrested, tried at the Nuremberg International Military Tribunal (IMT), and found guilty of conspiracy to commit aggressive warfare, crimes against peace, war crimes, and crimes against humanity. He was sentenced to death and hanged on October 16, 1946. That guaranteed him special recognition from extreme right-wingers in Germany and elsewhere, which is why to this day frequent references to his writings can be found in publications and on websites. Historians for the most part disregarded Rosenberg as a politically irrelevant oddball among more determined and brutal Nazis. But based on the available documentation there can be no doubt that Rosenberg played a key role in the planning and implementation of Nazi genocide in general and the Holocaust in particular.

Rosenberg, the "Jewish Question," and the War against the Soviet Union

From his earliest days as a right-wing journalist to his arrest by the Allies, Rosenberg left no doubt about his unshakable belief that something radical had to be done against Jews and Communists. In order to liberate the German Volk and the Nordic race, one had to lay the axe at the problem's roots.[16] For our topic it is interesting to see how his ideas evolved over time. In his 1920 book *The Tracks of the Jew throughout the Ages*, Rosenberg combined the call for severe anti-Jewish restrictions with a concession of rudimentary rights to Jews "as human beings"; in later editions of the book these concessions were purged, as were his earlier expressions of support for Zionism. But he remained consistent in his

2. Reichsleiter Alfred Rosenberg and Adolf Hitler confer at military headquarters, November 1941. (Credit: United States Holocaust Memorial Museum #75995, courtesy of Perquimans County Library.)

belief of German-Jewish incompatibility by demanding severe punishment—even the death sentence—for "race defilement" and racial slander.

The combination of firm ideological convictions and political flexibility was a defining feature of the Nazi leadership, and is characteristic of the extreme right in general. In the case of the Nazi party, this opportunistic feature became crucial once Hitler had been granted power and his movement started interacting with state bureaucracy and other social forces. Hitler's ability to shape and organize the complex structures of a modern state for the purpose of securing his rule was remarkable. While the regime constantly invoked established ideological tenets, its violent dynamic was largely driven by other factors, most notably military and economic interests that became radicalized over time. For Hitler, concrete circumstances and a variety of often short-term considerations determined the implementation of Nazi goals; the same applied to his lieutenants eager to advance their careers. The vaguer the Führer remained in describing future policy making towards these goals, the better inconsistent and sometimes blatantly contradictory measures could be justified. Tactical considerations as well as anti-Jewish animus influenced Hitler's notorious Reichstag speech of January 30, 1939, in which he threatened "the annihilation of the Jewish race in Europe" in the event of war.[17] One week later Rosenberg followed suit by providing his own future projection: for the Nazi regime, the "Jewish question" would be solved only "once the last Jew has left the territory of the German Reich."[18] He also called on the Western democracies to support the creation of a "Jewish reservation" (*jüdisches Reservat*) for roughly fifteen million Jews and to determine whether it would be in Madagascar or someplace else.

Once the war had started Rosenberg and other top Nazis were eager to use it as an opportunity to advance a solution to the "Jewish question" in conjunction with their own agenda. In the spring of 1941 Hitler supported Rosenberg's idea for creating an Institute for Research into the Jewish Question around the same time that he disallowed further deportations of Poles and Jews to German-occupied Poland—the so-called Generalgouvernement—due to transport difficulties and consulted Rosenberg on the planning for the imminent attack on the Soviet Union. Hitler assured his generals that, in what he planned as a war of annihilation, the "Jewish-Bolshevik intelligentsia ... must be eradicated (*beseitigt*)."[19] Meanwhile, the Nazi gaze was shifting away from Madagascar in a direction closer to home for its anti-Jewish initiatives. When on March 26, 1941, Reinhard Heydrich, the chief of the SS Reich Security Main Office (RSHA), presented Göring with a draft plan for the "solution of the Jewish question," they also discussed Rosenberg's as yet uncircumscribed responsibilities. Göring prompted Heydrich to prepare brief instructions for the invading army about "the threat from the Soviet secret police, political commissars, Jews etc., so that it would know whom to put up against the wall."[20]

Clearly, with the planning for Operation Barbarossa, Nazi leaders saw a solution to the "Jewish question" appear on the eastern horizon. In mid-March Hitler voiced his inclination to deport seventy thousand Jews from Berlin and Vienna and to make the Generalgouvernement "free of Jews" as soon as possible.[21] Simultaneously Rosenberg drafted a plan for radical expansion into Soviet territory, the redrawing of the region's political map, massive economic exploitation, and racial engineering. To him, parts of the soon-to-be-occupied territory seemed well-suited as a dumping ground for undesirable groups of people. Every Nazi leader agreed that the Soviet Union was to be dismembered, its leadership done away with, and its resources exploited; few, however, had a long-term concept, as Rosenberg did, for maintaining German dominance *and* advancing Nazi ideals. In the months prior to Operation Barbarossa, Himmler was arranging for his Einsatzgruppen and police units to "secure" the area conquered by the Wehrmacht, but Rosenberg was the man Hitler would talk and listen to on the broader issues of German rule in the East.[22]

The unprecedented violence of the German attack on the Soviet Union was propelled not only by military ruthlessness, expansionist ambition, and ideological fanaticism. There was also the key goal of extracting economic assets from the Soviet Union for the benefit of the German war effort. In early May 1941 policy planners of various Reich agencies met at the Wehrmacht High Command and agreed that continuing the war required stripping the conquered territory of agricultural products; as a result, they dryly stated, "umpteen million people (*zig Millionen Menschen*) will doubtless starve to death."[23] A month earlier Rosenberg had already stressed in a memo to Hitler that "securing the means essential for the Greater German Reich from the to-be-occupied territory" had to take precedent over more far-reaching political plans.[24] And in the pre-campaign guidelines to his representatives on the ground, he wrote that "this coming fight is a fight to ensure the supply of food and raw material for the German Reich as well as for Europe in its entirety, an ideological fight in which the last Jewish-Marxist foe has to be defeated, a war to determine state policy (*staatspolitischer Krieg*) towards a new order (*staatliche Konzeption*) and a decisive expansion of the true Europe towards the East."[25]

Antisemitic activism is a phenomenon sui generis, but it is also part of a broader mix of repressive or destructive ideas and interests. Even during this intense period of the war, the Nazi regime saw the "Jewish question" as inextricably linked with economic, military, and security planning and as part of the broad goal of massive and lasting conquest and ethnic cleansing in the East. Nazi economic goals coexisted with an ethnopolitical strategy that combined firm ideological commitment with openness to opportunities emanating from new, sometimes unforeseeable events and the diversity of situations on the ground. In the occupied Soviet territory administered by Rosenberg he issued his own guidelines, which called for the Germanization (*Eindeutschung*) of racially suitable locals, colonization by Germanic settlers, and resettlement (*Aussiedlung*) of "unwanted elements."[26] Regarding the "Jewish question," Rosenberg had little to say beyond recommending "a temporary transitional solution" that included forced labor and ghettoization but left future options open.[27] For the Baltic States, he favored a "complete exclusion of all Jews" (*restlose Ausscheidung des Judentums*); for Ukraine, he anticipated a "decisive solution" (*entscheidende Lösung*) from establishing ghettos and introducing forced labor.[28]

Clearly these guidelines did not amount to killing orders; in fact, they fell far short of the Wehrmacht's directives on the killing of Soviet army commissars and the deliberate, deadly neglect of Red Army prisoners. For all we know, Himmler's Einsatzgruppen had not received explicit orders on how to deal with Jews prior to the attack. Similarly, Rosenberg had sent his representatives into the occupied territories without clear directives regarding the "Jewish question," but they knew they were expected to deal with their new tasks based on general guidelines. Rosenberg's diary notes and other documents point to three characteristics of the thinking on the issue. First, he regarded a "solution," irrespective of its timing, as a matter of course, emanating as a quasi-natural consequence of the party's program: the Jews had to vanish. Second, after having pointed, years earlier, to different ways in which the desired vanishing act could be accomplished, Rosenberg saw the war in the East as a chance to develop new, more effective, and more radical methods by keeping an open mind to the possibilities offered by the course of events. And third, he was willing to leave the execution of at least some of these radical measures to others as long as they seemed equally committed to the overall goal and did not threaten his political prerogative. This also explains why Rosenberg limited his conflicts with Himmler and Heydrich to squabbles over competence whereas he never missed an opportunity to vigorously confront Nazi competitors who did not share his views.

Rosenberg was not only a dogmatic ideologue but also an eager opportunist. This is reflected in the propaganda guidelines his new office developed in the spring of 1941. The "Jewish question," the guidelines projected, could "be solved to a significant degree by giving free rein to the population for some time after the occupation."[29] Especially in Ukraine locals were expected to "perform Jewish pogroms and murders of Communist functionaries on a large scale"; thereafter, the only task left to the Germans would be "to take care of the remaining oppressors based on more in-depth knowledge." Rosenberg was not the only Nazi leader expecting locals to help bring the "Jewish question" closer to a "final solution" by way of pogroms and murder, but he was the first to translate these ideas into an action plan. It took Reinhard Heydrich until after the beginning of the German attack to instruct the Einsatzgruppen commanders in writing to encourage "self-cleansing measures by anticommunist and anti-Jewish circles."[30] By that time pogroms had already claimed the lives of thousands of Jews in the occupied Soviet Union while the Einsatzgruppen had started to embark on their own killing sprees.

Rosenberg, an Architect of Genocide

When, in the early hours of June 22, 1941, three million Wehrmacht men—soldiers as well as Himmler's ss—and police units carried the war to the East, Nazi leaders hoped to find there a solution to their immediate and long-term problems. Success depended, in their minds, on the swift and sustained "pacification" and exploitation of the area by eliminating "Jewish-Bolshevist functionaries," "snipers," and "useless eaters." Rosenberg's civil administrators started to arrive on the scene in late July, after Rosenberg's appointment as Reich minister for the eastern occupied territories, but months passed before even the key posts in the East were filled.[31] In the meantime, units of the Wehrmacht, Einsatzgruppen, ss, and police, along with troops deployed by Germany's ally Romania and collaborationist locals, had spread massive havoc behind the frontline. By January 1942, half a year into the campaign, roughly two million Soviet POWs had died in German custody and almost one million Jews had been murdered. This latter figure includes an estimated three hundred fifty thousand Einsatzgruppen victims as well as roughly ninety thousand Jews killed by Romanian units.[32]

It remains unclear when Rosenberg first learned about the surging violence behind the front line; his diary is silent on this issue. At the end of June, knowledge of the wave of mass murder in the East had spread beyond the SS leadership, and British officials had deciphered intercepted German execution reports.[33] In addition to the barrage of official reports on the fierce fighting and the swift German advance, soldiers and other Germans stationed on the eastern front sent or brought home accounts of violence against civilians. By mid-July Rosenberg must have been aware of the murder of Soviet Jews.[34] Still, some of the factors that shaped the measures Rosenberg's administrators adopted after assuming their posts in the occupied Soviet Union remain elusive. This applies to matters of general policy as well as the "Jewish question." Only recently have scholars acknowledged how decisive Rosenberg's civil administrators were in the escalation of anti-Jewish mass violence in the region. In his groundbreaking study on the Holocaust in Lithuania, historian Christoph Dieckmann points to the spike in mass executions in many districts in late July 1941 after the arrival of officials in the Reichskommissariat Ostland (RKO). Ninety percent of all Holocaust victims in Lithuania were murdered under the aegis of Rosenberg's civil administration.[35] In the following months, as more regions transitioned from military to civil administration—Latvia and the western parts of Belorussia in September and Estonia in December 1941—they were "cleansed" of their Jewish population; those deemed fit to work were exempt for the time being and confined to ghettos administered by Rosenberg's representatives.[36] Further south, in civil-administered Ukraine, German officials murdered 90,000 Jews in 1941; in 1942 more than 362,000 were killed—seven times the number of Jews murdered in Wehrmacht-administered Ukrainian territory.[37]

In the early phase of Operation Barbarossa, Nazi leaders seem to have convinced themselves that the locus for the implementation of a "final solution of the Jewish question" was the occupied Soviet Union. While German anti-Jewish policy in occupied Poland seemed stuck, more radical momentum was building every day further east, in the territory earmarked for Rosenberg's administration. One of the biggest problems Himmler and Heydrich faced resulted from Rosenberg's obstinate insistence on his prerogative. Although Hitler had granted them vast executive authorities, they could not simply ignore Göring's directive from March 1941 that said Rosenberg's responsibilities had to be taken into account in planning for a "final solution of the Jewish question." But the SS leadership saw a way out of this dilemma by utilizing Rosenberg's reluctance to be directly involved with making Jews "vanish" from the region. The more Himmler's units had been able to assert their role by taking violent action against "enemies of the Reich," the greater their advantage over Rosenberg's newly arrived representatives.

Even though Rosenberg preferred to leave matters regarding the implementation of the Final Solution vague, his administration did not stand idly by. The involvement of Rosenberg's men in anti-Jewish measures was a matter of active choice based on a perceived need, not an assigned onus. This became clear in early August 1941 when Rosenberg's chief administrator for the RKO, Hinrich Lohse, approached the higher SS and police leader (HSSPF) in Riga with "preliminary guidelines for the treatment of Jews" in the region.[38] By outlining a number of concrete discriminatory measures—from defining who was a Jew to regulating Jewish forced labor—these guidelines radicalized regulations developed earlier, first in the Reich and later in occupied Poland. At the same time, the civil administration claimed supreme authority to perpetuate and systematize more random and haphazard measures taken by the Wehrmacht and police agencies in the occupied Soviet Union: closed ghettos were to be created in all urban centers; all Jewish assets were at the civil administration's disposal; in the ghettos, Jews would receive "only that amount of food provisions that the rest of the population can spare, but not more than what suffices as bare supply" (*notdürftigen Ernährung*). The same applied to the provisioning of forced laborers; outside the cities, the "flat land has to be cleansed of the Jews" (*das flache Land ist von den Juden zu säubern*).

Tellingly, the guidelines made no mention of Himmler's apparatus. Although Lohse's combination of systematic starvation and intense exploitation could result only in the eventual death of the region's Jews, the ss leadership in the RKO objected vehemently to what they perceived as undue incursions onto their turf. In a draft response, Einsatzgruppe A-leader Walter Stahlecker did not offer a fundamentally different approach to Lohse's; instead, he pointed to the issue's broader implications and presented a shorter time line by highlighting what Lohse and Rosenberg already knew: that a "radical treatment of the Jewish question as a whole seemed possible for the first time in the east" (*die im Ostraum erstmals mögliche radikale Behandlung der Judenfrage*). According to Himmler's man in Riga, preventing the procreation of Jews "as early as possible" had to be a priority, and, as mass sterilizations seemed impractical, the only option was gender-segregated deportations to "Jewish reservations" (*Judenreservate*). Later, the "overall cleansing of Europe of all Jews" (*Gesamtreinigung des europäischen Raumes von allen Juden*) could be achieved somewhere beyond the continent.[39]

In the absence of clear directives from the Berlin central offices, conflicts over competences offered an opportunity for civil administrators and SS officers at the periphery to sharpen their own ideas concerning the "overall cleansing of Europe of all Jews." By pushing for radical approaches they could be certain their superiors would reward initiative and success on the ground, which in turn might even trigger praise and support from Hitler—the trump card in the struggle against institutional competitors. German institutions in the East clashed over ways and means, but agreed on the overall goal.[40] In mid-August Lohse amended his guidelines to stipulate that "further measures, especially by the Security Police" were not to be interfered with and that the civil administration would adopt "minimal measures" until "the final solution of the Jewish question" could be tackled.[41] Stahlecker in turn encouraged his subordinates to support the civil administration "especially in the

Jewish question," even if he and his men applied "very different means than the ones planned by the Reichskommissar."[42]

In focusing on the ss and police apparatus, historians tend to overlook the dual-track evolution of the Holocaust in the occupied Soviet Union: while Himmler's men targeted "enemies of the Reich" and "pacified" the area, Rosenberg and his civil administrators ensured the concentration and exploitation of the Jews within and outside the ghettos. When the Jews were considered to have outlasted their usefulness, both tracks converged at one destination: final solution by physical annihilation. At a time when, as Rosenberg confided in his diary, "history is looking us over the shoulder," his ideological convictions and his pragmatic flexibility made him as susceptible to the notion of a "radical treatment of the Jewish question" as Himmler's Einsatzgruppen-officers.[43] But the Nazi thinker looked beyond the immediate aspects of the issue. In September 1941 his ministry issued a set of administrative guidelines for the RKO with a section on the "Jewish question" perfectly attuned to the promise inherent in the escalation of violence in the region for an even more ambitious transnational solution:

> All measures on the Jewish question in the occupied Eastern areas have to be taken with a view towards the solution of the Jewish question after the war for all of Europe. Consequently, they are to be designed as preparatory partial measures and require coordination with other decisions taken on the issue. Conversely, the experiences gained in dealing with the Jewish question in the East can show the direction for solving the overall problem, due to the fact that Jews in these areas form, together with the Jews in the Generalgouvernement, the strongest contingent of European Jewry.[44]

With these guidelines Rosenberg had adapted his earlier ideas of a Europe-wide solution to the Jewish question to the new situation. Meanwhile, in the occupied Soviet regions, the cooperation between Rosenberg's civil administrators and Himmler's field officers increased the intensity of ghettoizing urban Jewish communities, weeding out "useless eaters," and "cleansing" rural areas, all of which caused a massive death toll among Jewish men, women, and children.[45] As German units expanded their mass execution actions and explored alternative killing techniques—including "solving the Jewish question by extensive labor utilization," for which the civil administration was responsible—earlier doubts by Nazi officials about the limited efficacy of this kind of physical violence subsided.[46]

Further west, the possibilities opening up in the East for a radical solution of the "Jewish question" were not lost on Nazi functionaries keen to "cleanse" their realm of Jewish influence. The last broad feature that I want to point to is particularly important for the radicalization of the Nazi regime's policy: internal competition and the urge to "work towards the Führer" that integrated individual functionaries into the system. Why wait until the end of the war for deportation when "de-Jewification" by mass murder was rapidly progressing behind the eastern front? What seemed like chaotic, uncoordinated efforts by rival institutions propelled systemic violence. At the German embassy in Paris officials expressed their hope in the summer of 1941 that the occupation of "the vast regions in the East" would "bring about a final, satisfactory solution in no time to the Jewish problem in Europe."[47] In the second week of September the German Foreign Office inquired at the RSHA whether the remaining Serbian Jews could not be shipped off to east Poland or Russia.[48] Shortly thereafter the pressure to deport prompted several waves of transports with Jews from the Greater Reich to Lodz as well as to Rosenberg's Ostland.[49]

Until the German advance towards Moscow stalled and further mass deportations of Jews were temporarily halted, expectations among Nazi leaders ran high. In a confidential press briefing in Berlin on November 18, 1941, following the official announcement of the Ostministerium's creation, Rosenberg articulated his goals more clearly than ever before:

> At the same time, this East is called up to solve a question that is posed to the peoples of Europe: it is the Jewish question. Around six million Jews still live in the East, and this problem can be solved only by a biological eradication of all of Jewry in Europe [*biologischen Ausmerzung des gesamten Judentums in Europa*]. The Jewish question is only solved for Germany when the last Jew has left

German territory, and solved for *Europe* when not a single Jew stands on the European continent up to the Urals.⁵⁰

It is hard to imagine Rosenberg not working towards the implementation of "a biological eradication of all of Jewry in Europe" first and foremost in his realm of influence. Yet military operations, the great distances involved, and the limited means of transportation derailed the planning. "The issue," Goebbels wrote in his diary about a meeting with Heydrich on November 17, 1941, "is really more difficult than we initially assumed," mostly because the Jews in the Reich could not be deported on the desired scale without disrupting the war economy.⁵¹ The failure to achieve a quick victory over Stalin increased the Nazi leadership's inclination to put military priorities first.⁵² Furthermore, the severe Russian winter prevented the digging of mass graves so that many mass executions in the region had to be postponed until the next spring.⁵³

When Heydrich sent out invitation letters in late November 1941 for what would become known as the Wannsee conference, he must have regarded Rosenberg's realm as a key site if not the only feasible option for a comprehensive final solution. As we know from summary notes drafted by Adolf Eichmann, the Berlin meeting aimed at "creating a unanimous understanding" (*Erreichung einer gleichen Auffassung*). It is an indication of the importance that the RSHA chief credited to the Ostministerium that Rosenberg's ministry was the only agency outside the SS from which two representatives were invited: the minister's deputy Alfred Meyer and political department head Georg Leibbrandt. The conference was originally planned for December 9, 1941, but Heydrich postponed it due to the United States joining the war. When the Wannsee meeting took place on January 20, 1942, SS Sturmbannführer Rudolf Lange, commander of the security police and the SD in Latvia, a part of Rosenberg's Ostland, provided not only an additional link between Himmler's apparatus and the civil administration but also firsthand experience with organizing mass executions in the East.⁵⁴

There the killers strove to improve the efficiency of the murder machine. Beginning in November 1941, German police killed tens of thousands of Jews in the occupied Soviet Union by carbon monoxide from trucks designed specifically for that purpose by RSHA technicians. Furthermore, initial steps were taken to create mass extermination camps for Jewish deportees. The SS placed a large order of Zyklon—a prussic acid used for disinfection and later for murder, in Auschwitz-Birkenau, in its "B" version—to be shipped to Mogilev and Riga, and developed plans for installing crematorium ovens in Mogilev. Yet, due to the changing conditions, no gassings with Zyklon seem to have taken place in either city. After the first crematorium ovens had been delivered to Mogilev on December 30, other oven parts were rerouted to Auschwitz in the annexed part of Polish Upper Silesia.[55] As much as "the East" appeared to Nazi leaders as the promised land of the "territorial solution" in the second half of 1941, by the time of the Wannsee conference the gravitational center of genocide had shifted further west, to the death camps under construction in occupied Poland, and thus away from Rosenberg's range of influence. Nevertheless mass killings in the occupied Soviet Union continued until the German retreat.

Where does this leave Rosenberg as a historical figure, and what aspects of his role seem most relevant today? The blend of obsession and opportunism that shaped his actions with regard to the Nazis' "Jewish question" stands out. Consistent in his racial beliefs from the 1920s until his execution, Rosenberg saw the need to reiterate and address this key item on his party's agenda. In so doing he acknowledged reality only when it supported his beliefs and thus ignored most of it. He also knew that the implementation of his agenda depended on opportunity, determination, initiative, and coordination. Rosenberg was not the only opportunistic ideologue within the Nazi elite, and this mix of motivating factors is not restricted to the Holocaust. The importance of Operation Barbarossa for the Third Reich's genocidal turn can hardly be overstated, and it was clearly not just Himmler and his Einsatzgruppen that drove the momentum. Similar to pre-war Nazi anti-Jewish policy, the Final Solution taking shape in the second half of 1941 did not advance on a single track and was not generated by a few Nazi leaders, but was propelled by cooperation and interaction on all levels towards the goal of conquering and "cleansing" the East.

To this day, antisemitic, xenophobic, and racist slogans remain rooted in dogmatic beliefs as well as in self-interest of one kind or another. Prejudices might be an integral part of the human condition, but they undermine that very condition when they are, instead of being critically scrutinized, used to channel social discontent and allowed to influence politics. Rosenberg, Hitler, and their fellow travelers would have remained vocal yet inconsequential hacks had they not been helped to power by established elites and kept in power by what Saul Friedländer called the "lure of authoritarian practices of ruling."[56] The resurgence of Rosenberg's writings on the websites of today's extreme right attests to the persistence of this lure. Blaming an imagined "other" and closing one's mind to facts remain the most powerful preconditions for genocide and other forms of man-made global disaster.

Questions for Further Discussion

1. The Nazis had many enemies during World War II but the Jews were "special in that they [were] seen as the driving force behind all other 'enemies.'" Discuss why having Jews as "enemy number one" was so important.

2. Alfred Rosenberg "processed information to find confirmation for preconceived notions that he never questioned." Explain why this is problematic.

3. Contrast *intellectual originality* with *repurposing old ideas*. How does Alfred Rosenberg succeed in doing the latter?

4. Define a dichotomist worldview. Give examples from both World War II and now.

5. Alfred Rosenberg had "a simple yet radical solution" to complex social problems. What was it? Explore the difficulties with the idea of simple answers to complex problems.

6. List the factors that made Nazi anti-Jewish policy take a genocidal turn. Were any factors more significant than others?

7. Discuss the relevance of these factors today. What lesson(s) can we take away from this?

8. Extension: What are the *Protocols of the Elders of Zion*? Do people still believe in this hoax? Why?

9. Why do you think conspiracy theories are so attractive to many?

Notes

1. The opinions presented here are mine; they do not reflect the opinions of the United States Holocaust Memorial Museum (USHMM). This essay is based on Jürgen Matthäus and Frank Bajohr, *The Political Diary of Alfred Rosenberg and the Onset of the Holocaust*, Documenting Life and Destruction: Holocaust Sources in Context (Lanham MD: Rowman & Littlefield in association with the USHMM, 2015), particularly parts 1 and 4.

2. See Fritz Nova, *Alfred Rosenberg: Nazi Theorist of the Holocaust* (New York: Hippocrene, 1986); Ernst Piper, *Alfred Rosenberg: Hitlers Chefideologe* (Munich: Blessing, 2005).

3. For an overview of post–World War I German history see Richard J. Evans, *The Coming of the Third Reich* (London: Allen Lane, 2003). For more on the strength of antisemitism during this era see Saul Friedländer, *Nazi Germany and the Jews: The Years of Persecution, 1933–1939* (New York: Harper Collins, 1997), 91–112; Peter Longerich, *Holocaust: The Nazi Persecution and Murder of the Jews* (Oxford: Oxford University Press, 2010), 10–26.

4. See Piper, *Alfred Rosenberg*, 116–21.

5. Lothrop Stoddard, *The Revolt against Civilization: The Menace of the Under-Man* (New York: Scribner's Son, 1922); Alfred Rosenberg, *Der Mythus des 20: Jahrhunderts: Eine Wertung der seelisch-geistigen Gestaltenkämpfe unserer Zeit* (Munich: Hoheneichen Verlag, 1930), 214.

6. See Alfred Rosenberg, *Das Parteiprogramm: Wesen, Grundsätze und Ziele der Nationalsozialistischen Deutschen Arbeiterpartei* (Munich: F. Eher, 1922). Point 4 of the program read: "None but members of the Volk can be citizens of the state. None but those of German blood, whatever their creed, can be members of the Volk. Therefore, no Jew can be a member of the Volk."

7. Rosenberg borrowed the term *Gegen-Rasse* from a book written by his longtime associate, fellow Baltic German, and college fraternity brother Arno Schickedanz, *Sozialparasitismus im Völkerleben* (Leipzig: Lotus Verlag, 1927).

8. William D. Bayles, "Hitler's Mystagogue: Alfred Rosenberg," in Bayles, *Caesars in Goose Step* (New York: Harper & Bros., 1940), 215.

9. With emphasis on anti-Jewish ideas as the driving force for the Holocaust: Phillippe Burrin, *Nazi Anti-Semitism: From Prejudice to the Holocaust* (New York: New Press, 2005); Jeffrey Herf, *The Jewish Enemy: Nazi Propaganda during World War II and the Holocaust* (Cambridge MA: Belknap, 2006).

10. For an overview see Patricia Kennedy Grimsted, *Reconstructing the record of Nazi cultural plunder: A survey of the dispersed archives of the Einsatzstab Reichsleiter*

Rosenberg (ERR) (Amsterdam: International Institute of Social History, 2011). Select archival material reproduced in *Files of the Einsatzstab Reichsleiter Rosenberg in Kiev* (Woodbridge CT: Primary Source Media, 2007); and "Navigating the Holocaust-Era Looted Cultural Property," National Archives, updated June 26, 2017, http://www.archives.gov/research/holocaust/international-resources/navigate.html.

11. Diary entry by Rosenberg for April 20, 1941, quoted in Matthäus and Bajohr, *The Political Diary*, 241–42.

12. See Timothy Patrick Mulligan, *The Politics of Illusion and Empire: German Occupation Policy in the Soviet Union, 1942–1943* (New York: Praeger, 1988); Andreas Zellhuber, *"Unsere Verwaltung treibt einer Katastrophe zu . . ." Das Reichsministerium für die besetzten Ostgebiete und die deutsche Besatzungsherrschaft in der Sowjetunion 1941–1945* (Munich: Vögel, 2006), 149–59. Still valuable: Alexander Dallin, *German Rule in Russia 1941–1945: A Study of Occupation Policies*, 2nd ed. (London: Macmillan, 1981); Gerald Reitlinger, *The House Built on Sand: The Conflicts of German Policy in Russia, 1939–1945* (New York: Viking, 1960). For more recent publications on German occupation policy in the Soviet Union see Alex J. Kaye, Jeff Rutherford, and David Stahel, eds., *Nazi Policy on the Eastern Front, 1941* (Rochester NY: University of Rochester Press, 2012).

13. See Raul Hilberg, *The Destruction of the European Jews* (New Haven CT: Yale University Press, 2003), 275–407; Christopher R. Browning (with a contribution by Jürgen Matthäus), *The Origins of the Final Solution: The Evolution of Nazi Jewish Policy, September 1939–March 1942* (Lincoln: University of Nebraska Press in association with Yad Vashem, 2004); Longerich, *Holocaust*, 179–255.

14. See Geoffrey P. Megargee, *War of Annihilation: Combat and Genocide on the Eastern Front, 1941* (Lanham MD: Rowman & Littlefield, 2006), 59–62.

15. See Jürgen Matthäus, "Antisemitism as an Offer: The Function of Ideological Indoctrination in the SS and Police Corps during the Holocaust," in *Lessons and Legacies VII: The Holocaust in International Perspective*, ed. Dagmar Herzog (Evanston IL: Northwestern University Press, 2006), 116–28.

16. On this line of thinking see Boaz Neumann, *Die Weltanschauung des Nazismus: Raum, Körper, Sprache* (Göttingen: Wallstein, 2010).

17. "Hitler Speaks before the Reichstag," January 30, 1939; trans. Jürgen Matthäus, http://www.ushmm.org/wlc/en/media_fi.php?ModuleId=10005175&MediaId=3108. Once the war had started, Hitler and his fiefs repeatedly referred to this "prophecy," but deliberately misdated it to September 1, 1939, the first day of what would become World War II.

18. Speech by Rosenberg, February 7, 1939, quoted in Matthäus and Bajohr, *The Political Diary*, 364–66.

19. Wehrmacht High Command war diary entry for March 3, 1941, quoted in Browning, *Origins*, 216.

20. File note by Heydrich for Himmler, March 26, 1941, quoted in Browning, *Origins*, 236.

21. See Longerich, *Holocaust*, 174–75.

22. See Megargee, *War of Annihilation*, 33–41.

23. File note on the results of the meeting on May 2, 1941, quoted in Browning, *Origins*, 235.

24. Memorandum "Betr. UdsSR," April 2, 1941 (1017-PS); printed in IMT, *Der Nürnberger Prozess gegen die Hauptkriegsverbrecher* Bd. 26 (Nuremberg: IMT, 1947), 547–54.

25. "Allgemeine Instruktion für alle Reichskommissare in den besetzten Ostgebieten," May 8, 1941 (1030-PS), printed in *Nürnberger Prozess* Bd. 26, 576–580 (here 580).

26. "Instruktion für einen Reichskommissar im Ostland," May 8, 1941 (1029-PS), printed in *Nürnberger Prozess* Bd. 29, 573–76.

27. "Eine allgemeine Behandlung erfordert die *Judenfrage*, deren zeitweilige Übergangslösung festgelegt werden muss (Arbeitszwang der Juden, eine Ghettoisierung usw.)." Memorandum Rosenberg re "Allgemeiner Aufbau und Aufgaben einer Dienststelle für die zentrale Bearbeitung der Fragen des osteuropäischen Raumes," April 29, 1941 (1019-PS), printed in *Nürnberger Prozess* Bd. 26, 560–66 (here 561; emphasis in the original).

28. "Denkschrift Nr. 2," quoted in Christoph Dieckmann, *Deutsche Besatzungspolitik in Litauen 1941–1944* (Göttingen: Wallstein, 2011), 794; "Instruktion für einen Reichskommissar in der Ukraine," May 7, 1941 (1028-PS), printed in *Nürnberger Prozess* Bd. 26, 567–573.

29. Propaganda guidelines by Rosenberg's office, n.d. (spring 1941), printed in Matthäus and Bajohr, *The Political Diary*, 373–75.

30. Heydrich to Einsatzgruppen commanders, June 29, 1941, quoted in Jürgen Matthäus, "Operation Barbarossa," in Browning, *Origins*, 272.

31. Reich commissariats for Ostland and Ukraine were established on July 25 and August 20, 1941, respectively.

32. Christian Gerlach, *The Extermination of the European Jews* (Cambridge: Cambridge University Press, 2016), 70.

33. Richard Breitman, *Official Secrets: What the Nazis Planned, What the British and Americans Knew* (New York: Knopf, 1998), 91–93.

34. See Otto Bräutigam's diary entry for July 11, 1941, printed in H. D. Heilmann, "Aus dem Kriegstagebuch des Diplomaten Otto Bräutigam," in *Biedermann und Schreibtischtäter. Materialien zur deutschen Täter-Biographie*, Götz Aly, Peter Chroust, H. D. Heilmann, and Hermann Langbein, eds. (Berlin: Rotbuch Verlag, 1987), 123–87 (here 134).

35. Dieckmann, *Besatzungspolitik*, 793–805.

36. Christian Gerlach, *Kalkulierte Morde. Die deutsche Wirtschafts-und Vernichtungspolitik in Weissrussland 1941 bis 1944* (Hamburg: Hamburger Edition, 1999), 609–743; Zellhuber, *Verwaltung*, 130–41.

37. Alexander Kruglov, "Jewish Losses in Ukraine, 1941–1944," in *The Shoah in Ukraine: History, Testimony, Memorialization*, Ray Brandon and Wendy Lower, eds. (Bloomington: Indiana University Press in association with the USHMM, 2008), 281.

38. RKO Office II to HSSPF, August 2, 1941; see Matthäus, "Operation Barbarossa," 285.

39. Draft letter by Stahlecker, August 6, 1941, quoted in Matthäus, "Operation Barbarossa," 285–86.

40. Rosenberg diary entries for September 1, 1941, and (retrospectively) December 28, 1941, printed in Matthäus and Bajohr, *The Political Diary*, 259–61, 270–83.

41. RKO II to Generalkommissare, August 18, 1941, quoted in Matthäus, "Operation Barbarossa," 286. See also Longerich, *Holocaust*, 232–35.

42. Stahlecker to Einsatzkommandos of Einsatzgruppe A, August 29, 1941, excerpted in Matthäus, "Operation Barbarossa," 286–87.

43. Rosenberg diary entry for September 7, 1941, printed in Matthäus and Bajohr, *The Political Diary*, 261–63.

44. "Richtlinien für die Zivilverwaltung in den besetzten Ostgebieten" (Braune Mappe), Teil I: RKO, n.d. (September 1941); USHMM Archives RG 18.002M (Central State Archive Riga, R70-5-7), reel 4, partly reproduced in *Einsatz im "Reichskommissariat Ostland." Dokumente zum Völkermord im Baltikum und in Weissrussland 1941–1944*, Wolfgang Benz, Konrad Kwiet, and Jürgen Matthäus, eds. (Berlin: Metropol, 1998), 33–37.

45. Longerich, *Holocaust*, 219–31.

46. Ereignismeldung 86, September 17, 1941, recommending "Lösung der Judenfrage durch umfassenden Arbeitseinsatz," printed in *Die "Ereignismeldungen UdSSR" 1941: Dokumente der Einsatzgruppen in der Sowjetunion I*, Klaus-Michael Mallmann et al., eds. (Darmstadt: WBG, 2011), 471–86 (here 479); see also Matthäus, "Operation Barbarossa," 283–84, 296.

47. Carltheo Zeitschel to Ambassador Otto Abetz, August 22, 1941; compare Browning, *Origins*, 323.

48. Browning, *Origins*, 341–42.

49. See Browning, *Origins*, 357–88.

50. Speech by Rosenberg at a press reception, November 18, 1941, printed in Matthäus and Bajohr, *The Political Diary*, 385–89 (emphasis in the original).

51. Diary entry by Goebbels for November 18, 1941, translated from *Die Tagebücher von Joseph Goebbels, Teil II: Diktate 1942–1945*, Elke Fröhlich, ed., vol. 2 (Munich: K.G. Saur, 1996), 309.

52. Browning, *Origins*, 333.

53. Gerlach, *Kalkulierte Morde*, 768–71.

54. See Mark Roseman, *The Wannsee Conference and the Final Solution: A Reconsideration* (New York: Metropolitan Books, 2002), 94–97.

55. See Browning, *Origins*, 354–56; Gerlach, *Kalkulierte Morde*, 764–67.

56. "Verlockungen autoritärer Herrschaftspraktiken," speech by Saul Friedländer at the German Bundestag, January 31, 2019, accessed December 28, 2020, https://www.bundestag.de/en/documents/textarchive/remembrance-2019-588924.

4

"Semites" on Display
David Gordon Lyon and the Jewish Other at Harvard University, 1889-1926

TIMOTHY TURNQUIST

In 1882 David Gordon Lyon assumed the Hollis Chair of Divinity (established in 1721) at Harvard University. A Protestant American Assyriologist, Lyon was a pioneering scholar of the recently deciphered Semitic languages of Mesopotamia, found between the Tigris and Euphrates rivers in modern-day Iraq and Syria. Lyon, who was interested in the origins of Western civilization, believed it was not solely Greek, Roman, and the Germanic Anglo-Saxon civilizations that had inspired American greatness, but also older Semitic cultures found in Babylon, Assyria, and Israel.[1] In drawing attention to Semitic languages—those belonging to an Afro-Asiatic language family that includes Aramaic, Arabic, and Hebrew—Lyon recognized Jewish contributions to Western thought. At the 1893 Parliament of World Religions he argued that American society "was produced and held together by Jewish thought."[2] After all, from among the Semites, Hebrew civilization had given monotheism, prophetic ideals of social justice, and the Jewish founder of Christianity to the West.

That such recognition hailed from Harvard, an emblem of Anglo-Saxon civilization—an "evolved" Germanic "race" of Britons and Anglo-Americans—was promising to Jacob Henry Schiff, a German Jewish immigrant and benefactor of Semitic research. Schiff hoped for a Semitic revolution in the American landscape, and helped Lyon to establish the Harvard Semitic Museum and the first American archaeological excavation of ancient Israel in Palestine. If expanding liberal education could demonstrate the genius of Semitic peoples, might Jewish immigrants realize themselves in higher education and redefine Anglocentric understandings of Americanism?

The significance of Lyon's career is more than his contribution to the scholarship of ancient Semitic languages; it is a window into larger European and American perceptions of Jewish racial otherness in narratives of Western civilization, which intersected with American racial anxieties and illiberal trends in higher education after World War I. In the early twentieth century, as Jewish immigration and university enrollment increased, culture wars between liberalism and reactionary conservatism framed the Jewish Other as essentially (un)American. Philosemitic liberals such as Lyon, Schiff, and Harvard president Charles T. Eliot extolled the virtues of the ancient Semitic "race"—particularly the Hebrews—to advocate for a Jewish place in the American republic, yet their liberal ideology objectified the positive "racial" traits of Jews while seeking to minimize their ethnic differences. On the other side were the nativists and antisemites such as Eliot's successor—President Abbot Lawrence Lowell—who framed Jewish and other non-Germanic immigrants as a demographic threat to Anglo-Saxon power. In 1922 Lowell proposed a Jewish admissions quota at Harvard, thus challenging the institution's liberal commitments to individualism, which had been favorable to Jewish education and social mobility. While Lyon opposed Lowell's illiberal maneuvers, he also contended with the president's attempts to limit funding for the Semitic Museum—Schiff's legacy. Wedged between hostile conservatism and inconsistent liberalism, the American "Jewish question" revealed cracks in the foundation of the American dream.

Lyon, Schiff, and a Jewish American Narrative

In 1879 Lyon was a budding American scholar who traveled to the University of Leipzig in the German Empire to earn a doctorate in Semitic philology, the academic study of Hebrew, Aramaic, Arabic, and the recently deciphered Akkadian—the Semitic *lingua franca* of the Babylonian and Assyrian empires and the focus of Assyriology. The nineteenth-century scholarly reconstruction of ancient Near Eastern civilizations stemmed from an imperial fascination with "Oriental" lands and the literatures of Mesopotamia, India, and Persia, whereby European orientalists undermined orthodox biblical and Greco-Roman readings of European civilization with alternatives based on forgotten or hitherto unintelligible civilizations.[3] The scholarly concern was about whence and from whom European greatness originated—or didn't. In the nineteenth-century marketplace of ideas, scientific philology had conflated language with race and mental attributes. Speakers of the family of Semitic languages, known collectively as the Semites, were stereotyped as having a crude and intolerant mentality incapable of developing advanced civilizations. In contrast stood the mentally superior Indo-European "Aryans," whose antagonistic relationship with the Semites in antiquity gave rise to the perception of European supremacy.[4] As Lyon entered his doctoral program, the Aryan-Semitic racial dynamic underlay the "scientific" antisemitism that permeated German political discourse, which had been popularized by journalist Wilhelm Marr (1819-1904) in his 1879 tract "Victory of Judaism over Germandom" (*Der Sieg des Judenthums über das Germanenthum*).

In Leipzig Lyon's doctoral advisor was Friedrich Delitzsch, a Semitic scholar and pioneering Assyriologist who later embodied an ethnic German nationalism that problematized "Semitic" or Jewish influences in a racial narrative of German Christendom. He was among prominent German academics, theologians, and journalists whose interpretations of ancient Semitic peoples mirrored contemporary theological and "scientific" biases against Jews, whom the German Reich had emancipated just before Delitzsch commenced his academic career. Now that Hebrew's older, possibly Aryan linguistic ancestors were emerging from hoary antiquity, what was the scientific relationship between European civilization, the Jews, and Judaism?

In 1902 Delitzsch commenced a provocative lecture series that sparked a transatlantic debate by undermining Christian orthodoxy, irking his patron, Kaiser Wilhelm II. Delitzsch's defiance of Judeo-Christian convention meant removing alien Semitic or "Judeo" influences from the German Christian state. The legitimacy of his Christian nationalism depended on how he reimagined the Mesopotamian ruins of Semitic Babylon and Nineveh. He claimed that the Old Testament was an immoral, degenerate product of an Aryan-infused Mesopotamian civilization, with whose sublime values German Christians could identify. By returning to Aryan roots, Delitzsch wanted to excise the Semitic Old Testament from German Christian consciousness.[5] Since he equated the Aryan racial mentality with spiritual idealism, Delitzsch claimed that Jesus was Aryan, as his German protégé, Paul Haupt (1858–1926), had similarly argued at the John Hopkins University.[6] Delitzsch opined that, in the modern era, the nationless, cosmopolitan Jew was a frightening danger (*eine furchtbare Gefahr*).[7]

American Semitists and orientalists looked to Near Eastern lands for the origins of progressive civilization, as had their European counterparts.[8] In the nineteenth century Christian dogmatism waned in American seats of higher learning, owing to the influences of German biblical criticism. In Lyon's field of Semitics, this translated to a scientific pursuit of the origins of Western civilization rooted in philology, archaeology, ethnography, and comparative religion. As Near Eastern lands became less alien to the Western mindset, Lyon saw Semitic civilizations as indispensable drivers of Western development: "Fifty years ago the times of Abraham seemed remote. Fifty years ago we knew of Assyrian history little beyond the names of a few rulers. . . . Fifty years ago the Assyrians seemed to be only a warlike tribe who made predatory assaults on inoffensive nations of the West. Today we see the whole current of western history directed by the statecraft of Nineveh and Babylon."[9]

In 1882 Lyon assumed the Hollis Chair of Divinity at Harvard, where an increasingly scientific and liberal spirit prevailed, fostered by Harvard president Charles W. Eliot, an upper-class Boston Brahmin who—inspired by intellectuals such as Ralph Waldo Emerson—upheld the sanctity of the individual, the perfectibility of the human race, and the universal brotherhood of man. Like many liberals, Eliot abhorred racial and religious discrimination and favored open immigration and diversity in higher education, believing that American institutions could assimilate ethnic differences into a transcendental American melting pot.[10]

Still, even theologically liberal scholars wrestled with German biblical scholarship that destabilized the Judeo-Christian foundation essential to the Puritan exceptionalism of American political and educational institutions. For Lyon, a Southern Baptist, the Bible—including the Hebrew scriptures—was central; to him, German biblical criticism "revealed the hidden life of Israel" and its "incomparable productions."[11] If the Israel idea was anathema to certain Gentile European orientalists, in the multicultural American landscape it seemed to offer Jews a nascent foundation in elite Protestant readings of Western civilization, outside the previous "scientific" attempts by German Jewish scholars to defend Jewish culture in the early nineteenth century, known as *Wissenschaft des Judentums*.

American Jews were attentive to antisemitic trends in Western Europe and therefore welcomed secular trends in higher education that were more receptive to Jewish scholarship, students, and patronage from the Reform Jewish community, whose German Enlightenment roots liberalized and adapted traditional Judaism with mainstream languages and political philosophies.[12] As Harold Wechsler notes, "a Jewish presence in [American] Semitics departments would assure that, unlike Germany, anti-Jewish findings would not emanate from universities."[13] Liberal education, assimilation, and Jewish recognition were of paramount importance to Lyon's Semitics benefactor, Jacob Henry Schiff, a German Jewish immigrant born in Frankfurt am Main in 1847. He hailed from a line of religious leaders, scholars, and philanthropists. At a young age Schiff developed a love of Judaism and Jewish learning and was a staunch advocate of American patriotism as the means to social acceptance. Naturalized as an American citizen in 1870, Schiff later headed the prominent New York banking firm Kuhn, Loeb, & Company, and played leading roles in the New York Chamber of Commerce and in the American Red Cross.[14]

By looking to ancient Israelite civilization Schiff hoped for his and other Jews' self-realization as American citizens, and Harvard seemed to make his vision possible. In the late 1880s Schiff formed enduring friendships with Lyon and Eliot, both of whom were eager to expand Harvard's role in Near Eastern exploration and research. In 1893 Schiff chaired the Harvard Semitic Committee and would contribute more than $275,000 toward the construction and collection of the Harvard Semitic Museum, its research library, and the 1908 watershed excavation of an ancient Israelite site in Palestine where Lyon uncovered Hebrew inscriptions.[15] Unbeknownst to Schiff, his investment in Palestine would lay the groundwork for the field of American biblical archaeology in Palestine.[16] Schiff's pursuit of Hebrew greatness within a Semitic revolution was an effort to resolve the so-called Jewish question prevalent in Euro-American discourse—one rooted in race, national identity, and fears of transatlantic antisemitism.

Eliot and Lyon certainly accommodated Schiff with philosemitic interpretations of Jewish history, although their race-conscious appropriation of Hebrew civilization revealed certain liberal blind spots. Eliot's positive assessment of Jews connected race with mental characteristics. On one hand he commended the "potency" of the "Jewish race" for its "lofty ideals," such as pure monotheism, the cornerstone of Western civilization. Yet, according to Eliot, successful Jewish assimilation necessitated the Jews' reconnection to their ancestral mentality to pass the American "test of liberty."[17] This meant avoiding crass materialism and "reliance on the power of money."[18] Later on, Eliot suggested that the American plurality of races—even Jewish citizens—should not intermarry. Immigration anxieties shifted Eliot from supporting assimilation to advocating a cultural pluralism intended to keep racial groups separate.[19] After all, what good was Jewish potency if it vanished into the American melting pot?

Lyon, too, helped Schiff construct a Jewish American narrative. Paradoxically, one needed to look to ancient Semitic monarchies and empires to transform the racial otherness of Jewish immigrants into a tale of individualist triumph. During the Columbian Exposition at the 1893 Parliament of World Religions, Lyon spoke to the audience about Jewish contributions to civilization, in which he reframed the question of Jewish otherness as a progressive march that culminated in a liberal democracy. Lyon spoke of Jewish mental traits and distinctive physiognomy; however, the Jewish mentality was not antithetical to American civilization. From a cosmopolitan perspective, Jews underpinned America's essential value system.[20] Of course, this meant objectifying Jewish historical characters familiar to Jews and Christians in the imperial sweep of history.

Lyon explained that Abraham—whom he erroneously dubbed "the first Jew"—had left Ur in Mesopotamia, whose "grandeur is just beginning to find due appreciation."[21] Here Lyon linked Abraham to the world of ancient Mesopotamia that archaeologists and linguists were deciphering. In Canaan, Lyon continued, Abraham established "in the distant West the foundations of the empire of faith" where great figures such as Moses—a "state-building patriot"—resided.[22] Because monotheism, the prophets, and a *Jewish* Jesus had originated in Israel, Lyon contended that American society was "produced and held together by Jewish thought."[23] He continued: "A Jewish empire does not exist, and Jerusalem is not the mistress of the world. And yet the dream of the prophet is true. A home for the oppressed has been found, a home where prosperity and brotherhood dwell together. Substitute America for Jerusalem and a republic for a kingdom, and the correctness of the prophet's dream is realized."[24]

Just before the advent of political Zionism, Lyon viewed the American republic as a New World haven for those suffering from Old World prejudice. Some scholars have noted Lyon's anti-Jewish tenor, but his liberal interpretation of Jewish contributions cohered with the assimilationist goals of Schiff, whom Lyon thanked for his generosity; it portended an "era of brotherhood" between Jew and Gentile in the recovery of a common heritage.[25] Lyon acknowledged Harvard's indebtedness to "the Jew" and "a Jewish carpenter," adding that the liberal Puritan institution employed "instructors without applying any tests of race or religion."[26] While Harvard emissaries had yet to explore the Middle East, in 1891—thanks to Schiff's largesse—Lyon obtained large casts of Assyrian and Babylonian monuments and cuneiform tablets from the Louvre, the British Museum, and Berlin.

On May 13, 1891, the Schiff-funded Semitic Museum debuted its collection on the second floor of the Peabody Museum. Discourse surrounding the museum's inauguration highlighted the influence of the Semitic race on the spread of Western civilization. According to Lyon, the museum would help the "inquisitive mind" to comprehend "that power whereby the Semites won their distinguished place in human history."[27] Speaking to two hundred

3. *North Platte (Nebraska) Semi-Weekly Tribune*, January 18, 1901, 7. (Credit: Library of Congress, Chronicling America: Historic American Newspapers.)

people, Schiff explained that Jews were the "modern representatives" of ancient Semites, and, because "anti-Semitism in Europe, social prejudice and ostracism in free America may for a time be rampant," he asserted the need to "combat" it with a deep "knowledge of Semitic history and civilization."[28] Only then would the world comprehend its debt to the Semites. At Harvard the Semites had a distinguished place, and Schiff positioned Jews as major players. Still, Lyon was not satisfied with the second floor of the Peabody Museum; he wanted an independent research institution where students, scholars, and the community could encounter the Semitic or biblical world, and accordingly framed the Bible and Jewish history as "the central interest in the whole Semitic field."[29]

That Harvard owed its heritage to the Semitic "race" was apparent in 1903 when the Semitic Museum debuted a three-storied brick building on Divinity Avenue in Cambridge. Designed by Alexander Wadsworth Longfellow—nephew of the famed American poet Henry Wadsworth Longfellow—the museum offered an alternative to antisemitic views of civilization's origins. Around two hundred fifty people attended the inaugural celebration, including members of the Board of Overseers, Schiff's family, scholars, and other donors. Notably, Jews articulated their contributions to Western civilization alongside Gentiles. Schiff spoke of his "deep attachment to my race," pondering, "Where did the history of my people begin?"[30] Cyrus Adler, who praised "the more liberal education of the student," contended that "modern man" owed his developed culture to "a few groups of peoples that lived about the Mediterranean."[31] Modernity was thus fundamentally Semitic. Adler was a Jewish American scholar involved in the creation of the Semitic Museum and the first recipient of a Semitics PhD in the United States.

Harvard's Gentile elite expressed their admiration for the institution's Semitic heritage. President Eliot underscored Harvard's "characteristic Puritan foundation" rooted in "Old Testamentarians" that would train "American youth in the sublime Semitic conceptions."[32] Lyon viewed the museum as a community institution to combat antisemitism—"that prejudice, both cruel and unjust, born of ignorance which in the minds of some still attaches to the name 'Semitic.'"[33] Charles Eliot Norton, an art professor and founder of the Archaeological Institute of America (AIA), surmised that Harvard "was founded on the rock of Semitic doctrine"—the Hebrew Bible—which had compelled the Puritans to create their civil government and social institutions. He celebrated a "fuller and more general recognition of the immeasurable debt which our Western civilization owes to the Jewish race."[34] In a letter read aloud, Crawford Howell Toy—who was Lyon's former mentor at the Southern Baptist Theological Seminary in Kentucky—explained that Western civilization arose in a dialectical give-and-take between Semites and Indo-Europeans. For him, it was not "worthwhile to ask what race contributed most to the final result."[35] The important thing was that at Harvard, as the museum attested, the Semite had found a place alongside the Indo-European Aryan. Such thinking compelled another patron to note in the *Boston Evening Transcript* that

> it is really an eye-opener for the Anglo-Saxon to find that there are other people in the world as bright as himself. We who think that all that is of any practical account dates from American, or

at the furthest from English history, may learn something to our advantage by contemplating the race qualities of these humble representatives of the Semites of the East. . . . If such Anglo-Saxons would heed the stately introduction of the dedication of the Semitic Museum at Harvard by Professor Lyon they would begin to get notions of what we owe the Jews. In every gathering, even of North End immigrants' children, are the qualities which have won the greatest achievements of the human race.[36]

The lines blurred between Anglo-Saxon and Jew, ancient and modern, American and immigrant, as the museum became a space to reimagine Americanism with respect to new geographic and racial possibilities.

Whereas Assyriology favored Mesopotamia over Palestine, the Semitic Museum gave Palestine greater representation for inquisitive patrons, who encountered diverse artifacts. On arrival to the Semitic museum, visitors encountered a progressive Semitic world that ranged from ancient Mesopotamian city-states to modern Near Eastern villages. Along the halls, and in the stairwells, Lyon displayed photographs from his sojourns in Palestine showing excavations, modern settlements, and geographical sites of religious interest.[37] While the Holy Land was already an object of American theological imagination, the museum turned the Levantine region and its "Semitic" inhabitants into an ethnographic object that portrayed diverse perspectives of Jews and Arabs; it was a space whereby Jews could empirically declare: we exist.

Lyon designated the third floor the Palestinian Room. It contained contemporary photographs, floral and faunal specimens, coins, glass vases, pottery, inscriptions, and bas-reliefs from Selah Merrill (a Congregationalist clergyman, amateur archaeologist, antisemite, and ardent anti-Zionist who served as the United States consul in Jerusalem from 1882 and 1907).[38] From a Jewish perspective, the Semitic Museum offered a sense of Jewish or Judean consciousness: "nowhere else in the United States can one get so complete an idea of Judaea as in this large room."[39] *The New Era Illustrated Magazine* construed the museum as reflective of the Jewish "race" and "spirit" known as Semitism: "the Semitic collections at Harvard may properly be called a Bible museum. Everything seems to group itself about the Jewish race and the Jewish spirit as a central fact in ancient civilization. All objects illustrate some phase of Biblical study. . . . Semitism, like every form of antique civilization, needs for its interpretation not merely the literary remains, but the relics that can be seen and handled."[40]

Such discourse offered a counter narrative to those who considered "Semitic civilization" oxymoronic. In fact, the Semitic Museum proved that Semitism was a civilizing force, though a belief in that idea—as evidenced by Selah Merrill—did not necessarily translate to pro-Jewish sentiment. Moreover, Harvard's search, beginning in 1908, for Hebrew origins at Samaria exposed a Western prejudice toward Palestinian Arab "Semites," whose idyllic primitiveness was seen to illustrate biblical times for Western consumption: "that lad on the rough mountainside piping to the flocks feeding about him might well be a David. That girl coming with the sheep to the well is surely Rachel. That scare at the well where Jacob first met her . . . is one of the most familiar in Palestine."[41]

Elsewhere Lyon lamented Palestinian "ignorance, superstition, and trickery," as well as "illegitimate digging" and "grave robbing" at excavation sites.[42] Lyon believed that establishing foreign-run archaeological schools in Palestine would "do much to abate this evil."[43] Insofar as Palestinian Arabs represented ancient Hebrews, they were edifying to Western onlookers; otherwise, as Arab Semites, they remained unintelligible.

For Boston's close-knit Jewish Reform community, the Semitic Museum offered a way to give back to Harvard—the *alma mater* of many. Lyon saw the Reform community as a natural ally for fundraising efforts. In the 1880s Lyon had promoted Semitic research among Jewish communities in New York and Boston and had lectured at the exclusive Jewish Elysium Club in Boston—once in 1893 to speak about Jewish contributions to civilization and again in 1899 to generate interest in a new museum building.[44] At the latter he upheld the Semitic Museum as a space to combat antisemitism: "By your help," Lyon exclaimed, "Harvard will do her part to drive it away with light."[45] Many Elysium patrons were members of the influential congregation Adath Israel, to which Lyon lectured at Harvard in 1906, noting a "large audience" and "good interest."[46]

Lyon's address to Adath Israel must have sparked interest in museum contributions. Though few matched Schiff, prominent Bostonian Jews—many from older waves of German immigration—donated to the museum's collection and operating expenses. In 1906 Mrs. Jacob Hecht (Lina) donated $185. Born in Baltimore, Maryland, Hecht established the Hebrew Industrial School in Boston's West End, with the goal of making eastern European Jewish immigrants "self-supporting."[47] Lina's husband, Jacob Hecht, was a German immigrant, Harvard alum, prominent merchant, and founding member of the Elysium Club. In the early 1900s the Hecht family established the Hecht Fund that would eventually apportion $5,000 to the upkeep of the "Schiff Semitic Museum" upon the passing of Jacob and Lina.[48] In 1906 Abraham Schuman donated $50. He was a clothier and founding member of the Elysium Club. Schuman's daughter married Carl Dreyfus, a 1895 Harvard graduate, who gave $10; his father's clothing firm, Jacob Dreyfus & Sons, donated $25. J. Koshland & Co., representing a prominent family of Jewish wool merchants, gave $150 in 1906. In the same year, the Eisemann family, another family of wool merchants, contributed $140.[49]

Other affiliates of the Semitic Museum achieved national and international renown. In 1906 Louis B. Brandeis, future Supreme Court justice, contributed twenty-five dollars to the museum.[50] He would later face opposition for his court appointment from Harvard president Lowell because of Brandeis's apparent Jewishness. Isidor Straus—co-owner of Macy's department store and a victim of the 1912 Titanic disaster—served alongside Schiff on the Semitic committee and donated ten fragments of Hebrew manuscripts from his sojourns in Istanbul.[51] Overall, while Schiff's patronage is well attested, other Jews and non-Jews ensured that the Semitic Museum would remain a testament to all things Semitic at Harvard, making it a space that linked the university, the wider community, and philanthropic circles in legitimizing Jewish American identity.

In the early 1910s, Schiff's hope for a Semitic revolution waned as waves of "new" immigrants arrived from eastern and southern

Europe, exacerbating racial anxieties among white Protestants. At Harvard, moreover, Eliot had retired in 1909, and Abbot Lawrence Lowell took his place. Reputed to be antisemitic, Lowell was cool toward the new immigration and Jewish self-expression on campus. Schiff, frustrated by the lack of interest in Jewish learning and Semitics by Harvard's Protestant donor base, threatened to withdraw from the Semitic committee in 1913. Lyon tried to appeal to Schiff, reminding him that the Semitic Museum

> is much visited by schools and colleges and by the general public and exercises therefore a unique function as a silent witness to the value of things Semitic. . . . If our subject has not yet the recognition which it deserves, we are sure that the tide will some time change. The Semitic peoples and the Hebrews in particular have been such leaders in the march of civilization that the world will gradually come to a recognition of its obligation.[52]

In 1914 Schiff withdrew from the Semitic committee. Though he distanced himself from Harvard, he continued to fund the publication of Lyon's excavation at Samaria, and later established the Jacob H. Schiff Behest, which apportioned funds to the purchase of objects for the Semitic Museum.[53] Unfortunately, Schiff never saw the delayed publication of the results of Lyon's work in Samaria, as he passed away in 1920.

In the post–World War I era, restrictions on Jews in higher education and immigration—but not Hebrew recognition—was forthcoming. Alongside the upheavals in European society were increasing Anglo-American fears of Bolshevism, labor unrest, increasing Jewish enrollment in elite universities, and nativist reactions to the perceived subversive, alien influences of non-northern European immigrants. In the culture wars of the "tribal twenties," congressional immigration quotas accompanied heated discourse on race and antisemitism, the latter disseminated by business magnate Henry Ford in the *Dearborn Independent* and echoed in rural districts by the Ku Klux Klan.[54] Subsequently, the abstract Jewish Other defined by liberalism encountered a reactionary conservatism rooted in Anglo-Saxon supremacy and the illiberal underbelly of an "enlightened" liberalism threatened by demographic change.

Lyon and the "Jewish Question" at Harvard, 1922-1926

Private education was a battleground for the Anglo-Saxon elite. Harvard, Yale, and Princeton—the Big Three—had educated the Protestant upper crust for centuries, and their elite "gentlemen" graduates enjoyed lucrative careers in politics, business, and law. Like Eliot, Lowell's worldview was rooted in a belief in the sublime mental capacities of the Anglo-Saxon race, which had manifested itself in stable self-government acquired over "centuries of discipline under the supremacy of law."[55] Lowell feared that growing racial heterogeneity would unravel the cohesion of traditional American institutions. Consequently, he advocated for restrictions on immigration from southern and eastern Europe, with their large Jewish and Catholic populations, and served as honorary vice president of the Immigration Restriction League, where fellow Harvard alumni opposed "unassimilable" immigrants—particularly eastern European Jews—about whom Harvard's traditional patrons and alumni grumbled. Lowell blamed Jewish immigrants themselves because of their "strong race feeling" imported from Europe.[56] In 1922, the year Lyon was to become professor emeritus, Harvard's Jewish enrollment had reached twenty-two percent, up from seven percent in 1900.[57] At stake was the American dream for Jewish applicants at Harvard and other major universities. Lyon's final years at Harvard reveal broader racial anxieties, contested notions of Americanism, and tribalistic challenges to liberal idealism.

In January 1922 Lowell maneuvered to weaken Jewish applicants and recognition at Harvard. In the following months he tried to reduce the number of Jews who received merit-based scholarships in line with their proportion in the freshman class. This required imposing character tests as well as advancing measures to limit the number of "Hebrews" from transfer and technical institutions.[58] Moreover, he went after the Semitic Museum. According to Lyon's diary, Lowell opposed any celebration honoring Schiff and opposed the installation of Schiff's portrait in the museum. He disapproved of efforts to fundraise for the museum.[59] Perturbed, Lyon spoke with Eliot, who assumed that Lowell's actions stemmed from his "fear" and "hostility" toward Jews.[60] Perhaps the

Semitic Museum—the legacy of a Jewish immigrant—proved too menacing to Lowell's Anglocentric interpretations of history, race, and politics. Amid concerns from some faculty members and the Board of Overseers, one of Harvard's governing bodies, the chairman of the admissions office urged Lowell to involve the Faculty of Arts and Sciences in Harvard's "Jewish question."

The faculty met four contentious times in the spring of 1922. On May 23, 1922, in the third faculty meeting, James Hardy Ropes, a professor of divinity, advanced a measure to cap "not easily assimilated" minority groups at fifteen percent of the incoming freshmen class. While not addressing Jews explicitly, according to Lyon, Lowell stated that the "object of the vote was to limit Jews in Harvard College."[61] In a stunning move—no doubt owing to Lowell's pressure—the faculty voted fifty-six to forty-four to grant the admissions office the capacity to determine the "proportionate size of racial and national groups."[62] In response Lyon urged the creation of an investigative committee consisting of "representative Jews" to find a solution "consistent with the liberal, democratic Spirit of the University."[63] In light of the "radical departure from the spirit and practice of the College," Lyon helped to forward a petition demanding another faculty meeting, at least giving the faculty time to study the matter; the petition had thirty-one signatures.[64]

Lyon also sought his students' perspectives on the "Jewish question." Before the May 23 faculty meeting he posed the following question to pupils in his ancient Assyrian history course: "Do you as Jews (non-Jew) [sic] object to non-Jews (Jews) in the class room or the association with them, or if so why?"[65] Jews and Gentiles were to give anonymous evaluations of each other, which Lyon was to read in front of the class and at the May 23 faculty meeting. The evaluations reveal diverse student perspectives on Jewish-Gentile relations, rooted in racial discourse. Of the nine archived responses, four did not object to associating with Jews. What separated these responses from the four negative ones? For two students, their proximity to Jewish students had a humanizing effect, which resulted in friendships. One had associated little with Jews in the past but had befriended a Jewish classmate—"a distinct Jewish type." She resolved to adopt a "fairer attitude toward them," given that Christians "as a class have treated our Jewish brothers most unfairly." Another student had befriended several Jewish boys in a dormitory and had found them quite affable. "Because of my connection to these boys," she declared, "I have learn [sic] much that I never knew before about the boys of this race." She mentioned one of the Jewish men had invited her to a party, which, while delightful, had "a different atmosphere . . . than at ones I have been accustomed to attending." Such evaluations show the complexities of intercultural exchange. One Jewish student found non-Jews "[no] different than Jews." While this student admitted to having mostly Jewish friends, he or she made "[no] distinction based on religions or national causes." For this student, "Character is what counts."

What about the four negative evaluations of Jews? For two students, while they had no personal objections to Jews in the classroom, in social circles, Jews and African American students should know their place in relation to white Christians. "Jews and negroes," wrote one, "affect me alike. Their place as companions is not next to a Christian." Other complaints cited stereotypes about Jewish foreignness, greed, lack of assimilation, and lack of cultural refinement. A male student felt that Jews did "not stand for the same ideals of manhood and well-rounded life" as befit a typical American male. Echoing nativist anxieties, another student surmised that Jews possessed "an independency of spirit that conflicts with adaptation." After reading the students' responses, Lyon asked his students who objected to Jews to write an anonymous response stating if they had inherited or acquired their prejudice in campus clubs and events. He received no follow-up responses.

Complicating Lowell's plans were leaks to the Boston press, subsequently featured in the *New York Times* on June 2 in an article headlined "Discrimination against Jews Suspected in New Harvard Policy on Admission."[66] Thus began a national conversation exposing racial anxieties about changing demographics. Some popular publications echoed Lowell's fears of foreign multitudes at Harvard. An article in *Life Magazine* opined, "it is not really a local trouble nor peculiar to Harvard. It is part of a large, difficult race problem which needs the carefullest handling. . . . If

Harvard can solve it, the whole country will be her debtor."[67] *The New Republic* commented that, although liberals of the "Harvard flavor" abhorred racism, they feared racial saturation: "No true Harvard man is prejudiced against the 'Jews as such'. . . . True Harvard men are liberals, in matters of race and religion at least." However, it continued, "five Jews to the hundred will necessarily undergo prompt assimilation. But twenty or thirty—no. They would form a state within a state."[68] Hence, a white liberal might embrace nativism if too many individuals of a particular ethnic background threatened majoritarian demographics.

Lowell called the fourth and final faculty meeting in the evening of June 2, 1922. The faculty overturned their May 23 decision by a new vote of sixty-nine to twenty-five. Lyon and Harvard liberals scored a victory; elated, Lyon noted he stayed up until 12:30 a.m. discussing "Lowell and Roper's humiliating defeat in their anti-Jewish campaign."[69] On June 5 the overseers expanded the investigation beyond the Faculty of Arts and Sciences to include other colleges. Designated the Committee on Methods of Sifting Candidates, it consisted of subcommittees to guide any future decision making about racial or national groups at Harvard. Still, for Julian W. Mack, Harvard overseer, federal judge, and son of German Jewish immigrants, Harvard's handling of the Jewish question was too narrow in scope. He wrote to Lyon that the "inquiry is a deeper one" because it involved "the place and function of Harvard, or indeed of any American college or university, in the life, present and future, of the American people." He concluded that "no subcommittee to deal with that problem has been appointed."[70]

Amid the fanfare *The Boston Post* interviewed Lyon, who, according interviewer David P. Shea, was especially "qualified to discuss the proposed restriction of Jewish students at Harvard" because he knew about "the history of the race, its traditions, ideals and has been in touch with hundreds of Jewish students."[71] Fearing social harm, however, Paul Sachs of the Investigation Committee discouraged Lyon from publishing the article, and he decided not to.[72] This did not deter Lyon from informing Jewish and Christian audiences about the events unfolding on campus. He met with the Harvard Menorah Society, a nationwide student organization devoted to

Jewish intellectual interests and cultural pluralism.[73] Lyon was its honorary vice president, and upon his retirement in June 1922 the Menorah Society gave him a silver vase with the engraved words

> To David Gordon Lyon
> Scholar, Teacher, and Courageous
> Upholder of Harvard Liberal Traditions[74]

If Lyon's liberalism viewed Jews as exceptional, it also put the onus on exceptional Jewish conduct to combat antisemitism. At a lecture at the B'nai B'rith Lodge in Brooklyn he reminded his Jewish listeners that the cure lay "in mutual understanding." To dispel doubts of their disloyalty, Jews needed to have "straight conduct" and be their "Brother's Keeper." Moreover, Jews should "frown on Jewish wrongdoing" and remain wholly cooperative. They were to accomplish "good works"—à la Schiff—and to be mindful of "their past" and the "duty of citizenship"—the "real glory of America."[75] At a Jewish fraternity at Harvard Medical School, Lyon again argued for "straight" Jewish conduct and for Jews to "frown on Jewish wrongdoing."[76] His biblical and patriotic appeals are deeply unsatisfying to modern ears. How would impeccable conduct have stopped institutional antisemitism? Harvard was determined to keep Jews out, model minority or not; in September 1922 Harvard's admissions application included new questions about race, color, religious preference, father's birthplace, and any changes to surnames.[77]

Despite the changes, Harvard's Jewish students and alumni defended themselves as American Jews. Harry Wolfson, a Russian Jewish immigrant and Lyon's brilliant former doctoral student, advised a Jewish student group to draft a letter advocating their position at one of the faculty meetings. Harry Starr, a law student and president of the Menorah Society, led the dissent of Jewish students. In his letter, he exclaimed that, "as Jews, we should feel humiliated at this apparently unprecedented expression of racial hatred in the United States, against a group that has been taught to consider itself an integral part of the larger American life."[78] Unfortunately Starr could not have foreseen that an appeal to "larger American life" would soon work against Jewish applicants.

On April 9, 1923, Mack informed Lyon that the overseers had adopted the "sifting" committee's findings reaffirming Harvard's liberal character. Harvard liberals and the press were elated; amid "great rejoicing," Lyon noted in his diary on April 9 that "Lowell thus has met his Waterloo."[79] The faculty adopted the report's findings, but experimented with a modification. Although the New Plan disavowed overt racial or religious discrimination, it democratized admissions by encouraging recruitment outside the urban region of the Northeast, where a majority of Jewish immigrants resided. Students from farms, towns, and cities in the American South and West could forgo the meritocratic entrance examination if they had graduated in the highest seventh of their class. As such, a supposedly democratic appeal to fairer geographical representation still restricted Jewish applicants.

To Lowell's chagrin, between 1923 and 1925 the New Plan failed to realize his Jewish quota. In 1925 Jews constituted forty-two percent of the 276 top-seventh students, prompting Lowell to work with the overseers and the admissions office in January 1926 to include character interviews and photographs in the application.[80] Additionally, Lowell watched the Semitic Museum languish. Denying funding, he pressed Lyon—now Curator Emeritus—to prepare lists of prospective donors, which included considerable outreach to Reform Jews. Lowell and his Corporation, Harvard's other governing body, reviewed Lyon's lists and crossed out 60 out of 63 "Gentiles." Of the 292 Jewish names, Lowell removed only two.[81] This sent a clear message to Lyon: leave Semitics to the Jews. According to Lyon, William Rosenzweig Arnold, who had assumed Lyon's position as Hancock Chair of Hebrew, called the move "idiotic" and cautioned that appealing to only Jews "would make the museum a sectarian affair and ultimately destroy it and the Department."[82]

That Jewish outreach might be destructively sectarian demonstrated how far the ideological currents had shifted at Harvard, from an idealistic universalism shared by Eliot, Lyon, Schiff, and others at the Semitic Museum's 1903 inauguration, to the implementation of Jewish immigration and educational quotas in the mid-1920s. If the Semitic Museum had once symbolized the triumph of the Semitic "race" and new frontiers of liberal education, the museum's decline in the 1930s mirrored wider reactions against immigration, Jewish learning, and meritocracy. Lyon died in 1935, and the US Army and Navy utilized the museum as a space for military purposes during the Second World War.[83] As American troops fought against the Nazified outcome of German philology—Aryan civilization—American higher education was reconciling its understanding of Western civilization with race- and religion-based discrimination rooted in transatlantic notions of white supremacy.

Conclusion

The significance of Lyon's academic journey is the transatlantic context in which it occurred—restless Western nations in search of their roots, their exceptionalism, and essential identity. In the United States, concurrent with the transatlantic movement of scholars, artifacts, and ideas, was an influx of European immigrants, expansive industrialization, and urbanization. As geographical, intellectual, and educational horizons expanded—alongside waves of new immigration—it was common to associate "races" with particular mental attributes, which in turn influenced the way scholars, university administrators, their patrons, and the public sphere interpreted present social and political realities. Whether one agreed with strict racial definitions or not, the concept of race was present everywhere. In Lyon's time, at the forefront of the transatlantic debates about race and national identity was the "Jewish question." In the pursuit of antiquity, how did the "Jewish" or "Semitic" mentality—or any foreign mentality for that matter—align with Euro-American identities and national narratives based on Aryan or Anglo-Saxon superiority? Thus, the nineteenth and early twentieth centuries witnessed the rise of "scientific" and political paradigms to comprehend a changing world. These advocated for either the inclusion or exclusion of ethnic and religious minorities.

For many nationalist liberals and traditionalists, the "Jewish question" and race were intertwined. At Harvard, the nineteenth-century expansion of liberal education and race-averse individualism tended to frame racial and religious heterogeneity more optimistically than their conservative counterparts. By nuancing Harvard's traditionally Anglo-Saxon Protestant character, liberal education promised to make the institution more representative of American plurality, whereby Jewish scholars, patrons, and students could assimilate into the cultural mainstream. If the United States, Harvard, and the West were exceptional, they owed something to Semitic or Jewish exceptionalism. If anything, the archaeological science behind the Semitic Museum reminded Anglo-Saxon Protestants—the spiritual heirs of ancient Israel—of their indebtedness to Jewish institutions, and a theoretical commitment to meritocracy promised to realize Jewish potential. Nevertheless, liberalism's blind spots objectified the biblically beneficial features of the Jewish-Semitic mentality for civilization, such as monotheism, while attacking stereotypes such as Jewish materialism. Furthermore, when faced with an influx of immigrants and Jewish students, liberal attitudes could turn illiberal. Still, liberalism was a starting point for Jews looking to articulate a sense of mainstream Jewish American identity—one reappropriated from Puritan exceptionalism.

Regarding traditionalists, Lowell's illiberalism stemmed from the fact that meritocracy, part of the American mythos, initially worked well for Jewish immigrants in secular higher education. The increased numerical and cultural representation of Jews and other immigrants in American life necessitated illiberal restrictions in immigration, education, and cultural representation for the sake of racial homogenization—that is, Anglo-Saxon or Germanic demographics. While many factors explain the interwar decline of Jewish learning in Semitics departments, Harold Wechsler notes that it was "conditioned by majority attitudes about the people represented by that learning, and by the role of knowledge in legitimating the place of Jews in the university and in American life."[84] In the aftermath of the Second World War, while Jewish immigration increased and the field of Judaic studies slowly emerged, the central debates and anxieties of Lyon's time—whence comes American greatness—remain with us today.

Questions for Further Discussion

1. Why was displaying Semitic people (i.e., Jews) in a positive light so important for their acceptance into society?

2. What role did academia in play in the development of modern racial antisemitism in the early 1900s? Would you say that its academic roots gave this form of antisemitism more acceptance?

3. Why would some see it as important that American Jews not adopt the concept of the melting pot but stay separate?

4. Would you argue that the Semitic museum served as a bulwark against the development of antisemitism in America, or did the museum aid in its development?

5. In the 1920s attitudes towards Jews in America seemed to become less positive. To what might this change be attributed?

6. Do you feel well informed about the history and presence of antisemitism? Have you heard about the events in Pittsburgh in October 2018?

7. What might account for a rise in antisemitism in the United States today?

Notes

I want to thank my MA committee, Susan Cohen, Robert Rydell, and James Meyer, and Adaliss Rodriguez, who helped my research efforts at Harvard; moreover, I thank my husband James Benes for his support, and Gerald Steinacher and Ari Kohen for involving me in the 2019 Sommerhauser Symposium at the University of Nebraska-Lincoln.

1. Germanic languages include the West Germanic dialects, German and English, and the North Germanic, or the Scandinavian (aka Nordic) languages. Anglo-Saxons were Germanic northern Europeans who colonized the British Isles beginning in the fifth century BCE. "Aryans" were largely synonymous with fair-skinned northern Europeans.

2. Lyon, "Jewish Contributions to Civilization," in *The World's Parliament of Religions: An Illustrated and Popular Story of the World's First Parliament of Religions Held in Chicago in Connection with the Columbian Exposition of 1893*, Rev. John Henry Barrows, ed. (Chicago: Parliament, 1893), 823.

3. See Suzanne Marchand, "German Orientalism and the Decline of the West," *Proceedings of the American Philosophical Society* 145, no. 4 (2001): 465–73.

4. See Jerrold S. Cooper, "Sumerian and Aryan: Racial Theory, Academic Politics, and Parisian Assyriology," *Revue de l'histoire des religions* 210, no. 2 (1993): 176–84.

5. Friedrich Delitzsch, *Die Große Täuschung: Zweiter (Schluss-)Teil* (Stuttgart: Deutsche Verlags-Anstalt, 1921), 4.

6. See Paul Haupt, "The Aryan Ancestry of Jesus," *Open Court* 23, no. 4 (1909): 193–204.

7. Delitzsch, *Die Große Täuschung: Erster Teil*, 105.

8. See Wade Meade, *Road to Babylon: Development of U.S. Assyriology* (Leiden: E. J. Brill, 1974), 7.

9. Lyon, "A Half Century of Assyriology," *Biblical World* 8, no. 2 (1896): 137–38.

10. See Jennings L. Wagoner Jr., "Charles T. Eliot, Immigrants, and the Decline of American Idealism," *Biography* 8, no. 1 (1985): 25–27.

11. Lyon, "The Results of Modern Biblical Criticism," *Old Testament Student* 3, no. 4 (1883): 110.

12. Leading Judaic scholars were Cyrus Adler, Richard Gottheil, Max Margolis, William Popper, Morris Jastrow, and Abram Isaacs. See Frederick Greenspahn, "The Beginnings of Judaic Studies in American Universities," *Modern Judaism* 20, no. 2 (2000): 209–25.

13. Harold S. Wechsler et al., "Jewish Learning in American Universities: The Literature of a Field," *Modern Judaism* 3, no. 3 (1983): 263, 265.

14. Naomi W. Cohen, *Jacob H. Schiff: A Study in American Jewish Leadership* (Hanover NH: University Press of New England/Brandeis University Press, 1999).

15. See Marcia Graham Synnott, *The Half-Opened Door: Discrimination and Admissions at Harvard, Yale, and Princeton, 1900–1970* (Westport CT: Greenwood, 1979), 11–12.

16. See Rachel Hallote, "Jacob H. Schiff and the Beginning of Biblical Archaeology in the United States," *American Jewish History* 95, no. 3 (2009): 225–47.

17. Eliot, "The Potency of the Jewish Race," *Menorah Journal* 1, no. 3 (1915): 144.

18. Eliot, "The Potency of the Jewish Race," 144.

19. Wagoner and Wagoner Jr., "Charles T. Eliot, Immigrants, and the Decline of American Idealism," 27–35.

20. Lyon, "Jewish Contributions to Civilizations," 817.

21. Lyon, "Jewish Contributions to Civilizations," 818.

22. Lyon, "Jewish Contributions to Civilizations," 818.

23. Lyon, "Jewish Contributions to Civilization," 822.

24. Lyon, "Jewish Contributions to Civilizations," 819.

25. Hallote, "Jacob H. Schiff and the Beginning of Biblical Archaeology in the United States," 234.

26. Lyon, "Jewish Contributions to Civilizations," 820.

27. Lyon's diaries are available online through the Harvard University Archives: https://hollisarchives.lib.harvard.edu/repositories/4/archival_objects/1077377. For 1891 address, see Diary Ephemera, 1891, Papers of David Gordon Lyon, HUG 1541, Harvard University Archives. (Lyon collection subsequently designated "Lyon Papers").

28. Schiff quoted in in Cyrus Adler, *Jacob H. Schiff: His Life and Letters* (Garden City NY: Doubleday, Doran, 1928), 21.

29. Lyon, "The Harvard Semitic Building," *Boston Evening Transcript*, February 16, 1899, 12.

30. Harvard University, *The Semitic Museum of Harvard University: Addresses Delivered at the Formal Opening of the Museum on Thursday, February 5, 1903* (Cambridge MA: Harvard University Press, 1903), 21.

31. *The Semitic Museum*, 15, 18.

32. *The Semitic Museum*, 26, 28.

33. *The Semitic Museum*, 5-6.

34. *The Semitic Museum*, 13.

35. *The Semitic Museum*, 20.

36. *Boston Evening Transcript*, April 29, 1903, 15.

37. Frederick Rice, Jr. "The Semitic Museum: A General Account of Its Interesting Collections and Statement of Its Needs," *New Era Illustrated Magazine* 4, no. 5 (1904): 230.

38. See Michael B. Oren, *Power, Faith, and Fantasy: America in the Middle East, 1776 to the Present* (London: W.W. Norton, 2007), 282-83.

39. Rice, "The Semitic Museum," 232.

40. Rice, "The Semitic Museum," 226.

41. Lyon, "Finds Proofs Today in Palestine," *Chicago Evening Post*, February 26, 1910.

42. Lyon, "On the Archaeological Exploration of Palestine: Presidential Address, 1910," *Journal of Biblical Literature* 30, no. 1 (1911): 2-3, 6.

43. Lyon, "Finds Proofs Today in Palestine."

44. Lyon, Diary Ephemera, 1893, Lyon Papers.

45. Lyon, "A Semitic Museum for Harvard," Address to the Elysium Club, May 23, 1899, Box 15, Lecture Series, Lyon Papers.

46. Lyon diary, April 15, 1908.

47. Meaghan Dwyer-Ryan et al., *Becoming American Jews: Temple Israel of Boston* (Waltham MA: Brandeis University Press, 2009), 63.

48. Mary Elvira Elliot et al., *Representative Women of New England*, ed. Julia Ward Howe (Boston: New England Historical, 1904), 335.

49. Harvard University, *Reports of the President and the Treasurer of Harvard College, 1905-06* (Cambridge MA: Harvard University, 1907), 27.

50. Harvard University, *Reports of the President*, 27.

51. Harvard University, *Annual Reports of the President and the Treasurer of Harvard College, 1899-1900* (Cambridge MA: Harvard University, 1901), 303.

52. Lyon to Schiff, November 11, 1913, Box 12, Correspondence Series, Lyon Papers.

53. See Joseph A. Greene, "A Complicated Legacy: The Original Collections of the Semitic Museum," *Journal of Eastern Mediterranean Archaeology and Heritage Studies* 5, no. 1 (2017): 66.

54. See John Higham, *Strangers in the Land: Patterns of American Nativism, 1860-1925* (New Brunswick NJ: Rutgers University Press, 1955), 264-99.

55. Lowell, "The Colonial Expansion of the United States," *Atlantic Monthly*, November 1899, 152.

56. "Lowell Tells Jews Limit Might Help Them," *New York Times*, June 17, 1922, 1, 6.

57. Synnott, *Half-Opened Door*, 19.
58. See Synnott, *Half-Opened Door*, 58–84.
59. Lyon diary, January 26, 1926.
60. Lyon diary, January 9, 1922.
61. Lyon diary, May 23, 1922.
62. Synnott, *Half-Opened Door*, 65.
63. In Box 16, Subject Files, 1894–1927 and Undated: Admission of Jews to Harvard, 1922–23, Lyon Papers, HUG 1541, Harvard University Archives.
64. Faculty Petition to President Lowell, May 28, 1922, Box 16, Admission of Jews to Harvard, 1922–23, Lyon Papers; see diary entry for May 28, 1922.
65. Lyon's narration of events and student evaluations all found in box 16, Admission of Jews to Harvard, 1922–23, Lyon Papers.
66. "Discrimination against Jews Suspected in New Harvard Policy on Admissions," *New York Times*, June 2, 1922, 1.
67. *Life Magazine*, July 6, 1922, 15.
68. See "The Flavor of Harvard," New Republic, August 16, 1922, 322–23.
69. Lyon diary, June 2, 1922.
70. Mack to Lyon, June 24, 1922, Box 16, Admission of Jews to Harvard, 1922–1923, Lyon Papers.
71. Unpublished Lyon interview, Box 16, Admission of Jews to Harvard, 1922–1923, Lyon Papers.
72. See Lyon diary, June 24, 1922.
73. See Daniel Greene, *The Jewish Origins of Cultural Pluralism: The Menorah Association and American Diversity* (Bloomington: Indiana University Press, 2011).
74. Lyon diary, June 20, 1922.
75. Lyon, Address to Lodge of B'nai B'rith, November 27, 1922, Box 16, Admission of Jews to Harvard, 1922–23, Lyon Papers.
76. Lyon, "The Jew and Education," November 24, 1922, Box 16, Admission of Jews to Harvard, 1922–23, Lyon Papers.
77. "Harvard Asks Race and Color of New Students," *New York Tribune*, September 20, 1922, 1.
78. See Starr, "The Affair at Harvard: What the Students Did," *Menorah Journal* 8 (1922): 263–76.
79. Lyon diary, April 9, 1922.
80. Synnott, *Half-Opened Door*, 106–10.
81. Lyon diary, March 3, 1926.
82. Lyon diary, March 7, 1926.
83. See Janet Tassel, "The Museum Trail: The Harvard Semitic Museum Rises Again," *Biblical Archaeologist* 46, no. 2 (1983): 101–8.
84. Wechsler, "Anti-Semitism in the Academy: Jewish Learning in American Universities, 1914–1939," *American Jewish Archives* 42 (1990): 11.

5

Use and Abuse of the Bible
German Christian Antisemitism in the 1930s and 1940s

LEONARD GREENSPOON

"For you are a people holy to the LORD your God; it is you the LORD has chosen out of all the peoples on earth to be his people, his treasured possession." (Deuteronomy 14:2)

"For the LORD has chosen Jacob for himself, Israel as his own possession." (Psalm 135:4)

"An account of the genealogy of Jesus the Messiah, the son of David, the son of Abraham." (Matthew 1:1)

"After eight days had passed, it was time to circumcise the child; and he was called Jesus, the name given by the angel before he was conceived in the womb. When the time came for their purification according to the law of Moses, they brought him up to Jerusalem to present him to the Lord." (Luke 2:21-22)

Imagine that you are a Lutheran pastor somewhere in Germany sometime in the mid- to late 1930s. In the best Protestant tradition, you base your sermons—and you'd like to think you base your life—on the Bible.[1] You are also a supporter of the National Socialists, though not a card-carrying member of the Nazi party. For you, as well as for most of your colleagues, these two affiliations, far from being contradictory, are mutually supportive.[2]

For this to be truly the case, governmental policies, including anti-Jewish rhetoric and actions, must be seen to be consistent with God's word as uniquely expressed in the Bible. When confronted with biblical passages like the ones above—two from the Old Testament and two from the New Testament—how is it possible to overcome the apparent dissonance between what appear to be the biblical messages of Jews as the Chosen People and Jesus being a

Jew and the demonization (in the secular and sacred realms) of twentieth-century Jews promoted by the Nazis?

In the first part of this chapter we will explore the ways in which the Bible was used (or, as I contend, abused) to support anti-Judaism. We will begin with some general considerations for both testaments and then move to reliance on specific themes or passages from the Old Testament. But this is only part of the story, as dismaying as this part is. The New Testament also contains passages criticizing, even demonizing, "the Jews." The history of their interpretation is an important one for Protestant clergy and faculty to know and is the subject of the second part of this chapter. In the third part we pay appropriate attention to those Christians, admittedly a small minority, whose encounters with the Bible led them to live, and sometimes die, in opposition to the Nazis.[3] Individuals' misreadings and misapplications of biblical text gained traction when supported by powerful groups that held sway over substantial segments of the population. But they did not go unchallenged. In the fourth and final part of this chapter, we will have the opportunity to compare and contrast this (ab)use of the Bible with two other instances in the nineteenth and twentieth centuries. This will also open us to the recognition of, and appreciation for, those whose identification with the Bible led them to uphold its authentic teachings.

Part 1: The Bible and Anti-Judaism

The Old Testament verses cited above were intentionally selected from many similar verses to demonstrate that the theme or trope of Chosen People was not restricted to one section of the Bible. If indeed the Israelites, forebears of the Jews, were uniquely marked by God as his "own, treasured possession," how could their persecution, to say nothing of their annihilation, be part of the divine plan?

A maximalist approach, if you will, would be to exclude the entire Old Testament as Sacred Writ for Christians, seeing it instead as an accretion to, and perversion of, God's true word as presented in the New Testament. Such an extreme view was in fact promoted by some in the early church, but the majority view adopted by Catholic, Orthodox, and Protestant Christians was that the Old Testament, while "perfected" by the New, was nonetheless part of God's authoritative revelation. The force of this tradition was, however, not strong enough to deter many German Christian supporters of Nazism from taking the extreme step of excision.[4]

But maybe only some of the Old Testament had been "contaminated" by Jews. In this case, passages indicating God's eternal promise to his people could be excluded. Definitely to be retained, on the other hand, were all of the passages—found with some frequency in the words of the prophets—that explicitly condemned Israel's behavior, thereby rendering the Israelites, and the Jews as their descendants, unfit to be regarded as God's people. There were also narrative sections, as for example the stories of the patriarchs and matriarchs in the book of Genesis, that implicitly criticized the founders of Judaism as flawed (we might say fatally flawed) individuals carrying odious traits that latter-day Jews had inherited and continued to exemplify.

A third option would be to retain almost all of the Protestant Old Testament (excluding the Apocrypha found in Catholic editions), but reassign or reidentify the heroes and villains. Along these lines, "true" Germans and others of Teutonic origins could become the Chosen People, the heirs of God's promises. Under this method, the ancient Israelites and modern Jews would become cursed, not blessed, and those who would punish them—the Egyptians, the Babylonians, the Assyrians, among others—morph into the Nazis and their political and ideological allies. As such, they become, to use a biblical turn of phrase, the "rods of God's anger."[5]

As we shall see, these options were often used in tandem and were buttressed by other arguments. But for the most part, they were not well crafted to deal with the central "problem" of the New Testament: namely, the pronouncement that Jesus was born, lived, and died a Jew. The New Testament verses cited above are among many that proclaim this.

It was not a theologically viable option to offer a Christian Bible without any New Testament. What is Christianity without Christ? That said, what was Christianity with a divine founder who was Jewish? In response to these concerns, some German Christians decided that authentic New Testament Scripture comprised only an edited version of the Gospel of Luke and most of Paul's letters in truncated form. Anything that connected or identified Jesus with Judaism was excluded.

A less drastic reconfiguring of the New Testament retained most of the Gospels by equating Jesus the Galilean with Jesus the Aryan.[6] This served to contrast him with his opponents, who were Judeans and Jews. In this scenario, Jesus had come not only to downgrade Judaism but also to overwhelm Jews. What the Nazis were doing, then, was fully in accordance with God's will—whether or not all of them recognized this.

Any of these approaches left unanswered one significant question: if the authentic New Testament promoted this absolute distinction between Jews and Jesus, how did it happen that subsequent editions of the New Testament read as they did? There was only one possible explanation: Jewish editors and scribes "infected" the original text by introducing malicious and misguided material ascribing a Jewish identity to Jesus. And they had, as even German Christian leaders had to acknowledge, been remarkably successful in this misdirection for almost two thousand years. Thus, purging Jewish elements from the New Testament was in reality cleansing it. What could be more pleasing to God?

For the most part I cite and discuss Old Testament examples in their canonical (Protestant) order. It would be a mistake to expect consistency in (mis)understandings, as the same verse or image could elicit different reactions in different circumstances. Equally fruitless would be the search for contextual interpretations—that is, interpreting passages within their immediate biblical context.

For some exegetes, the earliest reference to the true nature of Jews is found in Genesis 4, where Cain, "marked" by the Lord, is branded "a fugitive and a wanderer of the earth." Ignoring the statement that Cain's "mark" was actually for his protection, German Christian exegetes saw here the origins of the wandering or rootless Jew. Within the context of twentieth-century Germany, this status, understood as divinely ordained, excluded Jews as loyal citizens or residents of the land and devalued them as clannish foreign interlopers who should never be trusted to put national interests over their international dealings.

The very first patriarch, Abraham, though he had some admirable traits, was most often described as a serial liar. After all, he twice asked his wife Sarah to pretend that she was his sister in order to save his own skin (Genesis 12 and 20). From the very beginning Jews placed little importance on truth. And this, it was argued, continued to be one of their distinguishing characteristics.

Jacob was another unattractive figure. Because he was renamed Israel, his activities, especially the ethically questionable ones, could be applied to all of his descendants. In Genesis 25 Jacob is pictured forcing his brother Esau, nearing starvation, to hand over his birthright in return for a bowl of stew. And, just two chapters later, Jacob deceives his dying father into bestowing on him the blessing that Isaac had intended for Esau. It was no great leap of faith for interpreters to equate the supposedly notorious dishonesty of contemporary Jews with that of their eponymous ancestor. It was also reason enough for a number of Christian men named Jacob to change their name.

In addition to being untrustworthy, Jews were reputed to be consumed with a desire for wealth. In Exodus 32 the Jews in the wilderness had enough precious metals in store to construct a golden calf. Where did this wealth come from? According to some interpretations of Exodus 12 and parallel passages, the departing Israelites had asked "to borrow" gold and silver from the Egyptians. Since they had no intention of repaying it, this was another example of Israelite—that is, Jewish—deception in busy dealings of all types.

And so it went. For any figure who could be identified positively as a hero, there were one or more defining flaws. The vaunted King David? He ordered the death of his mistress's husband (Bathsheba and Uriah, 2 Samuel 11). And much of the second half of the book of 2 Samuel chronicles the dissolution of his family through incest, intrigue, and rebellion. David was indeed a paragon, but not of virtue, for all of the conniving and disloyal Jews who followed in his wake.

This held true even when David acted bravely and victoriously, as in his battle against Goliath in 1 Samuel 17. Improbably, from our perspective, German Christians identified with Goliath, a true Aryan warrior if there ever was one: "His height was six cubits and a span. He had a helmet of bronze on his head, and he was armed with a coat of mail; the weight of the coat was five thousand shekels of bronze. He had greaves of bronze on his legs and a javelin of bronze slung between his shoulders. The shaft of his spear was like a weaver's beam, and his spear's head weighed six hundred shekels of iron; and his shield-bearer went before him" (vv. 4–7). As for David, so puny he was unable to walk with helmet or sword, his weakness and seeming insignificance drew unfavorable comparisons with the mighty Goliath. Of course, for these identifications to work, the outcome of the battle—David's improbable victory over Goliath—had to be ignored. But once again the context that mattered for Christian supporters of Nazism was their own experience, not the full account in the Bible.

Any number of biblical characters could be pressed into service as precursors to Hitler. Once Germans, or more broadly Aryans, were identified as the authentically Chosen People, then Hitler's "deliverance" of Germany could be likened to Moses's role in liberating the Hebrew slaves from Egypt. Or, looked at from another perspective, Hitler's annihilation of the Jews was in line with Nebuchadnezzar's destruction of Jerusalem: both divinely ordained punishments for a people—actually the same people—who turned away from God.

This leads to another (mis)characterization of Hitler as a biblical prophet chastising the Israelites (Jews) for an almost endless list of individual and communal failings. Where German Christians retained the prophetic books and narratives in their Bibles, it was to bring out what they saw as a pattern of Jewish sin leading to divine punishment that was to play out in their own time as it had in antiquity. Not surprisingly, the other elements of the pattern—Israelite repentance and divine salvation—did not appear in church preaching or teaching.

As God's spokespersons, one of the primary goals of the biblical prophets was indeed to shake the Israelite community from its complacent belief that all was well. Thus prophets' criticisms of Israelites were not infrequent. For the sake of analysis, we can divide their targets into two categories: ritual sins and social sins. The former, which included, for example, the failure to offer sacrifices in the prescribed way, were of less interest to German Christians. Instead, they focused on Israel's failure, individual and communal, to practice justice among each other. To illustrate this, I will select representative passages from each of the following Minor Prophets: Amos, Hosea, and Micah, where these themes are especially prominent.

> Amos (chapters 4–6) God is against the Israelites, "who oppress the poor, who crush the needy . . . you trample on the poor . . . afflict the righteous and take bribes . . . lie on beds of ivory and lounge on your couches."

> Hosea (chapter 4) God is against the Israelites: "There is no honesty or goodness and no obedience to God in the land. [False] swearing, lying, and murder, and stealing and adultery break out; bloodshed follows upon bloodshed."

> Micah (chapter 2) Among the sins of Israel's leaders, they "plan wickedness and evil deeds on their beds; when the morning dawns, they do it, because it is in their power. They covet fields, and seize them; houses, and take them away; they defraud householders of their homes, and people of the land they should inherit."

Let us be clear: German Christians did not make up these accusations, nor were they alone in enhancing their force.[7] But they purposely removed these passages from their proper biblical context by omitting prophetic calls for repentance and God's positive response to such actions. Moreover, whenever it suited their purposes to do so, church leaders readily applied such characterizations (or, more accurately, misapplied such mischaracterizations) to the Jews of their day, who supposedly sought material gain at the expense of everyone else; lied, cheated, stole, and worse when it suited their purposes; and maneuvered from dawn to dusk to flaunt ethical and legal norms to gain what was not rightfully theirs. On behalf of God, so the argument went, the biblical prophets poured down divine wrath on the ancient Israelites. In like manner, God appointed, and anointed, Hitler and his henchmen to end Jewish perfidy by annihilating Jews.

Part 2: Demonizing "the Jews"

Throughout the New Testament Jesus's opponents are labeled "Jews." (The Greek term is *Ioudaioi*, to which we will return below.) In the traditional reading of such passages, to which German Christians subscribed, this group of people, individually and collectively, were hostile to Jesus. A more balanced view of the context of such passages would question this us versus them dichotomy, but in fact such nuanced interpretations were rare among Christians until well after World War II and had scant support among the Protestant theologians who held sway in Germany and elsewhere during the first half of the twentieth century.

What do these anti-Ioudaioi passages look like? I include here a representative sampling of such language. Although this and related themes are more frequent in some portions of the New Testament (see especially the Acts of the Apostles and the Gospel of John), it is crucial to acknowledge their presence in pretty much every part of the New Testament.[8]

The Gospels

(Matthew 8:11–12) Jews lack faith: "And Jesus said, 'Truly I tell you, in no one in Israel have I found such faith. I tell you, many will come from east and west and will eat with Abraham and Isaac and Jacob in the kingdom of heaven, while the heirs of the kingdom [that is, the Jews] will be thrown into the outer darkness, where there will be weeping and gnashing of teeth.'"

In Jesus's view, it is a Roman officer, a centurion, who embodies the faith that Jews lack. This contrast extends to the eschatological future: Gentiles like this centurion will gain admittance to the kingdom of heaven and eat (probably understood literally as well as metaphorically) with the patriarchs. By contrast, there will be no place in the kingdom for those who fancy themselves its heir—that is, the Jews. Only darkness and suffering await them.

(Matthew 27:20–26) Jews take responsibility for Jesus's death: "Now the chief priests and the elders persuaded the crowds to ask for Barabbas and to have Jesus killed. The governor again said to them, 'Which of the two do you want me to release for you?' And they said, 'Barabbas.' Pilate said to them, 'Then what should I do with Jesus who is called the Messiah?' All of them said, 'Let him be crucified!' Then he asked, 'Why, what evil has he done?' But they shouted all the more, 'Let him be crucified!' So when Pilate saw that he could do nothing, but rather that a riot was beginning, he took some water and washed his hands before the crowd, saying, 'I am innocent of this man's blood; see to it yourselves.' Then the people as a whole answered, 'His blood be on us and on our children!' So he released Barabbas for them; and after flogging Jesus, he handed him over to be crucified."[9]

In this scene, which is not found in any of the other canonical gospels, responsibility for Jesus's death is entirely the Jews'. Not only this, but these Jews are portrayed as willingly taking on this responsibility, and passing on the guilt to their descendants as well. This passage was regularly used by Christians to criticize Jews of their own generation as Christ killers. (Such inherited guilt is no longer part of the teaching or preaching of the Roman Catholic Church and many other Christian denominations.)

(Mark 11:18) Jews seek to kill Jesus: "And when the chief priests and the scribes heard Jesus's teachings against the Temple, they kept looking for a way to kill him; for they were afraid of him, because the whole crowd was spellbound by his teaching."

Jewish antipathy, even leading to murder, was evidenced by leaders such as the chief priests and scribes well before Jesus's crucifixion. It is not clear what particular aspects of Temple worship Jesus was objecting to when he "cleansed" it. But the destruction of the Jerusalem Temple in 70 CE was widely interpreted by Jesus's followers as a divine punishment that enabled Jesus to fully assume in his person the sanctity and promise the Temple had held as an institution.

(John 8:39–47) Jews are sons of the devil: "The Jews answered Jesus, 'Abraham is our father.' Jesus said to them, 'If you were Abraham's children, you would be doing what Abraham did, but now you are trying to kill me, a man who has told you the truth that I heard from God. This is not what Abraham did.' Jesus said to them, 'If God were your Father, you would love me, for I came from God and now I am here. I did not come on my own, but he sent me. Why do you not understand what I say? It is because you cannot accept my word. You are from your father the devil, and you choose to do your father's desires. He was a murderer from the beginning and does not stand in the truth, because there is no truth in him. When he lies, he speaks according to his own nature, for he is a liar and the father of lies. Whoever is from God hears the words of God. The reason you do not hear them is that you are not from God.'"

This designation of Satan as the progenitor of the Jews is the basis, historically and theologically, for much of the antisemitism Jews experienced. As in Matthew 8:11–12, discussed earlier, Jews who deny Jesus's claims may consider themselves descendants of Abraham. But, as Jesus counters here, nothing could be further from reality. All of God's promises would indeed be fulfilled, but not in the Jewish community whose descent from the devil was made especially manifest in their virulent rejection of Jesus.

Acts

(3:15) Jews killed Jesus: "Peter addressed the people: 'You Israelites killed the Author of life, whom God raised from the dead. To this we are witnesses.'"

Peter's statement succinctly characterizes the actions of Jews, who demanded Jesus's death before Herod, as the primary catalyst for his crucifixion. This verse neatly contrasts the life-giving powers of Jesus (the Author of life) and God (who raises from the dead) with the dire consequences of being Jewish (here, Israelite), namely, killing and death. This dichotomy between Jesus's bestowal of life and the Jews' fixation on death was absolute, beginning with Peter and Jesus's other disciples and continuing on to their followers through all generations.

Epistles

(1Thessalonians 2:14–16) Jews killed Jesus: "For you, brothers and sisters, became imitators of the churches of God in Christ Jesus that are in Judea, for you suffered the same things from your own compatriots as they did from the Jews, who killed both the Lord Jesus and the prophets, and drove us out; they displease God and oppose everyone by hindering us from speaking to the Gentiles so that they may be saved. Thus they have constantly been filling up the measure of their sins; but God's wrath has overtaken them at last."

In addressing the congregation at Thessaloniki, Paul first equates the possibility of their persecution in the future with the reality of past suffering of Jesus's followers in Judea at the hands of the Jews. What then follows, as part of Paul's diatribe, is a statement of the major anti-Jesus activities concocted by the Jews: the murder of Jesus and silencing of those who truly spoke words of prophecy, the forcible eviction of some of Jesus's followers from their homes, and turning against God in every possible way. Here the emphasis falls on opponents of Paul who stymied his mission to the Gentiles, whose conversion to the ranks of Jesus's followers they (that is, the Jews) adamantly opposed.

Revelation

(2:9) Synagogues are of Satan: "I know your affliction and your poverty, even though you are rich. I know the slander on the part of those who say that they are Jews and are not, but are a synagogue of Satan." (The expression "synagogue of Satan" also occurs in Revelation 3:9).

What is this reference to "a synagogue of Satan" frequented by those who claim (falsely, according to John, the reputed author of Revelation), to be Jews? Although certainty of interpretation is not possible here within the context of the book of Revelation itself, historically Jews who oppose Jesus constitute a group of what we might call delusional Jews. If this is so, then, in John's view, being a follower of Christ was the major and determinative factor for true Jews and authentic Judaism. Just as Jews were singled out as descendants of Satan in an earlier passage (John 8:39–47), so their distinctive institution, the synagogue, also belonged in some real sense to Satan.

The number and scope of these passages could be considerably increased by including, for example, those that refer to the Pharisees, scribes, or priests. In several of the passages cited above those terms do appear, but as part of a crowd or assembly.

Martin Luther (in *The Jews and Their Lies* [1543]) cited some of these passages, as well as others, in this vitriolic diatribe of his later years:

> Jesus did not call them Abraham's children, but a "brood of vipers" [Mathew 3:7]. Furthermore in John 8, he states, "You are of your father the devil." It was intolerable to them to hear that they were not Abraham's but the devil's children, nor can they bear to hear this today.

> Learn from this, dear Christian, what you are doing if you permit the blind Jews to mislead you. Then the saying will truly apply, "When a blind man leads a blind man, both will fall into the pit" [Luke 6:39]. You cannot learn anything from them except how to misunderstand the divine commandments.

> My essay, I hope, will have served to furnish a Christian with enough material not only to defend himself against the blind, venomous Jews but also to become the foe of the Jews' malice, lying and cursing, and to understand not only that their belief is false but that they are surely possessed by all devils.[10]

This biblically inspired hatred of Jews took many forms over the almost two millennia between the writing of the New Testament and the onset of the Holocaust. Frequently there were those (including the younger Luther himself) who offered conversion as a means of correcting the supposed flaws of Jews and Judaism. Such efforts ran the gamut from fairly benign (if insistent) preaching to demanding a literally life-or-death decision at gun- or knifepoint. Underlying all such efforts was the presupposition that individuals or communities could, via a series of oaths and actions, cease to be Jewish and become Christian. Throughout history there were Jews who, out of self-determination or self-interest, chose this path, which their children and other descendants typically followed.

There were often tangible benefits to renouncing Judaism and embracing Christianity (fully or only publicly), as full participation in the political and economic institutions of cities, regions, and nations throughout Europe was usually reserved for professing

Christians. Jews could survive, and on occasion thrive, but always at the whim of one or more protectors among the ruling political or religious leadership. Even when they were a piteously powerless minority, however, there were effective familial, social, and religious structures in place for the maintenance of Jewish identity.

In short, there were choices, often difficult and always constricted. But, for the most part, the extirpation of Judaism as a religion did not require the elimination of individuals who sought (or were perceived to be seeking) entry into the larger Christian world. And, in fact, for long periods of time the regnant interpretation of New Testament passages such as those cited above did not call for the abolition of Jews and Judaism. Basing their understandings on the teachings of St. Augustine, many Christian leaders (both lay and ecclesiastical) followed the early fifth century exegete in calling for the preservation of at least some Jews, who at an appointed time would be re-grafted (to use Augustine's agricultural imagery) onto the roots of true believers, thereby initiating the second and final coming of Jesus.[11] Clearly Jews, as individuals and as communities, were to be abased, if not abused, but their continued existence, as tenuous as it was, was perceived to be part of a divinely ordained plan. Even the massacres of European Jews in connection with the First and Third Crusades and the invention of anti-Jewish canards like the blood libel and desecration of the consecrated host were not universally accepted or encouraged.

For many scholars the distinction between anti-Jewish and antisemitic activities lies in the fact that those harboring anti-Jewish attitudes would typically welcome individuals who had been Jewish but converted to Christianity. With the rise of pseudoscientific theories in the nineteenth century, Judaism was reconceived as a race and perceived as an immutable and permanent condition. No one, so the argument went, could stop being Jewish—or Teutonic, for that matter. Moreover, distinctive physical, intellectual, and psychological traits characterized each "race."

It is less well known that the earliest manifestations of Judaism as a racial category date back to the late fifteenth century in Spain as a byproduct of the Inquisition. Under threat of expulsion, many Jews on the Iberian Peninsula accepted baptism as a rite of conversion to Christianity. But a substantial percentage of those who did so retained their connection to Judaism in private. It was these "hidden" Jews that the Inquisition targeted, among other victims. Its perpetrators presumed, not incorrectly, that there was an essential part (or combination of parts) of Jewish identity that conversion would not, or could not, change. Even though the elements of comparison differed, this view shared with the late, "racial" designation the basic premise "once a Jew, always a Jew."[12]

It is worth noting that the Nazi conception of Jews as a race, with its dependence on such features as physiognomy and blood typing, played a substantial role in the development of what we generally call the Confessing Church (as opposed to German Christianity), who on the whole merit their characterization as courageous opponents of Hitler. But their opposition was not always directed toward what we might consider optimal goals. Many in the Confessing Church opposed the designation of Jews as a race not because of some biblically derived view of the equality of all humans, but rather as a defense of the Christian practice of baptism. The Nazis' contention that Jews remained Jews even after converting to Christianity would negate the traditional belief that an individual was reborn or born again as a result of baptism. Although it is for this reason correct to see much of the Confessing Church's interest as self-interest, it nonetheless served to keep some Jews alive, even those who did not formally join the Church.[13]

To return to the issue of anti-Judaism, if not antisemitism, in the New Testament, we should observe that even in the late nineteenth-early twentieth century there were options beyond interpreting every reference to Ioudaioi as a divinely ordained, unchanging, and essentially permanent stigma that attached itself to every Jew from Jesus's time until the present. Although admittedly not all of these options were well developed or articulated in, say, the 1930s, the critical study of the Bible was nonetheless a hallmark and bedrock of Protestant biblical studies at German universities.

We noted above that the term *Ioudaioi* is ambiguous in that it could be a geographical or religious designation.[14] In the context of this part of our discussion, this uncertainty allowed for the criticisms by Jesus and others to be accounted for as intra-Jewish conflict, with Galilean and Judean Jews at odds on any number of rituals or beliefs, perhaps centered on the Jerusalem Temple.

Among other approaches were those that saw the origins of critical comments about Ioudaioi within the contexts of the Gospel writers' eras rather than in the time when Jesus lived. This stance is especially popular in explicating the intensity of the animosity expressed by Jesus in the Gospel of John against his seeming contemporaries, whose "Jewishness" decisively separated them from him.[15] Since nineteenth-century critical scholarship had already discerned several separate layers of composition within the Gospels (the life of Jesus, a period of oral transmission, and the periods in which each Gospel was committed to writing), such an approach removed this material from Jesus's sayings, although not from the New Testament itself.

A more traditional yet quasi-critical approach asserts that the "red-letter" words were in essence Jesus's, but their intended application was limited to a specific audience under specific circumstances as determined by the literary context of a given passage. Since many of Jesus's words and activities are paralleled, but not replicated, in more than one New Testament book, Jesus's sayings would not necessarily be limited to one instance, but with equal validity we would maintain that their application is not fruitfully expanded to all audiences at all times.

To sum up, German Christian pastors had access to a number of New Testament passages about "the Jews." In tone they ranged from mildly critical to wildly adversarial. Although the more learned Church men had access to multiple exegetical tools, their negative assessments of Jews and Judaism, from Jesus's time to their own day, dictated what they would teach and how they would preach. Their adherence to this approach made them useful to Nazi propagandists, whether or not such propagandists self-identified as Christian.

Up to this point we have evaluated members of the Confessing Church as narrowly focused opponents to Nazi racial policy, but this alone does not do justice to the much wider and principled stances they and other Christians took. It is to this topic that we now turn.

Part 3: The Bible and Opposition to the Nazis

I do not know of any statistics that provide more than rough estimates for the percentage of German Protestants who actively opposed the Nazis' racial policies on the basis of their exegesis and application of the Bible. Among other reasons for this uncertainty is the documented inflation of numbers by pro-Nazi Christians who repackaged themselves as philo-Semites after the war. But no matter! Though of little influence, it was in these individuals that moral courage resided.

Among the most renowned of these theologians was Dietrich Bonhoeffer, who, with his allies, formed what came to be known as the Confessing Church.[16] It was not a monolithic or even meticulously structured organization. Membership changed, motives changed, methods of opposition varied. Not all, perhaps not even most, of those who identified with the Confessing Church did so out of a sense that Jews too were God's people, whose religious beliefs and practices functioned as valid ways of worshipping and living. Rather, they continued to adhere to the relatively benign instruction of St. Augustine, according to which at least some Jews needed to stay alive until the moment (perhaps not far off) when their conversion would signal the Second Coming of Jesus and the millennial age. Others opposed the persecution of Jews as anti-Christian, which indeed it was. For such individuals, however, the purity of Christians rather than the security of Jews was preeminent.

Let us look at a few of the passages that impelled some German Christians to be supportive of Jews. Interestingly enough, the story of Cain and Abel from Genesis 4 was regularly cited. In interpreting this passage, Jews were equated with Abel, and the Nazis and their supporters were identified with Cain. When Cain asks, "Am I my brother's keeper?," the only valid reaction for the sensitive reader is "Yes, you are." God's response, as recorded in the Old Testament, would have been seen as especially poignant as well as pointed: "Your brother's blood is crying out to me from the ground! And now you are cursed from the ground, which has opened its mouth to receive your brother's blood from your hand."

In the 1930s and 1940s, the blood shed by one brother was immeasurably multiplied—as was the curse.

Earlier we observed that pro-Nazi exegetes took the story of David and Goliath out of its biblical context when they fashioned Goliath, who was humiliated by David, as an archetypal Teutonic hero. Here we can observe that philo-Jewish interpreters concluded their account before the ending of Genesis 4. Cain ultimately received a mark from God that was intended to keep him safe from anyone who would try to kill him. It is most unlikely, to say the least, that members of the Confessing Church had any such deliverance in mind for the Nazis.

At the same time, sympathetic Protestant scholars may have been familiar with a rabbinic midrash on Genesis 4 that could not have been more applicable to their own age. Observing that the Hebrew word for "blood" always appears in the plural—in such expressions as "your brother's blood"—the rabbis responsible for this midrash calculated that the murder of even one person deprived the world of countless others, that is, the children, grandchildren, and so on, whose births would no longer be possible. No more need be said about this analogy when it comes to the Holocaust.

Confessing Church members sometimes used 2 Samuel 16:17 to indict Christians who were indifferent to the plight of the Jews, to say nothing of those who took an active part in inciting or carrying out atrocities. The query cited—"Is this your loyalty [or kindness] to your friend? Why did you not go with your friend?"—is situated biblically within a complicated series of maneuvers involving King David, but was applied with equal (if not greater) aptness to the twentieth century.

The prohibition against killing, or more precisely murder, was regularly ignored by those who engineered the taking of Jewish life on a massive scale. Some Confessing Church members expanded the prohibition to cover any action that would diminish the worth of a human life from God's perspective. This was taken to include such common Nazi practices as confining large numbers of Jews to ghettoes or other constricted neighborhoods, forcing Jews from their jobs, and subjecting them to ridicule or defamation. Inherent in this broad application of the prohibition was the insight that the Nazi persecution of Jews often began with what at first seemed to be far from life-threatening actions.

Bonhoeffer was among those who annotated his copy of the Old Testament to demonstrate his solidarity with the Jews as the apple of God's eye, a people set apart through their covenantal relationship with the Lord. So, in connection with Psalm 74, which describes an attack on Mount Zion, Bonhoeffer boldly and directly identified the Nazis and their supporters as "your foes [who] have roared within your holy place / they set up their emblems there. . . . They said to themselves, 'We will utterly subdue them' / they burned all the / meeting places of God in the land" (vv. 4 and 8).

Bonhoeffer made this connection as early as the pogrom of November 1938 (Kristallnacht). Reflecting on the same events, another sympathetic preacher used Jeremiah 22:29—"O land, land, land / hear the word of the Lord"—as the starting point for his Repentance Day sermon. Surely, just as individuals reap what they sow, so a dreadful harvest for Germany would result from the planting of seeds of hatred that were already producing the destruction of synagogues, the closure of Jewish businesses and schools, and the murder of Jews. Unfortunately, this preacher was like the one Isaiah (40:3) described as "a voice crying out in the wilderness." But even such a lone or lonely voice could have changed the attitudes and actions of the few who were willing to listen.

Zechariah 2:12 was among the other prophetic passages Bonhoeffer and his colleagues adduced to counter charges that persecution of the Jews was in accordance with divine will. The text there reads, "The Lord will inherit Judah as his portion in the holy land, and will again choose Jerusalem." Even if some members of the Confessing Church proved obdurate in their antipathy toward Jews as a group, they might be persuaded to disassociate from the worst of Nazi practices by passages such as Jeremiah 7:1–9, addressed to those who "trust in deceptive words to no avail . . . stealing and murdering": "Amend your ways and your doings . . . do not trust in deceptive words. . . . Do not oppress the alien, the orphan, and the widow, or shed innocent blood." I would characterize these as calls to Christian charity in its broadest sense.

A singular instance of communal support for the Jews was

offered by the Huguenots, Protestants who lived in the village of Chambon-sur-Lignon in southern France. Led by their pastor, André Trochmé, the residents of this small, somewhat isolated community consistently risked their own lives to shelter and save Jews. Their experiences, and their ancestors', of persecution at the hands of the majority-Catholic population of France was undoubtedly a factor leading to their almost instinctive identification with fleeing Jews who ended up in Chambon. But beyond, or perhaps behind, these biographical similarities lay a sympathetic reading of the Old Testament. The villagers actually took to speaking of their Jews as "Old Testaments."[17]

Central to the task they undertook was their deliberate designation of Chambon as a city of refuge. The concept of such cities was developed biblically in Numbers 35 and Joshua 20. Here, as elsewhere, even sympathetic readers of the Bible took liberties in their application of ancient institutions to contemporary circumstances. Biblically speaking, the cities of refuge were established as places of safety for those who committed manslaughter (that is, the unintentional taking of a human life) from family members of the deceased who might seek revenge. The key element the Huguenots took from the biblical designation was the city as refuge or sanctuary for those who were unjustly pursued. Even as rank amateurs in the art of subterfuge, vis-à-vis the Germans and their French Vichy collaborators, the residents of Chambon were remarkably successful in saving perhaps as many as three thousand Jewish lives.

A later visitor to what had been Pastor Trochmé's church found a Bible opened to Psalm 119: "Blessed are those whose way is blameless / who walk in the law of the Lord! / Blessed are those who keep his decrees / who seek him with their whole heart. . . . Remember your words to your servants / in which you have made us hope. / This is our comfort in our distress / that your promise gives us life." Perhaps it was just serendipitous that someone had left the Bible open to this psalm. But it is certainly apposite as a biblical description of the motivations and accomplishments of the entire village of Chambon-sur-Lignon during World War II.

Part 4: Compare and Contrast (Ab)Uses of the Bible

For a number of years I taught a course at Creighton University titled The Bible and the Holocaust in Historical and Theological Context. It was listed under the rubric of Senior Perspectives, which is no longer a requirement of our undergraduate core.[18]

When I first proposed this course, my colleagues suggested expanding its coverage to include one or two other examples of how the Bible was used or abused in reference to what we might speak of as morally questionable pursuits. As it happened, one of my students had written a relevant paper for a previous course, "300 Years of Divine Guidance: The Transformation of the Dutch Reformed Church's [DRC] Theology in Response to the Rise of Afrikaner Christian-Nationalism."[19] It critically examined how the Church justified many of its practices with reference to its reliance on God's absolute sovereignty as made manifest in the Bible. To this was added the distinctively Calvinist understanding of predestination.

For example, Afrikaners (early Dutch settlers in South Africa) saw in their early victories a sign that they, as God's chosen people, were divinely protected even as they wandered in the wilderness. The indigenous African population was seen as unalterably heathen and inferior. Because of this judgment, native populations that at first were offered baptism were now excluded from this rite, which would otherwise have elevated them above their pre-destined status as slaves. This us versus them mentality served to distinguish Afrikaners not only from non-white (European) populations, but also from non-Afrikaners such as the British, whose monarch they styled as a pharaoh. Such an application of biblical imagery is, to say the least, inexact. But this is a phenomenon we have seen before from both sides of an argument.

In their struggles against the Zulus, the Afrikaners reckoned themselves martyrs for the Christian (that is, DRC) cause against heathenism. As instruments in the hands of God to put an end to hated Zulu practices, Afrikaner leaders sought to exterminate native Africans, taking their lead (so they argued) from the extermination of Canaanites by the Israelites as they entered the Promised

Land. As it happens, Genesis 10 designates Canaan as the eponymous founder of these nations and places him in the lineage of Noah as a grandson whose father was Ham. For the Afrikaners—and in this they were far from alone—blacks were devalued as the accursed sons of Ham, so that, in a sense, the Afrikaners sought to complete the process of annihilation that had eluded Joshua and his generation. After all, it was God "Most High who had apportioned the nations, when he divided humankind" (Deuteronomy 32:8).

In a sense the Afrikaners had gone full circle in applying (or, I would say, misapplying) their interpretation (I would say, misinterpretation) of primary biblical texts to justify their own racial, cultural, and religious superiority. This emboldened leaders such as Paul Kruger to address his soldiers in the words of general Joshua (Joshua 24:15): "Choose this day whom you will serve," secure in the knowledge that they would follow him. Nor should the Afrikaners despair if the forces they faced were more numerous and better equipped. In such circumstances, the Afrikaners could be likened to David. As in the victory over Goliath (the British), God, all-governing and mighty, once again revealed his most wondrous deliverance and help.

Even a defeat at the hands of their enemies was foreseen and preordained, as in Malachi 3:4. "God is like a refiner's fire and like fuller's soap, he will sit as a refiner and purifier of silver, and he will purify the descendants of Levi and refine them like gold and silver" was cited as proof that such losses, or trials by fire, served to make the surviving remnant that much closer to the ideal as God's people. It was this sort of people, the refined Afrikaners, of whom the Psalmist wrote, "Happy is the nation whose God is the Lord / the people whom he has chosen as his heritage" (Psalm 33:12). Not without good reason did a young journalist named Winston Churchill single out the hymns the Afrikaners sang on the battlefield for divine inspiration.

In early January 1861, on the initiative of President James Buchanan, preachers, pastors, and rabbis throughout the United States presented sermons on the hotly contested issue of slavery. From the pulpit abolitionists declared that what mattered most was the broad principle of common equity within the Bible. At the time, most attention was paid to the thundering rhetoric of Protestant abolitionists such as Henry Ward Beecher, whose sermon was printed in full on the front page of *The New York Times*. For them, slavery was inconsistent with the biblical principles of justice and righteousness. Pro-slavery advocates, on the other hand, placed the greatest emphasis on what they saw as the pro-slavery implications of specific biblical texts as well as the demonstrable fact that there was no clear-cut, forthright prohibition against this practice.

I have examined sermons by rabbis on each side of the argument.[20] First is Morris Jacob Raphall, who was at the time rabbi at Manhattan's Greene Street Synagogue. To the question of whether slaveholding was a sin before God, his response was an unequivocal no. Among other sources of support, he cited the Ten Commandments, in which Israel was instructed to give rest on the Sabbath to male and female slaves and to be resolute against coveting the male or female slaves of a neighbor. Slavery, Raphall reasoned, was just a part of life to which the Commandments attached no opprobrium or vilification.

Moreover, as Raphall saw it, no less impressive biblical characters than Abraham, Isaac, Jacob, and Job were all slaveholders who faced no condemnation for their status. If, Raphall queried, slaveholding was lawful in biblical times, how had it now become a sin? He concluded his sermon with both a personal disavowal of slavery and an affirmation that this institution was indeed biblically sanctioned: "But I stand here as a teacher in Israel . . . to propound to you the word of God, the Bible view of slavery."

On that same day, Bernard Illowy, a traditional rabbi in Baltimore, also spoke in favor of slavery, albeit with infrequent direct appeals to the Hebrew Bible. For the most part, he asked questions of those who "pretend to be more philanthropic than Moses": "Why did Moses not prohibit the buying and selling of slaves from and to other nations?" And, "Why did Ezra not command the Babylonian exiles . . . to set their slaves free and send them away?" The rhetoric of these two rabbis can be summed up this way: It was good enough for Abraham, Isaac, Jacob, Moses, Ezra, and Job. Why should we hold ourselves to higher standards, or be held to them?

Probably the best known of Raphall's interlocutors was a Reform rabbi, also in Baltimore, named David Einhorn. Interestingly, he delivered his sermon in German, but it was soon translated and widely circulated in English. For the German-born Einhorn, "the question simply is: Is Slavery a moral evil or not?" Responding in the positive, he also took direct aim at Raphall, who "concocted the deplorable farce in the name of divine authority . . . to designate slavery as a perfectly sinless institution sanctioned by God!"

Starting at the beginning, as it were, Einhorn observed that "God created man in His image" (Genesis 1:28), with no mention of dominion over the negro. After arguing that there was in fact no connection between the negroes and Canaan or Ham, Einhorn offered this rejoinder to Raphall: "No matter how this may be—the negroes must decline the honor of having been destined by Noah, who plated a vine-yard, but not cotton, to be slaves!" Einhorn continued by characterizing Scripture's position on slavery in this way: it merely tolerated the institution as an evil not to be disregarded, but eventually to be dissolved through the mild spirit of its legislation. This is far from the contention that Scripture favored, approved of, or justified any sort of slavery. If, as Raphall pointed out, Jews (Israelites) had once been slaveholders, shouldn't they always enjoy this status? Nonsense, Einhorn retorted: do Jews still accept bigamy or blood-vengeance?

Einhorn, as did others, called to mind "all of Israel's prophets who proclaimed . . . that all human beings on the whole wide globe are entitled to the service of God." Einhorn concluded that he was "no politician and I do not meddle in politics." Nonetheless, he fervently called upon the Jewish press and Jewish American leaders to raise firm objections to the proclamation of "slavery in the name of Judaism to be a God-sanctioned institution."

Conclusion

I have heard it said that you can prove anything from the Bible. I don't agree, unless the standards of proof being offered are entirely separated from rigor, morality, and faith. What I do think is true—but by no means beneficial—is that you can try to prove just about anything on the basis of the Bible.

This chapter has examined the process in several contexts, mostly related to the Holocaust. It is important to recognize that I am not contending that German Christian misuse or abuse of the Bible was the only or even the most significant rationale for the horror that was the Holocaust. But we err if we fail to acknowledge how people's perceptions of (in this instance) Jews and Judaism were shaped by what they read, or more likely heard, as the Bible's message—that is, God's word. This is especially true for Protestants, among whom frequent contact with the Bible and essentially literal understandings of its text predominate. When churchgoers heard the same teachings of contempt and condemnation week in and week out, it was bound to make an impression.

In this work I have studiously avoided assigning blame, except where there is, frankly, no other reaction to contemptible words and acts. Would that more pastors had stood up for the Jews, not as potential converts but as fellow believers! But they didn't.

In this chapter I have also attempted to convey some of the destructive power that propelled otherwise pious Christians toward unspeakable impieties. My goal has not been to ask readers to imagine what they would have done in similar circumstances. After all, we can all be the heroes of our own tellings and retellings of the past. Rather, I humbly request that all of us make use of our God-given talents (yes, I do describe them in this way) to avoid precipitous judgments or actions even—or perhaps especially—when we are assured that the Bible says it's so. Maybe it is. But then again, maybe it's not. And, as we've seen, that difference can have life-and-death implications far beyond a given educational or religious institution.

Questions for Further Discussion

1. What is the difference between Christian and "modern" racial antisemitism? Are there common elements or are they completely separate ideas?

2. Antisemitic Germans rationalized their readings of the Bible by claiming that Jewish editors "infected" the original text and its true meaning. What other tactics did Nazis and anti-Jewish

Germans use to promote their version of the truth about the Bible? Why do you think people of the era were so accepting of propaganda?

3. While no one is portrayed as perfect in the Old Testament, the negative attributes of the Hebrew/Israelite figures were skewed until Jews were seen as fatally flawed people who needed to be punished. What role did the Christian clergy of the time play in this? What should they have done differently to better represent humanity as a whole?

4. As referenced in the text, there are clearly many passages in the New Testament that are antisemitic and demonize Jews. How do contemporary Christians deal with these passages as they conflict (one hopes) with their present-day views of Jews?

5. Members of the Confessing Church (German Lutherans) risked their own lives to save Jews during the Holocaust. Does it matter that the motives of some of the members may have been to keep Jews around so they could convert to Christianity for the second coming of Christ, or did their deeds outweigh any motives?

6. Does the contemporary Lutheran Church or Catholic Church in Germany actively work for the conversion of Jews? What are their views on Judaism?

7. Are there still Christian communities, in the United States or elsewhere, that pray and hope for the conversion of Jews? Why?

Notes

1. The biblical text here and in all other passages is taken from the New Revised Standard Version (NRSV), with occasional revision by the author.

2. For an overview see Richard Steigmann-Gall, *The Holy Reich: Nazi Conceptions of Christianity, 1919–1945* (Cambridge: Cambridge University Press, 2003).

3. A particularly compelling case is that of the Austrian conscientious objector Franz Jägerstätter. A farmer and an observant Catholic, he refused to bear arms for the Nazi regime, which he saw as evil. He ultimately paid the highest price for his stand. The 2019 film *A Hidden Life* is a sensitive portrayal of his life and that of his family in the years before his execution.

4. Some elements in the German Protestant and also the Catholic churches found common ground with the Nazis, at least in part because of their vocal antisemitism.

For more about this see Susannah Heschel, *The Aryan Jesus: Christian Theologians and the Bible in Nazi Germany* (Princeton NJ: Princeton University Press, 2008) and Kevin P. Spicer, *Hitler's Priests: Catholic Clergy and National Socialism* (DeKalb: Northern Illinois University Press, 2008).

5. For an overview of these options and their implications, see Doris L. Bergen, "Old Testaments, New Hatreds: The Hebrew Bible and Antisemitism in Nazi Germany," in *Sacred Text, Secular Times: The Hebrew Bible in the Modern World*, ed. Leonard J. Greenspoon and Bryan F. LeBeau (Omaha NE: Creighton University Press, 2000). Also available online at http://www.bibleinterp.com/articles/bergen_033001.shtml.

6. On this and related issues see especially Heschel, "Draining Jesus of Jewishness," 26–66. She places these efforts within the context of the activities of the Institute for the Study and Eradication of Jewish Influence on German Church Life. See also Susannah Heschel, "The Aryan Jesus in Nazi Germany: The Bible and the Holocaust," April 2013, lecture, Creighton University, https://www.youtube.com/watch?v=hnnggA-miji.

7. For an accessible introduction to the history of the interpretation of passages such as those cited here, see Edward Kessler, *An Introduction to Jewish-Christian Relations* (Cambridge: Cambridge University Press, 2010). See also Eugene B. Korn et al., eds., *Two Faiths, One Covenant?: Jewish and Christian Identity in the Presence of the Other* (New York: Sheed & Ward, 2004); and Amy-Jill Levine and Marc Zvi Brettler, eds., *The Bible with and Without Jesus: How Jews and Christians Read the Same Stories Differently* (New York: HarperCollins, 2020).

8. Helpful in this process are the annotated New Testament texts collected in Amy-Jill Levine and Marc Zvi Brettler, eds., *The Jewish Annotated New Testament*, 2nd ed. (New York: Oxford University Press, 2017); and Shaul Magid, ed., *The Bible, the Talmud, and the New Testament: Elijah Zvi Soloveitchik's Commentary to the Gospels* (Philadelphia: University of Pennsylvania Press, 2019).

9. On this and related passages see Amy-Jill Levine, "Proclamation, Translation, Implication: Addressing the Vilification of 'the Jews,'" in *Found in Translation: Essays on Biblical Translation in Honor of Leonard J. Greenspoon*, ed. James W. Barker, Anthony Le Donne, and Joel N. Lohr (West Lafayette IN: Purdue University Press, 2018), 267–89, 878.

10. See, among other studies, Thomas Kaufmann, *Luther's Jews: A Journey into Anti-Semitism* (Oxford: Oxford University Press, 2017); and Christopher J. Probst, *Demonizing the Jews: Luther and the Protestant Church in Nazi Germany* (Bloomington: Indiana University Press, 2012).

11. See Paula Fredriksen, *Augustine and the Jews: A Christian Defense of Jews and Judaism* (New Haven CT: Yale University Press, 2010).

12. See Paul Johnson, *A History of the Jews* (New York: Harper & Row, 1987), 217–30.

13. For an analysis of what was at stake here, see Doris L. Bergen, "Non-Aryans in the People's Church," in Doris L. Bergen, *Twisted Cross: The German Christian Movement in the Third Reich* (Chapel Hill: University of North Carolina Press, 1996), 82–100.

14. For an overview, see Leonard Greenspoon, "Translating 'Jesus' and 'the Jews': Can We Eradicate the Anti-Semitism without also Erasing the Semitism?," in *Sound-

ings in the Religion of Jesus: Perspectives and Methods in Jewish and Christian Scholarship, ed. Bruce Chilton, Anthony Le Donne, and Jacob Neusner (Minneapolis: Fortress, 2012), 11–27.

15. For a full explication of relevant issues, see Anthony Le Donne, "Translating Poliscentrism: The Politics of Ethnicity and *Ethnos* Related to Defining *Ioudaios*," in *Found in Translation: Essays on Biblical Translation in Honor of Leonard J. Greenspoon*, ed. James W. Barker, Anthony Le Donne, and Joel N. Lohr (West Lafayette IN: Purdue University Press, 2018), 243–65.

16. An excellent analysis of the Confessing Church is among the topics covered in Robert P. Ericksen and Susannah Heschel, eds., *Betrayal: German Churches and the Holocaust* (Minneapolis: Fortress, 1999). See also Christiane Tietz, *Theologian of Resistance: The Life and Thought of Dietrich Bonhoeffer* (Minneapolis: Fortress, 2016) and Victoria Barnett, *For the Soul of the People: Protestant Protest Against Hitler* (New York: Oxford University Press, 1992).

17. For a sensitive narrative of these events along with a careful exploration of what motivated Pastor Trochmé and his colleagues, see Philip P. Hallie, *Lest Innocent Blood Be Shed* (New York: Harper Perennial, 1994).

18. For my experiences in teaching this course at Creighton University and a comparison between it and a course I taught at Spertus Institute for Jewish Learning and Leadership, see Leonard Greenspoon, "Reflections on a Course: 'Judaism and Early Christianity: The Parting of the Way—When? Where? Why?," in *Teaching the Historical Jesus: Issues and Exegesis*, ed. Zev Garber (New York: Routledge, 2014).

19. The student's name is J. P. Rankin.

20. I initially conducted research on this topic for a paper titled "The Bible Says It's So . . . But, It Ain't Necessarily So," that I delivered in 2011 during a conference on Jews, slavery, and the Civil War at the College of Charleston in Charleston, South Carolina.

6

The Forgotten Jewish Atlantis
Poznań and the Legacy of Antisemitism

ŁUKASZ W. NIPARKO

Atlantis is a mythological city-state, rich in development, history, and culture, that perished under the sea. Similarly, the history and culture of Jews in Poznań in western Poland was covered with water when the Nazi occupiers transformed the city's biggest synagogue, the so-called New Synagogue, into a swimming pool. Atlantis is almost all that is left of one of the most important European Jewish *gmina* (communes) of the sixteenth century, the home of great rabbis including Akiva Eger and Judah Löw ben Bezalel, Jewish traveler Gaspar da Gama, and philosopher Zygmunt Bauman.[1]

Since 1945, multiple generations in Poznań have grown up in a city where there was no visible Jewish presence or culture. For many of them, Poznań's urban landscape had very little to say about its magnificent Jewish past, except for a collapsing synagogue in the city center. Poznań's residents heard a lot about the Jews from Łódź, Warszawa, Kraków, and little *shtetls* all over Poland, but not from Poznań. Things are changing, however, and the best example is that the first Hanukkah light was put on the Poznań headquarters of the Jewish gmina to mark the Jewish holiday only in 2009 (seventy years after the outbreak of World War II). This light is out there to show the way for those who still believe that finding Atlantis is possible.

Poznań is Poland's fifth largest city and the capital of the historical region of Greater Poland (*Wielkopolska*), one of the sixteen administrative regions (*voivodeship*) in Poland. The population is roughly 540,000, but together with Poznań Agglomeration it totals approximately one million. It is a vivid site for Polish culture, history, education, and business. Located on the crossroads, Poznań is a hub where, in the past, the West and the East met.

More than eighty years ago Poznań, like any other place in Poland, was inhabited by a multiethnic society, including ethnic Jews, Poles, Germans, and others. Today, all that remains of the Jewish community is a group of fewer than forty people and many more stones: stones from the destroyed synagogue; stones of the old Jewish District; and destroyed *macewy* (gravestones), used as concrete reinforcement by the Nazis in Rusałka Lake. Jews were present in the Polish state from its beginning, and, even when many places like Poznań were stripped of their Jewish past by totalitarian brutality and antisemitism, this past is a part of every living Pole, consciously or not. Jewish tradition and culture are part of the mosaic that constitutes what we know today as Poland.

My own connection to Jewish Poznań began in 2004, when I was invited to accompany my uncle to the seventh National Annual Days of Christian-Jewish Dialogue in Poznań. One of the events took place in the destroyed New Synagogue. Candles were placed on the surface of the water in the shape of the Star of David, and the entire event was called "Atlantis" by the artist and professor Janusz Marciniak. This performance opened my eyes to the lost presence of Jews in Poznań. Now that presence, its thousand-year history, has begun to move back to the surface like those floating candles. It became clear to me that we, old and young historians of Poznań, cannot discuss its history if we do not fully embrace its diverse identity. And the Jewish aspect of this identity is indispensable to understanding Poznań's past.

The Medieval Times and the Commonwealth (966–1772)

In Polish, the word commonwealth, *Rzeczpospolita*, originates in the Latin *res publica*, which means public or common thing. This notion, developed in the Jagiellonian dynasty, implies a Golden Age of Poland in which the country, the Polish-Lithuanian Commonwealth, grew not only in economic prosperity along with its splendid cities but also in tolerance and religious freedom not seen at that time in the rest of Europe, though even then pogroms and other conflicts existed. Until the time of Partitions in the eighteenth century, Polish Jews were under the immediate protection of the Catholic Polish king—a protection that was guaranteed by

4. Artistic performance and installation titled "Atlantis" in the former building of the New Synagogue in Poznań. (Credit: Janusz Marciniak, University of Fine Arts, Poznań, 2004.)

the statutes given and confirmed by monarchs since the time of the Piast dynasty. Statutes covered not only personal and property freedoms but also extended to the judiciary system. Jews could not be adjudicated by the municipal court, but only by the king or his official—the *wojewoda*, equivalent to a governor.[2] Polish Jews

5. Artistic performance and installation titled "Atlantis" in the former building of the New Synagogue in Poznań. (Credit: Janusz Marciniak, University of Fine Arts, Poznań, 2004.)

received religious freedom and had a degree of self-governance over religious and societal life, as well as the ability to establish their own courts for cases concerning Jews. It was an unprecedented degree of freedom that, years later, resulted in Poland being the country with the largest Jewish population. Of course, Poland was not a paradise for its Jews, but there was no other country at that time where life could be better. In Europe, cleaved by religious wars, Poland was an outlier.

In the tenth century Poland's first historical ruler, Mieszko I, the founder of the Piast dynasty, unified the western Slavic tribes and Christianized them and himself. In doing so, he established the state, whose name would be taken from the old word for the people inhabiting the fields (*Polanie*). He built the first royal palace and the first Christian church in Poznań. In 965 his new wife Dobrawa, a Czech princess, came to Poland. It is believed that she brought with her the first Poznań Jews.[3] Mieszko's new state was first described by the Sephardi Jew Ibrahim ibn Jakub, who traveled around Europe and was involved in the slave trade for Khanate in Cordoba.[4] Additionally, from the time of the Piast dynasty comes the oldest inscription in Hebrew found in Poland, imprinted on the coin of the prince of Wielkopolska, Mieszko III the Old, at the turn of the thirteenth century.[5]

The following centuries brought more Jewish newcomers to Wielkopolska and Poznań, as Jews from other parts of Europe sought refuge and shelter and Polish rulers were mostly welcoming toward Jewish settlers and inhabitants. Poland's first Jewish Laws were introduced by the Piast rulers: the Statut Kaliski (1264), which was based on previous laws appearing in other parts of central Europe, and the Statute of Casimir III the Great (1356).[6] The Statut Kaliski, issued by Bolesław the Pious, who is buried in Poznań, provided a framework for the Jewish gmina in Poznań by outlining the prerogative for Jews to have their synagogue and a cemetery.[7] It also guaranteed a separate, independent judiciary system for Jews.[8] Many of the thirty-six articles were concerned with how loans could be provided and debts executed between Jews and Christians, but this statute also stated that a Jew could not be accused of any form of ritual blood-drinking and obliged others to provide help in case of emergency in a Jewish household.[9] Unfortunately, neither monarchical nor papal documents could stop people from raising many accusations against the Jewish communities of kidnapping Christian children, drinking Christian blood, or profaning the Holy Communion.

The most vivid example of such an accusation that is still pres-

6. The antisemitic fresco in the Church of the Most Precious Blood of Jesus by Adam Swach, from the eighteenth century. The fresco showcases fictitious events from 1399, when Poznań Jews were accused of "hosts desecration." (Credit: Photo by Łukasz Niparko, 2020).

ent in the urban memory is an event from 1399 called the Three Hosts Accident.[10] It was a calque of similar accusations that can be traced to thirteenth century Paris.[11] In the church of the Dominican order (today's Jesuits Church at Dominikańska Street), one woman preserved the Host in her mouth after Holy Communion and sold it to Jews. These Jews, according to legend, took the Host to the basement at Żydowska Street, where they crucified and stabbed it until the blood of Jesus came out.

As a result of this story Jews were attacked. In a similar case from Sochaczew the local court sentenced an unknown number of Jews to death.[12] However, the Polish monarchs did not stay silent in those cases, and reacted by passing laws protecting Jews from such accusations. The last king of the Jagiellonian dynasty, Sigismund II Augustus, issued a special rule for Poznań's gmina in 1556 to prosecute anyone who claimed that Jews committed any ritual murders of Christian boys or profanation of the Hosts. One year later, Sigismund Augustus asked the Poznań court to release every Jew who was arrested for such irrational accusations and stated that such cases had to be disputed in front of the Royal Court.[13]

One of the Largest Gminas in Europe

A *gmina* was a regional form of self-government by Jews in the Polish-Lithuanian Commonwealth. Not many know that Poznań's (in Yiddish: Pojzn) Jewish gmina was one of the biggest in Poland and Europe in the sixteenth century. The Hebrew word for Poland, *Polin*, means "here I will stay," which reflects the protection offered to Jews living in the Polish Kingdom and the relative religious freedom they enjoyed.[14] Yet this freedom often bothered the non-Jewish majority. The Roman Catholic Church's synod in Wrocław (1267), for example, requested a new settler law, which would inscribe in the urban space quarters for Jewish consolidation.[15] Although we cannot compare these efforts with the later ghettoization, this is an example of orchestrated separation within cultures and ethnicities in medieval and Renaissance Poznań. On the other hand, we need to keep in mind that pressure to separate the Jewish population back then also came from the rabbis, who perceived a potential danger for the cultivation of the Jewish religion and traditions in increased contact with non-Jews.[16]

The fifteenth century saw a growing number of Jewish settlements in Poznań that can be confirmed with historical sources, including documented transactions in 1443 and 1460 of selling properties between Jewish and Christian Poles, and a bid from 1464 that ordered the construction of a well.[17] By the latter part of the seventeenth century, 32.3 percent of Poznań inhabitants were Jewish.[18] The degradation of the monarch's power and rise in the power of the nobles made Poznań Jews more and more dependent on local laws that were influenced by the Wielkopolska nobility. All of these laws and previous ones were banned in 1793 with the Second Partition of Poland.

After the Jagiellonian dynasty, Poland was ruled by elected kings of various European dynasties as well as the noble houses of Poland. The second elected king, Stefan Batory, following the Jagiellonian line of religious tolerance, enhanced the law by the creation of the

Council of Four Lands, in which Wielkopolska played an essential role.[19] This council met in Lublin and discussed issues concerning Polish Jewish gminas, including social care and education, and also regulated the collection of taxes. The council also served a judiciary role in disputes between different gminas, and tried to reconcile the needs of a gmina and its people.[20] This council was unique in Europe and as such confirms the special role Poland played in the history of the world's Jewish community.

The gmina self-government was overseen by a *kahał*, which was a board of the oldest and often wealthiest members of a particular gmina. The kahał supervised schools, cemeteries, and public baths; the kahał also could decide who would be admitted to the Jewish community and receive gmina citizenship.[21] By fulfilling all these roles, the kahał was very similar in its function to the Poznań city council, which was reserved for Christian inhabitants.

History gives many accounts of different attitudes toward the Jewish community in Poznań. Seeing how much the gmina was contributing in taxes to the Polish crown, we may wonder if the intentions of the monarchs were so pure in granting special rights for Jews. However, those monarchs were guarantors of the relatively peaceful cohabitation between Jews and Christians.[22]

The Poznań gmina repeatedly faced financial problems, mostly following the impoverishment caused by the Chmielnicki Cossacks' uprising in the east of Poland and the Swedish Deluge that affected the entire country.[23] These events marked the approaching fall of the Polish-Lithuanian Commonwealth a hundred years later. Chmielnicki, a Ukrainian *hetman*, slaughtered many Jews in eastern Poland. Although these events seemingly did not affect Poznań directly, many Jews sought refuge from the uprising and often ended up in Poznań.[24] The Swedish Deluge of 1655–1660 had a direct impact on Poznań Jews, as they were accused of sympathizing with the Swedes and therefore persecuted.[25]

Additionally, the Counter-Reformation deepened the conflict with the Church. There are multiple examples of the Catholic Church's involvement with the active persecution of Jews in Poznań. For instance, in 1639, during one of the religious processions, clergy entered the Jewish District with their followers, resulting in an open conflict that left many people wounded.²⁶ In 1736, after a Christian child was found dead, the leaders of the gmina were accused of ritual murder and four of them were executed. While this was condemned by King Augustus III, this kind of bittersweet relationship between Jews and Polish monarchs (in which Jews were de jure protected but de facto exposed to threats, accusations, and pogroms) lasted until the abdication of Stanisław August Poniatowski, the last king of Poland, in 1795.²⁷

Rabbis, Travelers, and Moneylenders

Beginning in the fifteenth century Poznań was the site of a renaissance in terms of the Jewish academy with the establishment of Lamdej Posna, the Talmudic school that included such rabbis as Jorna Turek, Judah from Oborniki, Pinchas from Vienna, Moses from Halle, and Isaac Mintz (Menz) from Bamberg.²⁸ Although the school was an innovative project, Poznań could not easily compete with other sophisticated schools in central and eastern Poland, including the biggest yeshiva in the world, located in Lublin. Poznań Jews often chose to study at the university in Frankfurt an der Oder (Germany) to pursue their interest in non-religious studies. The overall number of students was low, as the dominant orthodoxy of Poznań discouraged many young Jews from pursuing scientific or humanistic paths in academia, instead solely focusing on religious studies. In the Jewish primary schools, called *cheder*, children were taught to write and read as well as how to translate the Torah from Hebrew to Yiddish; they studied Talmud and basic mathematics. In comparison to their Christian counterparts, a higher percentage of Jewish boys enrolled in schools, but the situation was worse for Jewish girls.²⁹ Girls went to special schools limited to the basic teaching of reading and writing skills.

In his book *The Jews of Poznań*, Zbigniew Pakuła lists Poznań's rabbis. The first known rabbi of Poznań was Pechno, who led the gmina between 1389 and 1393.³⁰ Between 1474 and 1508 we know about Rabbi Moses Minz, who led the Lamdej Posna.³¹ A particular characteristic of the rabbinate of that time in Europe is the mobility of rabbis all over the continent, which is why some rabbis who were born in Poznań served in Prague or other central Euro-

The Forgotten Jewish Atlantis   159

pean cities. In 1580 Eliezer Aszkenazi ben Elia Roef was elected as a new rabbi of Poznań after studying in Thessaloniki and serving in Egypt, Venice, and Prague.[32]

The most fascinating rabbi in Poznań's history was Judah Löw ben Bezalel, also known as De Hohe Rabbi Löwe or the MaHaRal. In addition to his knowledge of astronomy, alchemy, and mysticism, his metaphysical skills made him the protagonist of one of the most popular Jewish stories in Europe: Rabbi Löw created the clay monster known as the golem.[33] Today, in the city center of Poznań at Marcinkowskiego Avenue, there is a statue of the golem made by an artist from Czechia, David Černỳ.[34]

Despite Löw's mystical abilities and his significant presence in European history, the most important rabbi in the history of Poznań is Akiva Eger (1761–1837), who started his tenure in 1815.[35] Eger grew up in the Austrian Empire, where from early childhood he learned Talmud. While traveling to Wielkopolska, Eger impressed Rabbi Icyk Margolioth from Leszno (eighty kilometers from Poznań), who decided to marry his daughter to Eger and finance Eger's further Talmudic studies. Rabbi Eger opposed the reform of Judaism in the nineteenth century and prevented more liberal Jews, who wanted to allow children further studies, from closing *cheder* schools. After *cheder*, some of the most qualified students could further their education only in yeshivas like Lamdej Posna.[36] It was during Eger's lifetime that Poznań (then called Posen) became part of the kingdom of Prussia in 1793. Eger died at the age of seventy-six and was buried in Poznań's Głogowska Street Cemetery (Głogowska 26/26a). His son Salomon succeeded to the rabbinic seat in Poznań.[37]

In the nineteenth century Salomon Plessner became the new rabbi of Poznań. He was inspired by Rabbi Eger and followed the orthodoxy of Poznań Jews in his attitude and approach.[38] At the same time, many Poznań Jews were becoming more liberal. Those Jews established a new gmina—the Gmina of Brothers—which also raised its own synagogue. In 1862 this new gmina also got a new rabbi, Joseph Perles. Rabbi Plessner became outraged by such developments and created a new group called the Gmina of Unity, which was similar in its mission to the counterreformatory forces within the Roman Catholic Church.³⁹ Perles soon obtained a new post in Munich and was replaced by Rabbi Phillipp Bloch, who maintained his position until 1921.⁴⁰ The Gmina of Unity kept Wolf Feilchenfeld as the rabbi until 1913; he was followed by Ajkob Freimann, who in 1928 became a new rabbi in Berlin, leaving the gmina without a rabbi for almost a year.⁴¹ In that time, Dawid Szyje Sender became the acting rabbi. Sender was the only candidate when the rabbinic election finally took place in 1935, and he died with his Poznań sisters and brothers in the tragedy of the Holocaust.⁴² Today the rabbinic post of Poznań is overseen by the general rabbi of Poland, Michael Schudrich.

Jews of Poznań played an important role in trade, but they could not join any of the traditional guilds reserved for Christians, which were a very influential force in the city—often as powerful as the city council, and sometimes more so. In response, Poznań Jews—about half of whom were involved in business—created their own guilds to represent Jewish interests.⁴³ However, many Jews preferred to live in cities slightly smaller than Poznań, where there was less competition between Polish and German businesses.⁴⁴ Those who did live in Poznań were highly educated and skilled in comparison to Jews from other regions, which also contributed to the growth of Poznań's economy over those of other cities in Poland. Many Jews were also involved in businesses, such as kosher butcheries, that reflected their religion; many Jews worked as moneylenders.⁴⁵ There is also an account of Jonasz from Sambor, who was Poznań's Billy the Kid and was prosecuted multiple times for crimes committed against both Jews and Christians and ultimately exiled from the city in 1457.⁴⁶ Some links connect people from the past to us—Hartwig Kantorowicz, for example, created the recipe for the most delicious Polish vodka, Wyborowa [Selected], which is still produced in Poznań today.⁴⁷

Finally, the most exciting story to tell concerns Gaspar da Gama, who was not only a believer in Judaism but later became a Muslim and finally converted to Christianity.⁴⁸ Gaspar became the first hand to Vasco da Gama and served in the Portuguese overseas campaigns. Polish historian Joachim Lelewel wrote, "Without the Jew from Poznań who was going around India, and after baptism called Gaspar da Gama; Vasco da Gama (1498) and Pedro Álvares Cabral (1500) would not be that successful in their journeys as thanks to him."[49] Gaspar is believed to have been crucial in the voyage to "discover" Brazil, as well as in supporting Vasco da Gama in his confrontations with Malayalis in Kerala, India. Gaspar most likely died after the Battle of Calicut (today's Kozhikode) and is buried somewhere in Kerala. Maybe he was buried in St. Francis Church in Kochi along with his master Vasco before Vasco's body was shipped to Lisbon in 1539.

The Longest War of Modern Europe (1772–1918)

For some, the time during which Poland was under the Partitions after the Congress of Vienna (1815) was the longest time of peace in modern Europe, but for the Poles it was not a peaceful time. Instead it was the time of uprisings and organic work for a nonexistent country. The Prussian partitioners were shrewd, and, having some experience with the *Haskalah* in Germany, the so-called Jewish Enlightenment, they quickly used it as an excuse to transform the Poznań "Polish" Jewish gmina into a "German" one by putting the Jewish *Kahał* under the strict control of the Prussian government.[50] The enlightened Prussian monarchy brought a lot of freedom to the Poznań Jewish community, and many Jews quickly noticed improvements over the collapsing, corrupted, and impoverished Kingdom of Poland. Most importantly, the Partition brought citizenship rights for many Poznań Jews.[51] Moreover, the followers of the Haskalah in Poznań, the Association of the Friends of Charity, found their natural allies in the heart of the Haskalah movement in Berlin.[52] Poznań Jews quickly assimilated into the German population to the extent that a Poznańer, Philipp Jaffé, became one of the editors of the *Monumenta Germaniae Historica*.[53]

Until 1848—the time of the Spring of Nations in Europe—Jews did not have civil rights. Those rights were introduced by the Prussian government, which started its quest for assimilation of Jews with the German bourgeoisie inhabiting Poznań and other towns under the Prussian Partition.[54] Jews could then participate in elections to the city council, and two Jewish members were elected in the first elections.[55] As Elizabeth A. Drummond explains in her work "On the Borders of the Nation":

> Despite having lived under the rule of the Commonwealth of Poland-Lithuania for centuries, Poznań Jewry transformed itself from a Polish Jewry into a truly German Jewry over the course of the nineteenth century.... With the exacerbation of the German-Polish conflict, however, the opportunities for Jews to function as a bridge between the German and Polish communities largely evaporated.... The demands of national solidarity increasingly forced Poznań Jews to choose between the two opposing national groups. Faced with such a choice, they overwhelmingly embraced Germandom; only a few individual Poznań Jews embraced Polonism as a national identity or supported Polish political movements.[56]

Many Poznań Jews also became members of the German nationalistic societies that later became imbued with racial and antisemitic ideology. At the same time, for Christian Poles, it became clear that the Jewish population of Poznań was not Polish, especially as Jews were excluded from Polish patriotic organizations; alongside Germans, these non-Polish Jews became targets in the Polish push for independence.[57] For example, when Polish Christians boycotted German products, they also boycotted the products of Polish Jews.[58] And when Germans boycotted Polish products, the majority of Poznań Jews joined them.

All of that, I argue, happened due to one particular reason. During the medieval Polish kingdom and later in the Polish-Lithuanian Commonwealth, Jews were directly protected by the monarch and had an incomprehensible number of liberties compared to Jews in the rest of Europe. When the Enlightenment led to the inclusion of Jews in European nation-building, the Polish kingdom was already in collapse, and the Prussian partitioners, in opposition to Tsarist Pale of Settlement laws, made good use of such progressive developments. The result was that, by the time of the First World War, neither the Christians of Poznań nor the Jews themselves considered Poznań Jews to be Polish. This later became an immense issue that put Jews in the middle of the conflict over independence between ethnic Poles and ethnic

Germans.[59] Wealthy Jews, who for the most part identified with German language and culture, could move to Germany once the Wielkopolska region was part of the new Poland after February 1919; those who were poorer, mostly living in the Jewish quarter around Żydowska Street, stayed.[60]

Jews leaving for Germany did not alter the demographics of the Poznań gmina; for instance, in 1926, 144 Jews left Poznań, but 325 arrived.[61] However, socially it was the end of a vibrant community, as its character changed dramatically.[62] The 1931 statistical review of Poznań shows that among all members of the gmina only fifteen percent of Jews lived in Poznań before Poland regained her independence in 1918.[63] Those who came, mostly from the eastern regions, felt strongly affiliated with Polish statehood.

The Phony Times (1919-1939)

In his interview for *Gazeta Wyborcza*, one of the most popular Polish newspapers, Bronisław Bergman stated that, going back in his memory to pre-1939 Poznań, the city was not free from nationalism and antisemitism.[64] In 1919, following the request of the Jewish Schooling Council, the Polish government opened a public school for Jewish youth in a private house at Małe Garbary Street.[65] Initiatives of this sort were the first steps taken by the government in Warsaw, under the leadership of the author of Poland's regained independence, Marshall Józef Piłsudski. Later, attitudes changed and, especially after the elections of 1928, were clearly antisemitic.[66] Indeed, from May 1926, when the so-called Sanacja (Healing) took power under the leadership of Piłsudski and later his political heir, Ignacy Mościcki, the environment in Poland became worse and worse for Jews.[67]

It was in Poznań on December 4, 1926, that the Camp of Great Poland, a political organization advocating for a Poland "only for Poles," was established.[68] Edward D. Wynot describes the situation:

> Like the majority of the Sanacja, the nationalists (National Democracy led by Roman Dmowski) believed firmly in a powerful, centralized government, asserting the supremacy of the Polish nation and the Catholic Church over the national and religious minori-

ties that comprised nearly one-third of the country's population; unlike most of Piłsudski's associates, however, the nationalists were dedicated [antisemites]. The Socialism of Piłsudski, emphasizing the state, and the National Democracy of Dmowski, with its stress upon the Polish nation—it is hardly surprising that antisemitism was envisioned as the main bridge spanning the chasm between the two rivals.[69]

At the same time, Poznań became a home for nationalistic and chauvinistic publications, including *The Voice of Homeland*, established in 1924 by Mieczysław Noskowicz, who was the chairman of the Board of Directors of the Anti-Jewry League of Protection of Homeland and Faith.[70] Another group, The Society of Social Self-Defense—"Progress," had a "black book" in which the names of people who were buying from Jews were published. The 1930s brought other antisemitic magazines, such as *Under the Pillory*, *Spider*, *National Self-Defense*, and the National Democracy Party newspaper *Poznań Courier*. The latter newspaper reused the old antisemitic accusations of ritual blood-drinking and wrote about them zestfully. The labels of Jews as greedy bankers, communists, and heartless capitalists (sometimes all at the same time), were reproduced within these publications.

In this reborn Poland, the Poznań gmina was very well developed, with twenty full-time workers, including a rabbi, a secretary, cantors, a butcher, a custodian of the synagogue, a teacher in the Jewish school, and workers in the Jewish cemetery and baths. The gmina was in possession at that time of two synagogues on Dominikańska Street and Szewska Street.[71] It also owned a rabbinic house and a library at 10 Stawna Street that is today used as the center of the recreated Jewish universe in Poznań and has been, since 2003, the headquarters of the Poznań Jewish gmina. Moreover, the gmina's possessions at that time included a cemetery at Głogowska Street, a Jewish Orphanage for Girls at Noskowskiego Street, and the Rohr's Hospital at Wieniawskiego Street. Other institutions connected with the Jewish gmina included the Salomon ben Latz Elderly Shelter next to Żydowska Street and the Baron Kotwitz Orphanage at Stawna Street. Additionally, vibrant

Jewish charity organizations were active within the city, such as the Israeli Society for Sickly Care and Funeral Organization, the Society of Welfare and Support for Jewish Women in Poznań, and Achi Eser Society for Jews in Poverty.[72]

Poznań's Jewish population between the wars was dominated by the petite bourgeoisie, whose socioeconomic situation was much better than that of the petite bourgeoisie in other parts of Poland, thus attracting many migrants to settle in Poznań. Data from the 1935 rabbinic election shows that 54 percent of the electorate were merchants, 13 percent were craftsmen, 10 percent were intelligentsia, and 5.5 percent were physical workers.[73] Before World War II Jews were owners of about two hundred shops in Poznań, and Jewish businesses hired many Christians. Moreover, the Jewish community had two banks belonging to the Society of Jewish Cooperative: Shares Bank at Szewska Street and Commerce Bank at December 27th Street.[74]

The Jewish Public School's first year (1919–1920) saw an enrollment of seventy-one children, though some Jewish children went to other public schools.[75] In 1932, another Jewish school was opened next to Noskowskiego Street, Primary School No. 14, and it operated until the outbreak of the Second World War.[76] Each year about two hundred students attended, including those who lived in the dormitory for mostly underprivileged children. A separate kindergarten existed at 5 Szewska Street.[77] The number of Jewish students who wanted to further their education was so high that, in 1937, the Jewish Education Association asked the superintendent's office to establish a special junior high school for Jewish students. Poznańers also had access to the Jewish Society Libraries as well as other two Jewish libraries on Szewska and Żydowska streets.[78]

In 1935 *The Voice of Poznań*, a weekly magazine, appeared for the first time. It was printed in Kalisz, and included two pages in Polish and four in Yiddish. Poznań Jews also had their sports club, called Bar Kochba.[79] Twentieth-century Poznań witnessed the growth of Jewish organizations and Jewish political parties, including Zionist groups such as the General Zionistic Organization, the Society of Revisionist Zionists, the Jewish Socialistic Workers Party—Poalej Zion (The Workers of Zion), the Bund, and the Orthodox *Aguda*.⁸⁰ Poznań had two Jewish Masonic lodges on Stawna Street and Marcinkowskiego Avenue, both of which were liquidated on November 22, 1938, following the decree of the Polish president Ignacy Mościcki.⁸¹

Hashomer Hatzair (Young Guard) was especially popular among young people who were fascinated by the paramilitary character of the group. The membership consisted of secondary school and university students and some older primary school students. In separate groups they could study Jewish history, the Hebrew language, and the geography of Palestine, and participate in many sports activities.⁸² The leader of the Society of Revisionist Zionists, Ze'ew Żabotyński, often visited Poznań to present lectures.⁸³ The Poznań Zionists who lived under the German Partition, like their group's founder, Dr. Max Kollenscher, did not consider themselves Zionists in the strict sense. As "Western Jews," they were collecting money to support the desire of "Eastern Jews" to migrate as settlers to Palestine.⁸⁴ All of these organizations portray a diverse Jewish community that contributed significantly to the entire city of Poznań, an energetic community that was about to perish.

Five Years from a Thousand

In September 1939 the German army invaded Poland. Troops took over the city on September 10 and, in five days, confiscated books from Jewish libraries. On September 16 they closed all Jewish schools, and on September 20 closed all Jewish shops and confiscated Jewish property for the National Socialist People's Welfare (Nationalsozialistische Volkswohlfahrt or NSV).⁸⁵ On 5 November, a concentration camp was established on Bałtycka Street in the Główna District of Poznań. One week later, SS Gruppenführer Wilhelm Koppe ordered the removal from the city of all Poznań Jews and thirty-five thousand Poles.⁸⁶ In the process, my mother's family was evicted from Poznań and moved to the Generalgouvernement. Starting on November 29, Poznań Jews had to wear a yellow Star of David attached to their clothes and a yellow band attached to their forearm.⁸⁷ On December 12 the remaining Jews, about fifteen hundred people, were ordered to come to Główna District, where their belongings were taken from them. They were put into barracks and, within a couple of days, moved to the Generalgouvernement, where they were sent first to the ghettos and ultimately to their death. From then until April 1940, Nazi authorities worked to change the New Synagogue into a swimming pool, covering the Jewish District of Poznań with its waters.

Heinrich Himmler, the Reichsführer-ss, envisioned Poznań as an integral part of the Reich. For this reason, he instated his colleague Arthur Greiser as the *gauleiter* (a Nazi term for governor) of the Warthegau, as they called the Poznań region. Himmler visited the city on a number of occasions. In speeches given in Poznań to fellow Nazi officials on October 4 and 6, 1943, Himmler openly talked about the Final Solution. Such public discussions of the ongoing genocide by a top Nazi leader were extremely rare.[88]

On October 20, 1939, Benno Rindfleish and Juliusz Tychauer were killed in Fort VII, also known as Konzentrationslager Posen, the first Jews to be murdered there.[89] Fort VII, part of the Prussian fortification system built during the Partition, became the first Nazi concentration camp on Polish soil, established on October 10, 1939.[90] The first mass murders using carbon monoxide gas in Nazi-occupied Poland occurred in that first month, when 400 patients and the medical personnel of Owińska Psychiatric Hospital were executed. This fact is omitted by the literature, and it is hard to find even the name Fort VII or Konzentrationslager Posen represented in works on this topic. Yet its gas chamber became the testing ground for what later happened in Auschwitz-Birkenau and other places. It is estimated that about 18,000 people were imprisoned in Fort VII and that about 4,500 of them died before it was closed on April 27, 1944, and its remaining prisoners moved to a new facility in Żabikowo.[91] It is estimated that about 21,624 prisoners were kept in Żabikowo; the number of those who perished is unknown because the bodies were burned at the Poznań Medical University crematorium and the city landfill incinerator, or dumped into a nearby pond.[92]

By the end of February 1940 almost all Wielkopolska Jews were removed from the region. However, at that point, the Germans were in need of a labor force and established a camp at the city stadium on Dolna Wilda Street.[93] About one thousand Jewish

7. The opening ceremony of the New Synagogue in Poznań on September 5, 1907, and the present-day (2011) view of the building. (Credit: Janusz Marciniak, University of Fine Arts, Poznań.)

prisoners worked at construction sites, cleaned, or gardened. The majority of Jews imprisoned at the stadium lived under the open sky, and suffered from adverse weather conditions, famine, and epidemics, as well as the cruelty inflicted upon them by the Germans.[94] By the time the camp was liquidated in early 1943, and the remaining four thousand to five thousand prisoners moved to Krzesiny-Piotrowo Camp, more than twenty smaller camps were established; these included Antoninek, Dębiec, Franowo, Golęcin, Żabikowo, Kobylepole, Krzesiny, Krzesinki, Krzyżowniki, Malta, Piotrowo, Smochowice, and Strzeszyn.[95]

What is truly devastating is that few of those who orchestrated and carried out mass killings in Poznań were prosecuted and punished. As Ian Kershaw lists,

> head of the Posen SD Rolf-Heinz Höppner was sentenced in March 1949 in Poznań to life imprisonment and released under an amnesty in April 1956. . . . Arthur Greiser was condemned to death by a Polish court and hanged in Poznań (this was the last public execution conducted in Poland). . . . Wilhelm Koppe escaped after the war

The Forgotten Jewish Atlantis

and lived under a pseudonym for over fifteen years as a successful businessman, becoming director of a chocolate factory in Bonn before being captured in 1960 and finally, in 1964, being arraigned for his involvement in mass murder in Poland. He was deemed unfit to stand trial. He died peacefully in his bed on 02 July 1975.[96]

Poznań's Lost Synagogues

From the beginning of the Poznań gmina until 1939, in the area of Żydowska Street, there were about twenty different synagogues founded by various gminas as the result of conflicts between orthodoxy and enlightenment, as well as by private donors and societies. The first Poznań synagogue was built in 1367 and was later replaced by a synagogue belonging to the Gmina of Brothers located at the crossing of Szewska and Dominikańska streets.[97] The so-called Old Synagogue appeared in the block of Żydowska, Mokra, and Wroniecka streets that gave rise to a new Jewish microcosm in the middle of Poznań, adjacent to the Wroniecka City Gate (one of the four main city gates of medieval and Renaissance Poznań).[98] In the nineteenth century this synagogue was rebuilt and enlarged to address the needs of the growing gmina.[99] More synagogues in Poznań were built at the end of the sixteenth century, when the gmina had its most prosperous time, and also because the fire of 1590 destroyed many buildings in the Jewish quarter. Based on the laws issued by King Sigismund III Vasa, Jews could erect non-wooden buildings in Poznań. Therefore, when they started to rebuild their homes, they also decided to build the New Synagogue, which was adjacent to the Old Synagogue and finished by 1618.[100]

Poznań is full of memories of other synagogues, such as the Nehemiasz Synagogue, first mentioned in sources from 1735, which was most likely built after the fire of 1717 that affected the Jewish quarter.[101] In 1883 Nehemiasz Synagogue was rebuilt in the neo-Romanesque style. It was torn down in 1928, disappearing forever from the landscape of Poznań (along with all city synagogues).[102] In 1856–1857, the progressive Jews of the Haskala built their synagogue (called the Temple) at Dominikańska and Szewska streets.[103] This project was funded by the affluent Jewish intelligentsia of that time. It could hold about nine hundred people and had a partial glass roof, unique for that era.

At the end of the nineteenth century Poznań's synagogues were again in need of rebuilding. Modernizations occurred between 1883 and 1884, and cost the gmina 70,000 marks.[104] Along with giving buildings new neo-Romanesque façades and zinc roofs, they also created more space for women. The New Synagogue was needed due to a lack of space for praying among the Orthodox Jews. Its construction, at a cost of about 700,000 marks (about $4M today), dwarfed that of every other synagogue in Poznań.[105] On March 6, 1906, the cornerstone was laid, and on September 5, 1907, more than a year later, the synagogue was consecrated. Two kinds of granite and two kinds of bricks were used, the dome and *matroneum* (the space for women) were built with metal, and the entire building was stylized to resemble a Byzantine temple. The first floor had seating for 650 men, and about 650 women could be seated on *matroneums*.[106] The last service took place in Poznań's New Synagogue on September 9, 1939.[107] That day, Rabbi Szyje Sender prayed for the victory of the Polish army and freedom for Poland.[108] The New Synagogue became a swimming pool for *Wehrmacht* soldiers during the occupation. After the war, the municipal government kept it as a swimming pool until 2002, when it gave back the building to the Poznań gmina, which kept the swimming pool open for the next nine years.[109]

Conclusion

In this chapter, I briefly looked at nearly one thousand years of the history of Poznań's Jews. What is left today is the hidden landscape of that history and culture, best portrayed by the synagogue that the Nazis turned into a swimming pool—a symbolic Atlantis, the city that disappeared under the water. In the case of Poznań, what disappeared was the culturally diverse urban space that was destroyed by nationalism, totalitarian ideologies, war, and genocide. In Poland today, there are about twenty thousand people who consider themselves Jews, and only about six thousand are members of the religious gminas. Only one Jew living in Poznań today was born there before the Second World War.[110]

Like most Polish cities, Poznań has today's city landscape and the city landscape of the past that perished during the Second World War. This hidden, underground city is a repository of memories and scars from the past. Only a few choose to see these two dimensions of past and present simultaneously, yet everyone is able to do so. What is needed in order to make it happen is the awareness that has to come from home, school, or extracurricular activities and extraordinary teachers.

It was from January 11 to January 19, 2004, that I first had a chance to participate in Poznań Days of Dialogue between Jews and Christians. Watching people singing, praying, and experiencing spirituality, as well as eating delicious Jewish foods, I started to imagine the lost Atlantis. I began to think about that lost city and its culture and its history—but even more about the people who are gone. Of course, we cannot recreate the past as it was, but we can embrace the past and shape the future together. By participating in the Days of Dialogue, I also witnessed the artistic project of Janusz Marciniak that tried to discover lost Atlantis. I saw the archbishop of Poznań and the rabbi of Poland praying together and saying to the people, "become the blessings for each other."[111] As one of the best-known Poles, Pope John Paul II, said, "We cannot cut the roots from which we are growing."[112] A strong, democratic Poland in a more united Europe should be a country that remembers the past and is willing to learn from it. Every day we have new chances to prove that there is no place in Poland for intolerance and antisemitism.

Today we can observe the rejuvenation of the Jewish landscape of Poznań. In addition to the preserved elements of the past—including the Kronthal Fountain, one of the most beautiful fountains in Poznań—new elements have been added, such as the sculpture of the golem and the graffiti by Rafał Betlejewski that reads "I miss you, Jew."[113] Since 2005 there has been a monument on Królowej Jadwigi Street commemorating Jews who died at the concentration camp the Nazis established at the old city stadium. Piece by piece, the incompleteness is being filled by everyone who dares to dream about Jewish Poznań.

Antisemitism is still a problem in Poznań and it needs to be addressed. Awareness of past wrongs is a necessary beginning. The Israeli ambassador to Poland, Szewach Weiss, said, "the third generation begins looking for their roots, asking where are their neighbors?"[114] I am a member of the third generation that finally asks, "what is my identity and what is the identity of my place? Where are my neighbors?" My grandparents' was the generation of war and genocide, and my parents' was the generation under a totalitarian regime; I hope my children and the generations to come will know and cherish their complete history and heritage. I hope they will embrace the words of Janusz Korczak: "We are the Brothers [and Sisters] of one Earth. Centuries of common good and bad, and a long journey together—one Sun is shining for us."[115]

Questions for Further Discussion

1. In your own words, describe the author's use and meaning of The Lost City of Atlantis in relationship to the Polish city of Poznań.

2. Another metaphor the author uses to begin and end the chapter is that of a tree with many roots. Explain the significance of this to the city of Poznań.

3. The author points out that history happens to everyone but is usually told from only one point of view. List as many points of view as you can think of (gender, ethnic, religious, political, and socio-economic). How would having a complete history of all of these be of use to us now?

4. Did Christian Poles attack Jewish Poles repeatedly during the centuries? If yes, why?

5. The antisemitic myth of the Three Hosts persisted and evolved for over six hundred years. What are the essential elements of such an urban legend and what is its purpose over time?

6. Do you know any other accusations of blood libel from history?

7. Define *Haskala* and explain its impact on the Jewish population of Poznań.

8. Poland lost its sovereignty for 123 years during what the author refers to as "longest war of modern Europe." What is the significance of Haskala happening at the same time?

9. How did the changing of borders and rulers affect the identity of the Jews of Poznań? How did it affect the non-Jewish people of Poznań?

10. Briefly describe Jewish life in Poland (and in Europe) today. Are there more Jews in the United States than in Europe?

11. Identify a major theme of "The Forgotten Jewish Atlantis" and explain what we can take away and apply to our lives today.

Notes

I would like to thank the following persons for their motivation, inspiration, and unconditional support while conducting this research project: Prof. Ari Kohen (University of Nebraska—Lincoln), Prof. Gerald Steinacher (University of Nebraska-Lincoln), and Prof. Elun Gabriel (St. Lawrence University), as well as Laura Keeler and Ann Baker, whose suggestions helped tremendously improve this manuscript. Moreover, I am thankful to Prof. Janusz Marciniak (University of Fine Arts in Poznań) for his continuous strive to bring Atlantis back to the surface of Poznań and for sharing his artistic work and photographs.

1. Lech Muszyński and Bronisław Bergman, "Sylwetki Poznańskich Rabinów" [Profiles of Poznań's Rabbis], in *Poznańscy Żydzi—Kronika Miasta Poznania* [Poznań Jews—The Chronicle of the City of Poznań], ed. Jacek Wiesiołowski and Andrzej Niziołek (Poznań: Wydawnictwo Miejskie, 2006), 18.

2. "1334–1499, Polska Złota Wolność Żydowska" [1334–1499, Polish Golden Jewish Freedom], in *Historia Narodu Żydowskiego* [The History of the Jewish Nation], 2012, accessed December 6, 2012, http://www.izrael.badacz.org/historia/wolnosc.html.

3. There is no historical nor archeological evidence for this legendary statement. What we know is that Jews were on Polish territory before 966—those who were involved in the ancient trade routes. They were very likely also present in the area of Poznań before the location of the city in 1253 by Prince Przemysł I. Rafał Witkowski, "Kalendarium Dziejów Poznańskiej Gminy Żydowskiej" [The Timeline of the History of the Poznań Jewish Community], in *Poznańscy Żydzi II—Kronika Miasta Poznania* [Poznań Jews—The Chronicle of the City of Poznań], ed. Jacek Wiesiołowski (Poznań: Wydawnictwo Miejskie, 2009), 284–85. Jerzy Topolski, Krzysztof Mochelski, *Żydzi w Wielkopolsce na przestrzeni dziejów* [Jews in Greater Poland throughout History] (Poznań: Wydawnictwo Poznańskie, 1995).

4. Urszula Rajewska-Lewicka, *Arabskie opisanie Słowian: źródła do dziejów średniowiecznej kultury* [Arabic Description of the Slavs: Sources for the History of Medieval Culture] (Wrocław: Polskie Towarzystwo Ludoznawcze, 2004).

5. Zbigniew Pakuła, *The Jews of Poznań* (London: Vallentine Mitchell, 2003), 1.

6. Jacek Wiesiołowski, "Bolesław i Jolenta, czyli początki polskiej tolerancji. Przywilej kaliski księcia wielkopolskiego Bolesława Pobożenego z 1264 roku" [Bolesław and Jolenta, or the Beginnings of Polish Tolerance. Kalisz Privilege of the Duke of Greater Poland Bolesław the Pious from 1264], in *Poznańscy Żydzi—Kronika Miasta Poznania* [Poznań Jews—The Chronicle of the City of Poznań], ed. Jacek Wiesiołowski and Andrzej Niziołek (Poznań: Wydawnictwo Miejskie, 2006), 7–13.

7. Witkowski, "Kalendarium," 285

8. Wiesiołowski, "Bolesław i Jolenta," 7–13.

9. Wiesiołowski, "Bolesław i Jolenta," 7–13.

10. Witkowski, "Kalendarium," 285–86; Pakuła, *The Jews of Poznań*, 4.

11. Jacek Wiesiołowski, Z okien rezydencji Karmelitów [From the windows of the Carmelites' residence], in *Poznańscy Żydzi—Kronika Miasta Poznania* [Poznań Jews—The Chronicle of the City of Poznań], ed. Jacek Wiesiołowski and Andrzej Niziołek (Poznań: Wydawnictwo Miejskie, 2006), 124.

12. Pakuła, *The Jews of Poznań*, 5; Topolski and Mochelski, *Żydzi w Wielkopolsce na przestrzeni dziejów*, 46–47.

13. Pakuła, *The Jews of Poznań*, 5.

14. Pakuła, *The Jews of Poznań*, 1.

15. Bernard D. Weinryb, *The Jews of Poland: A Social and Economic History of the Jewish Community in Poland from 1100 to 1800* (Philadelphia: Jewish Publication Society of America, 1973), 26.

16. Weinryb, *The Jews of Poland*, 256.

17. Witkowski, "Kalendarium," 287.

18. Pakuła, *The Jews of Poznań*, 7.

19. Note that there is also a legend of a Jew, Saul Wahl, who was briefly the leading candidate to become a king of Poland after the death of Stefan Batory (Weinryb, *The Jews of Poland*, 336).

20. Witkowski, "Kalendarium," 290–91.

21. Witkowski, "Kalendarium," 291.

22. Weinryb, *The Jews of Poland*, 312; Rafał Witkowski, "Księga protokołów elektorów gminy żydowskiej w Poznaniu" [Book of Reports of Electors of the Jewish Community in Poznań], in *Poznańscy Żydzi—Kronika Miasta Poznania* [Poznań Jews—The Chronicle of the City of Poznań], ed. Jacek Wiesiołowski and Andrzej Niziołek (Poznań: Wydawnictwo Miejskie, 2006), 86–89; Zofia Wojciechowska, "Akt Rewizji Kamienic, Domów i Placów Żydowskich w Poznaniu w 1641 r." [Act of the Searches of Tenement Houses, Houses and Jewish Squares in Poznań in 1641], in *Poznańscy Żydzi—Kronika Miasta Poznania* [Poznań Jews—The Chronicle of the City of Poznań], ed. Jacek Wiesiołowski and Andrzej Niziołek (Poznań: Wydawnictwo Miejskie, 2006), 95–106.

23. Witkowski, "Kalendarium," 294.

24. Weinryb, *The Jews of Poland*, 181–90.

25. Pakuła, *The Jews of Poznań*, 7.

26. Witkowski, "Kalendarium," 294.

27. Witkowski, "Kalendarium," 296.

28. Pakuła, *The Jews of Poznań*, 3; Muszyński and Bergman, "Sylwetki Poznańskich Rabinów," 14–38.

29. Zofia Borzymińska and Rafał Żebrowski, *Polski słownik judaistyczny: Dzieje, Kultura, Religia, Ludzie* [Polish Judaic Dictionary: History, Culture, Religion, People] (Warszawa: Wydawnictwo Prószyński i S-ka, 2003), 281–83.

30. Pakuła, *The Jews of Poznań*, 6–7; Muszyński and Bergman, "Sylwetki Poznańskich Rabinów," 14–38.

31. Muszyński and Bergman, "Sylwetki Poznańskich Rabinów," 14–38.

32. Muszyński and Bergman, "Sylwetki Poznańskich Rabinów," 14–38.

33. Muszyński and Bergman, "Sylwetki Poznańskich Rabinów," 14–38.

34. "Golem stanął w centrum Poznania" [Golem Stood in the Center of Poznań], in *Gazeta Wyborcza*, 05 May 2010, accessed January 6, 2013, http://wiadomosci.gazeta.pl/wiadomosci/1,114873,7847576,_Golem__stanal_w_centrum_Poznania__zdjecia_.html.

35. Rafał Witkowski, "Rabin Akiva Eger" [Rabbi Akiva Eger], in *Poznańscy Żydzi—Kronika Miasta Poznania* [Poznań Jews—The Chronicle of the City of Poznań], ed. Jacek Wiesiołowski and Andrzej Niziołek (Poznań: Wydawnictwo Miejskie, 2006), 44–50.

36. Witkowski, "Rabin Akiva Eger," 44–50.

37. Poznańska Gmina Wyznaniowa Żydowska, "Rabin Akiva Eger," accessed January 6, 2012, http://poznan.jewish.org.pl/index.php/wydarzenia/Rabin-Akiva-Eger.html; "Macewa rabina Egera przy ul. Głogowskiej," in *Gazeta Wyborcza*, June 3, 2008, http://wiadomosci.gazeta.pl/kraj/1,34309,5275004.html#ixzz11u10VhSP.

38. Pakuła, *The Jews of Poznań*, 8; Muszyński and Bergman, "Sylwetki Poznańskich Rabinów," 14–38.

39. Pakuła, *The Jews of Poznań*, 8; Witkowski, "Kalendarium," 313.

40. Pakuła, *The Jews of Poznań*, 8.

41. Pakuła, *The Jews of Poznań*, 8; Witkowski, "Kalendarium," 319, 321–22.

42. Muszyński and Bergman, "Sylwetki Poznańskich Rabinów," 14–38.

43. Sophia Kemlein, *Żydzi w Wielkim sięstwie Poznańskim: Przeobrażenia w łonie żydostwa polskiego pod panowaniem pruskim* [Jews in the Grand Duchy of Poznań—Transformations in the Womb of Polish Jewry under Prussian Rule] (Poznań: Wydawnictwo Poznańskie, 2001), 209; Topolski and Mochelski, *Żydzi w Wielkopolsce na przestrzeni dziejów*, 54.

44. Topolski and Mochelski, *Żydzi w Wielkopolsce na przestrzeni dziejów*, 38–39.

45. Witkowski, "Kalendarium," 285.

46. Pakuła, *The Jews of Poznań*, 3.

47. Witkowski, "Kalendarium," 313, 315.

48. "Gaspar da Gama" in *Jewish Virtual Library*, accessed January 10, 2013, http://www.jewishvirtuallibrary.org/jsource/biography/GaspardaGama.html; Poznańska Gmina Wyznaniowa Żydowska, "Gaspar da Gama—Żydowski Podróżnik z Poznania" [Gaspar da Gama—Jewish Traveler from Poznań], accessed December 6, 2012, http://poznan.jewish.org.pl/index.php/Zasluzeni/Gaspar-da-Gama-zydowski-podroznik-z-Poznania.html; Radosław Nawrot, "Gaspar da Gama—odkrywca Brazylii z Poznania" [Gaspar da Gama—the Discoverer of Brazil from Poznań], in *Gazeta Wyborcza*,

December 19, 2010, http://poznan.gazeta.pl/poznan/1,37175,8837848,Gaspar_da _Gama-_odkrywca_Brazylii_z_Poznania.html; Ryszard Badowski, "Pod Portugalską Banderą" [Under the Portuguese Flag], *Wiedza i Życie* no. 6 (1998).

49. Joachim Lelewel, *Polska. Dzieje i rzeczy Jej* [Poland. Her History and Her Things] (Poznań, 1858).

50. Lelewel, *Polska*.

51. Edward David Luft, *The Naturalized Jews of the Grand Duchy of Posen in 1834 and 1835* (Bergenfield: Avotaynu, 2004).

52. Luft, *The Naturalized Jews*, 304–5.

53. Luft, *The Naturalized Jews*, 313.

54. Topolski and Mochelski, *Żydzi w Wielkopolsce na przestrzeni dziejów*, 140.

55. Topolski and Mochelski, *Żydzi w Wielkopolsce na przestrzeni dziejów*, 140–41.

56. Elizabeth A. Drummond, "On the Borders of the Nation: Jews and the German-Polish National Conflict in Poznania, 1886–1914," *Nationalities Papers* 29, no. 3 (2001): 464.

57. Drummond, "On the Borders of the Nation," 460, 462, 468.

58. Drummond, "On the Borders of the Nation," 465, 468; William Hagen, "National Solidarity and Organic Work in Prussian Poland, 1815–1914," *Journal of Modern History* 44, no. 1 (1972): 48.

59. Drummond, "On the Borders of the Nation," 468.

60. However, there is also evidence of Jewish support for the Polish cause. See Pakuła, *The Jews of Poznań*, 9; Witkowski, "Kalendarium," 310.

61. Pakuła, *The Jews of Poznań*, 9; Witkowski, "Kalendarium," 310.

62. Kemlein, *Żydzi w Wielkim sięstwie Poznańskim*.

63. Pakuła, *The Jews of Poznań*, 12.

64. Bronisław Bergman and Jerzy Janowski, "Wspomnienia" [Memories], in *Gazeta Wyborcza*. June 13, 2003; June 20, 2003; January 9, 2004.

65. Pakuła, *The Jews of Poznań*, 16; Anna Skupień, "Miejska Izraelicka Szkoła Powszechna w Poznaniu" [Miejska Izraelicka Szkoła Powszechna w Poznaniu], in *Poznańscy Żydzi—Kronika Miasta Poznania* [Poznań Jews—The Chronicle of the City of Poznań], ed. Jacek Wiesiołowski and Andrzej Niziołek (Poznań: Wydawnictwo Miejskie, 2006), 261–68.

66. Alexander J. Groth, "Polish Elections 1919–1928," *Slavic Review* 24, no. 4 (1965): 664.

67. Groth, "Polish Elections 1919–1928," 653–65.

68. Arkadiusz Meller and Patryk Tomaszewski, *Życie i śmierć dla Narodu: Antologia myśli narodowo-radykalnej z lat trzydziestych XX wieku* [Life and Death for the Nation: An Anthology of National and Radical Thought from the 1930s] (Toruń: Druk-Tor, 2009), 19.

69. Edward D. Wynot Jr., "A Necessary Cruelty: The Emergence of Official Anti-Semitism in Poland, 1936–39," *American Historical Review* 76, no. 4 (1971): 1036.

70. Pakuła, *The Jews of Poznań*, 17.

71. Pakuła, *The Jews of Poznań*, 17.

72. Pakuła, *The Jews of Poznań*, 13; Waldemar Karolczak, "Żydzi Stowarzyszeni. Życie organizacyjne gminy żydowskiej w Poznaniu na przełomie XIX i XX wieku" [Associated Jews. Organizational Life of the Jewish Community in Poznań at the Turn of the 19th and 20th Century], in *Poznańscy Żydzi—Kronika Miasta Poznania* [Poznań Jews—The Chronicle of the City of Poznań], ed. Jacek Wiesiołowski and Andrzej Niziołek (Poznań: Wydawnictwo Miejskie, 2006), 223-42.

73. Pakuła, *The Jews of Poznań*, 13; Karolczak, "Żydzi Stowarzyszeni," 223-42.

74. Pakuła, *The Jews of Poznań*, 13; Karolczak, "Żydzi Stowarzyszeni," 223-42.

75. Skupień, "Miejska Izraelicka Szkoła Powszechna w Poznaniu," 261-68; Pakuła, *The Jews of Poznań*, 16.

76. Pakuła, *The Jews of Poznań*, 16.

77. Pakuła, *The Jews of Poznań*, 16.

78. Karolczak, "Żydzi Stowarzyszeni," 239; Pakuła, *The Jews of Poznań*, 16.

79. Pakuła, *The Jews of Poznań*, 17.

80. Pakuła, *The Jews of Poznań*, 14-15; Noach Lasman, "Dzieciństwo Poznanskiego Żyda: O poznańskich Żydach i organizacji Haszomer Hacair w przedwojennym Poznaniu" [The Childhood of a Poznań Jew: About Poznań Jews and the Organization of Hashomer Hatzair in Pre-war Poznań], in *Poznańscy Żydzi—Kronika Miasta Poznania* [Poznań Jews—The Chronicle of the City of Poznań], ed. Jacek Wiesiołowski and Andrzej Niziołek (Poznań: Wydawnictwo Miejskie, 2006), 330-73; Karolczak, "Żydzi Stowarzyszeni," 223-42.

81. Pakuła, *The Jews of Poznań*, 16.

82. Pakuła, *The Jews of Poznań*, 14-15.

83. Pakuła, *The Jews of Poznań*, 14-15.

84. Drummond, "On the Borders of the Nation," 464.

85. Pakuła, *The Jews of Poznań*, 18; Anna Ziółkowska, "Żydzi Poznańscy w pierwszych miesiącach okupacji hitlerowskiej" [Poznań Jews in the First Months of the Nazi Occupation], in *Poznańscy Żydzi—Kronika Miasta Poznania* [Poznań Jews—The Chronicle of the City of Poznań], ed. Jacek Wiesiołowski and Andrzej Niziołek (Poznań: Wydawnictwo Miejskie, 2006), 378-93; Ian Kershaw, "Improvised Genocide? The Emergence of the 'Final Solution' in the 'Warthegau,'" *Transactions of the Royal Historical Society*, 6th ser., vol. 2: 1992.

86. Ziółkowska, "Żydzi Poznańscy," 378-93.

87. Ziółkowska, "Żydzi Poznańscy," 387.

88. Witkowski, "Kalendarium," 330.

89. Witkowski, "Kalendarium," 330; Leszek Wróbel, *Niemiecki Obóz Koncentracyjny w Forcie VII w Poznaniu* [German Concentration Camp in Fort VII] (Poznań: Wielkopolskie Muzeum Walk Niepodległościowych, 2007).

90. Witkowski, "Kalendarium," 330; Wróbel, *Niemiecki Obóz Koncentracyjny*.

91. Witkowski, "Kalendarium," 330; Wróbel, *Niemiecki Obóz Koncentracyjny*.

92. Anna Ziółkowska et al, *The Prison of the Security Police and the Educational Labour Camp in Żabikowo* (Żabikowo: Muzeum Martyrologiczne, n.d.).

93. Pakuła, *The Jews of Poznań*, 19.

94. *Stadion* (Żabikowo: Muzeum Martylorogiczne, 2010).

95. Anna Ziółkowska, "Obozy Pracy Przymusowej Dla Żydów w Poznaniu w latach okupacji hitlerowskiej" [Forced Labor Camps for Jews in Poznań during the Nazi occupation], in *Poznańscy Żydzi II—Kronika Miasta Poznania* [Poznań Jews II—The Chronicle of the City of Poznań], ed. Jacek Wiesiołowski and Andrzej Niziołek (Poznań: Wydawnictwo Miejskie, 2009), 394-412; Pakuła, *The Jews of Poznań*, 19.

96. Kershaw, "Improvised Genocide?" 77-78.

97. Weinryb, *The Jews of Poland*, 75; Pakuła, *The Jews of Poznań*, 3.

98. Poznańska Gmina Wyznaniowa Żydowska, "Stara Synagoga" [The Old Synagogue], accessed December 8, 2012, http://poznan.jewish.org.pl/index.php/Synagogi-pozn.wielkop./Stara-Synagoga-przy-ul.-Zydowskiej.html.

99. Witkowski, "Kalendarium," 313, 318.

100. Witkowski, "Kalendarium," 286-87.

101. Witkowski, "Kalendarium," 296.

102. Witkowski, "Kalendarium," 296.

103. Pakuła, *The Jews of Poznań*, 5-6.

104. Rafał Witkowski, "Poświęcenie Nowej Synagogi na Pl. Stawnym" [Consecration of the New Synagogue at the Pond Square], in *Poznańscy Żydzi—Kronika Miasta Poznania* [Poznań Jews—The Chronicle of the City of Poznań], ed. Jacek Wiesiołowski and Andrzej Niziołek (Poznań: Wydawnictwo Miejskie, 2006), 243-49.

105. Witkowski, "Poświęcenie Nowej Synagogi na Pl. Stawnym." Online currency conversion available at http://www.history.ucsb.edu/faculty/marcuse/projects/currency.htm and http://www.usinflationcalculator.com/, [viewed on 10 January 2012].

106. Witkowski, "Poświęcenie," 243-49.

107. Witkowski, "Poświęcenie," 328.

108. Witkowski, "Kalendarium," 328.

109. "Pływalnia w Synagodze zamknięta: wielkie plany!" [The swimming pool in the synagogue closed: big plans], *epoznan.pl*, accessed April 26, 2020, epoznan.pl/news-news-27744.

110. Poznańska Gmina Wyznaniowa Żydowska, "Nasza Gmina kim jesteśmy?" [Our Community who are we?], accessed 10 January 2012, http://poznan.jewish.org.pl/index.php/Nasza-gmina-kim-jestesmy/.

111. Jerzy Stranz, *Czerpiąc z korzenia szlachetnej oliwki. Dzień Judaizmu w Poznaniu 2000-2007* [Deriving from the Root to Trace the Ethereal Olive. Judaism Day in Poznan 2000-2007], Seria Teologiczna no. 7 (Poznań: Wydawnictwo Naukowe UAM, 2007).

112. John Paul II, *Homilia in Kraków*, June 10, 1979, http://ekai.pl/biblioteka/dokumenty/x579/homilia-w-czasie-mszy-sw-odprawionej-na-bloniach/.

113. "Tęsknię za tobą Żydzie . . ." [I miss you Jew . . .], January 20, 2010, http://www.sztetl.org.pl/pl/article/poznan/20,kultura-projekty-spoleczne-i-edukacyjne/17839,20-01-2010-tesknie-za-toba-zydzie/.

114. Anna Plenzler, *Jewish Culture Trail through Wielkopolska*, Wielkopolska Organizacja Turystyczna, 2012, 1.

115. Janusz Korczak, "Trzy prądy" [Three Currents], *Społeczeństwo* 42 (1910).

Part 2

Contemporary Antisemitism

7

Antisemitism and Its Transnational Inhibitions
1930s Europe and Now

R. AMY ELMAN

To seasoned observers of antisemitism, comparisons between the 1930s and now inevitably involve the question: what's new? Although the vectors of the "new antisemitism" include left-wing antisemitism, Islamic antisemitism, Holocaust denial, and Israel's demonization and delegitimization, the long history of each complicates antisemitism's novelty.[1] What has changed, according to historian Jonathan Judaken, is the geopolitical context within which each manifestation functions.[2] This chapter considers European integration as a key geopolitical site within which contemporary antisemitism is at once manifest and swiftly denied.

Despite the crucial importance of geopolitics, few scholars of contemporary antisemitism pay sufficient attention to transnational actors in general and the European Union (EU) in particular.[3] The EU is an economic and political international organization that currently comprises twenty-seven member countries, and has the stated objective of achieving "an ever closer union among the peoples of Europe" through the economic integration of those states. Established in 1957 through the Treaty of Rome, and renamed the European Union in 1994, its proponents believed that the economic prosperity that would result would promote unity and help prevent future wars. Despite its various challenges, the EU remains a powerful transnational institution.

In those fleeting moments in which globalization makes a cameo appearance, transnational institutions appear indistinguishable and their particular powers are misunderstood.[4] By contrast, those attentive to the history of Europe's integration and the intricacies of EU institutions rarely address antisemitism. This includes those whose stated concern is racism. This is especially ironic given that the horrors of the Holocaust helped legitimize Europe's founding narrative and subsequent policies to counter racism.

This chapter concentrates on the response of EU officials to just two of the above-noted vectors of the "new antisemitism"—Islamic antisemitism and Holocaust denial. While EU officials often elide Islamic antisemitism, their references to the Holocaust sometimes stagger into inversions that bolster the very antisemitism they may wish to counter. Otherwise referred to as "soft-core denial" by historian Deborah Lipstadt, Holocaust inversion is less about the blatant denial of the Holocaust than about the transformation of Jews into Nazis such that others (e.g., Palestinians or Poles) are mythologized as the real victims of Jewish genocide.[5] For Lesley Klaff, Holocaust inversion also involves the "inversion of morality" insofar as "the Holocaust is presented as a moral lesson for, or even a moral indictment of, 'the Jews.'"[6]

Holocaust inversion's increased popularity stems, in part, from its compulsive anti-Zionism, which bridges Europe's left-leaning populace with Islamic antisemites to provide a blistering portrait of Jews as exemplars of racism (e.g., against Muslims)—a stance that frees European gentiles (and their Arab allies) from the burdens of European history.[7] That record includes, but is not limited to, the ghettoization, expulsion, forced conversion, and attempted eradication of Jews.

In his bone-chilling account of just one decade of that history, the 1930s, Benjamin Carter Hett's *The Death of Democracy* looks beyond the weakness of the Weimar Republic and its flawed statesmen to emphasize the Nazis as a violent (nationalist) protest movement opposed to the globalization that Europe's integration came to represent.[8] Several of Hett's observations helped guide my own in considering the present against this historical backdrop. In his final chapter, Hett introduces us to former German chancellor Franz von Papen's conservative speechwriter, Edgar Julius Jung.[9] Jung's solution to the challenge of minority rights in Europe was closer ties to other countries through federalism and a common economic zone. In 1934 he insisted that Germany's foreign policy pursue "European justice" to transcend national conflicts that had been exacerbated by the Nazi emphasis on "racial and national exclusivity." Ironically, Jung's position cost him his life within the year, and later helped acquit Papen of all charges in 1945 at the Nuremberg Trials. According to Hett, the "farsighted" Jung "thought an integrated federal Europe would make 'wars of extermination' impossible."[10] Jung's insistence that Germans are "a people among peoples in the middle of Europe" made its way into the conclusion of Papen's last public speech as vice chancellor under Hitler.[11] And, though Hitler's propaganda minister, Joseph Goebbels, blocked the dissemination of that speech, its pan-Europeanism eventually took root through the establishment of the European Economic Community, a forerunner of today's EU.

Political Complexities of the 1930s

By 1930 Europeans had come to think of themselves as civilized. The Weimar Republic entered the League of Nations and liberal internationalists celebrated. Four years earlier they had awarded the 1926 Nobel Prize to the three foreign ministers (of Britain, France and Germany) who made the League possible.

Mass electoral politics had also emerged. Most European countries had just extended universal manhood suffrage and over a third of today's EU member states granted the vote to women as well (although France did so in 1945 and Italy the next year). Transnational women's organizations proliferated between 1919 and 1938, and suffragists who had won the vote understood their work was far from complete if women anywhere remained disenfranchised. Women from countries struggling to free themselves from colonial subjection embraced nationalism. But nationalism cut the other way as well. Women from imperial states condemned nationalist rivalries between states. Additionally, countless feminists and prominent pacifists, such as the distinguished German American Alice Salomon, identified as citizens of the world and were later disillusioned.[12]

Jews, too, had reason for guarded optimism. Several of the wide-ranging restrictions that had existed throughout most of European history had been lifted, and the Zionist quest for a homeland both relied on and was in step with the self-determination and the "new spirit of international law" that the League of Nations represented.[13] For German Jews even the state seemed on their side. The Weimar Republic (Germany's first full democracy after centuries of monarchical rule) adopted hate speech laws and applied them frequently against leading Nazis, including Joseph Goebbels. Insulting communities of faith and inciting class warfare or acts of violence was a punishable offense for which Nazi propagandist Julius Streicher, among others, served time in prison. From 1923 to 1933 the democratic authorities either confiscated or brought suits against Streicher's antisemitic newspaper, *Der Stürmer*, no fewer than thirty-six times. Yet, far from serving as a deterrent, the charges galvanized Nazi supporters into a mass protest movement. In 1930 Streicher was met by thousands of followers when he was released from prison; Hitler was among those who greeted him. As Danish journalist Flemming Rose explains, "the German courts became an important platform for Streicher's campaign against the Jews."[14] Moreover, antisemites sometimes successfully defended themselves against accusations of incitement by arguing that their opposition to Jews was premised neither in class nor religious hatred. Instead, they insisted their campaigns were aimed at Jews as a "race," which was not then a punishable offence.[15]

It was within this seemingly more benevolent political context that the "hatreds, prejudices, and superstitions that civilized Europeans thought belonged to the distant past had reemerged."[16] If the pervasiveness of antisemitism made it nearly imperceptible to many, including Communists, for whom Jew-hating was a distraction from authentic (class) conflict, others remained more critical.[17]

Biddy Barlow, a young relation of Charles Darwin, spent her teenage years in Germany and found it a remarkable "paradox of the thirties that parents with liberal left wing views almost invariably send their children to Nazi Germany when they wanted their minds broadened by a spell abroad."[18] While there were certainly some returning students who endeavored to alert their families and friends to Nazism's dangers, it is chilling that many of those coming back home seemed as enthused about Germany as the parents who sent them.

Even when indifference to escalating antisemitism does not appear to have prevailed, men in positions of political authority, including the American secretary of state Cordell Hull, insisted that antisemitism belonged to a bygone era. In 1933 Hull declared that "mistreatment of Jews in Germany may be considered virtually terminated."[19] Within a decade most German Jews had either emigrated or been murdered. Far from being discredited by this blunder, Hull received the Nobel Peace Prize in 1945 for helping to establish the United Nations.

As author Julia Boyd explains, "All travelers to the Reich, no matter who they were or what their purpose, were subjected to constant propaganda: the inequities of the Versailles treaty, the astonishing achievements of the Nazi revolution, Hitler's devotion to peace, the need for Germany to defend itself... and so on."[20] In a letter to the English newspaper publisher Lord Rothermere in 1933, Hitler wrote, "Just as we [Germans] are fanatically determined to defend ourselves against attack, so do we reject the idea of taking the initiative in bringing about a war. I am convinced that no one who fought in the front trenches during the world war, no matter in what European country, desires another conflict."[21] This and similar subterfuges helped mask Hitler's massive military escalation. Thus, after his meeting with Hitler in 1936, Britain's prime minister at the time, David Lloyd George, insisted Germany had abandoned its militarism and lacked any desire to rule Europe.[22] Such wishful thinking hinged on an inability to grasp Nazism's threat.

Still, like Biddy Barlow, some people proved less susceptible to misguided optimism and the Reich's messaging. Consider the renowned African American professor William Du Bois. His youthful admiration of Germany's intellectual treasures beckoned him to return as a senior scholar to explore the possible benefits for "Negros" of that state's programs for industrial education.[23] Yet, soon after arriving in Germany at the height of the Reich, he found Hitler's National Socialism nearly indistinguishable from communism under Stalin.

Not one to embrace received wisdom, in 1936 Du Bois was reluctant to reach conclusions about Germans as individuals, though he viewed Hitler's new government with clear contempt and declared it a facsimile of the Soviet Union. Hitler's tirades against Bolshevism made little impression on this scholar. For Du Bois totalitarianism was totalitarianism regardless of its ideological trappings. He cited the Third Reich's "ownership and control of industry; its control of money and banking, its steps toward land ownership and control by government; its ordering of work and wages, its building of infrastructure and houses, its youth movement and its one-party state at elections."[24]

More impressive is Du Bois's recognition of antisemitism as the distinguishing feature of Hitler's reign. He wrote, "The campaign against the Jews surpasses in its vindictive cruelty and public insult anything I have ever seen; and I have seen much."[25] For him it was "comparable only to such horrors as the Spanish Inquisition and the African slave trade."[26] That Du Bois enjoyed his five months in Germany was undeniable. He stated that he had "been treated with uniform courtesy and consideration" during his stay.[27] However, this did not dissuade Du Bois from concluding that Nazism was "an attack on civilization."[28] Just how immense and devastating this attack became, he could not have imagined.

Whether—unlike Du Bois and like the optimistic liberal Europhiles who saw only the best in Europe—one harbors similar illusions about the contemporary political landscape and the prospects of barbarity's reemergence matters less than the strength of Europe's leaders and the transnational institutions ostensibly established to inhibit it. As we will soon note, Europe's postwar elites were similar to Jung in that they regarded the economic integration among their countries as an appealing remedy for the ethnic antagonisms and antisemitism that turned their tumultuous continent of the 1930s into a necropolis by 1945.

Origins of the European Union

Europe's common market was advanced by politicians who presumed that a cohesive economic union between their once warring countries would diminish the rabid nationalism that helped foster genocide. Indeed, the preamble of the European Community's founding treaty requires member states to "substitute age-old rivalries ... by establishing an economic community" that could unite "peoples long divided by bloody conflicts." In accepting the Nobel Peace Prize on behalf of the EU in 2012, the president of the European Commission (the EU's executive arm) explained, "The genius of the founding fathers was precisely in understanding that to guarantee peace in the 20th century, nations need to think beyond the nation-state."[29]

As to the place of Jews in this newly constituted Europe, Robert Wistrich, one of the world's foremost scholars of antisemitism, stated that "the growth of the European Union and the extension of a democratic consensus based on antifascism and antiracism should have created the best of all possible worlds for Jews."[30] He continued, "What more could Jews have asked for than a fully democratic Europe?—especially those Jews interested in integrating into a peaceful, prosperous, and cosmopolitan civilization with special concern for its minorities."[31] Europe's integration held promise, though it is unclear whether peace through prosperity provided Jews with an *effective* antidote to hate.

If, as nationalism's primary losers in the early twentieth century, Jews now appear among the EU's key beneficiaries—think again. That the Holocaust now functions as a founding narrative that helps legitimize Europe's integration is nothing if not paradoxical. The EU may be the world's largest single market and its largest trader of goods and services, but its cosmopolitan transnationalism has scarcely cured antisemitism. The same year that the EU was feted for its ability to guarantee the peace, its Fundamental Rights Agency (FRA) was conducting what was then its most extensive survey on antisemitism.

The FRA was asked to provide the EU and its member states with objective, reliable, and comparative data, and its 2012 survey offered an ominous glimpse into conditions for Jews throughout Europe. After enduring antisemitic harassment and discrimination, nearly a third of the 5,847 self-identified Jewish respondents from eight member states stated they had considered *emigrating* from their country of residence.[32] Within a year of the report's release the Islamic State of Iraq and Syria (ISIS) first struck in Belgium. They targeted the Brussels Jewish Museum. Of the four slain, one was a French woman who had left for Belgium two months prior to escape France's escalating antisemitism.[33]

In 2018, the FRA implemented a follow-up survey of 16,395 Jewish respondents from across twelve member states. The survey revealed a 13 percent uptick in antisemitism since 2012. In 2012, 76 percent of respondents perceived an increase in antisemitism over the last five years in their own country.[34] By 2018, 89 percent of respondents stated this was their perception.[35] Between these two surveys the FRA found that "the categories of perpetrators of antisemitic harassment remain consistent" and noted they were more likely to be "someone with an extremist Muslim view" (30 percent) than "someone with left-wing political views" (21 percent) or right-wing politics (13 percent).[36] In response to the insecurity these perpetrators cause, a similar percentage of respondents (34 percent in 2012 and 38 percent in 2018) in each study considered emigrating.[37]

As in the first survey, thousands of the respondents noted again that they had grown leery of either using or wearing anything that might identify them as Jews. These items included, but were not limited to, kippot, Jewish themed jewelry (e.g., Stars of David), and mezuzahs affixed to (external) doorframes. Moreover, they feared the consequences of attending synagogue, purchasing kosher food, or frequenting Jewish cultural events. This fear is paramount for Europe's younger Jews, many of whom are more religiously observant than their elders. In 2019 the FRA released a report that distilled the 2018 survey data from those aged sixteen to thirty-four. It reasoned these respondents "hold the keys to the future of Jewish life in Europe" and thus have the potential to bring the tradition's culture and insights to forging Europe's future.[38] When one considers that younger Jews are more likely to experience antisemitism than their elders and that a higher percentage of them (forty-one percent) are considering emigrating, Europe's future looks dim indeed.[39]

In early 2012 a French jihadist murdered three children and their rabbi outside a Jewish day school in Toulouse. Jews throughout France, home to Europe's largest Jewish community, were rattled. That summer, a suicide bomber with suspected connections to Hezbollah murdered five Israeli tourists and their bus driver in Bulgaria. By fall, two jihadists had tossed a grenade into a French kosher market, injuring one shopper and terrifying countless others. These conditions, no doubt, informed the first survey, but more tragedy followed.

By the 2018 survey, the death toll mounted with jihadist slayings of Jews in three major European capitals. The year 2015 opened with a security guard slain outside his Copenhagen synagogue, and closed with Islamist attacks in Paris at the Bataclan Theatre and a French kosher market.[40] Months later, in March 2016, the suicide bombings in Brussels were no less motivated by antisemitism. According to Mohamed Abrini, who accompanied the terrorists to the Brussels airport, the initial plan was to detonate the bombs in the "departure areas for flights to Tel Aviv, the United States, and Russia."[41]

The 2012 survey registered the profound and eerily prophetic fears of Jewish respondents to escalating antisemitism, but both FRA surveys exposed the limited confidence that respondents had in any authority or organization—national or transnational—to counter it. In fact, over half of those surveyed in 2012 (sixty percent) and in 2018 (fifty-two percent) claimed that reporting antisemitic discrimination would be of no consequence, a finding that suggests that Europe's Jews recognize the public's general acceptance of their abuse and the disinclination of Europe's authorities to move against it.[42] Moreover, twenty percent of the 2012 respondents and twenty-five percent of those from 2018 claimed they did not trust the police.[43] Distrust of law enforcement was especially pronounced among younger Jews, eighty percent of whom did not report harassment incidents to authorities. Of those who suffered antisemitic violence, fifty-one percent chose not to contact law enforcement.[44]

These findings are unsurprising given several highly publicized incidents, including the refusal by the French police to recognize antisemitism's role in the 2006 kidnapping and eventual murder of a young man, Ilan Halimi, by a criminal gang. The gang believed that because Ilan Halimi was Jewish, his family would be wealthy and willing to pay a large ransom for his release.

In 2017, French prosecutors took ten months before officially recognizing the savage murder of Sarah Halimi (no relation to Ilan) by her Muslim neighbor as antisemitic. The assailant, Kobili

Traore, was heard calling Halimi a "devil," and witnesses stated that he shouted "Allahu Akbar" as he tossed her battered body from her third-story apartment. Then, in 2019, a French judge found that Traore could not be criminally responsible for his actions because he was under the influence of marijuana.

In a case reminiscent of Sarah Halimi's murder, another elderly French Jewish woman was murdered by her young Muslim neighbor in 2018. Mireille Knoll was eighty-five years old and a Holocaust survivor, and the man who murdered her stabbed her repeatedly before setting her on fire in her apartment. French president Macron attended Knoll's funeral and declared that the attacker "murdered an innocent and vulnerable woman because she was Jewish, and in doing so profaned our sacred values and our history."[45] Officials from Paris's main mosque also expressed support for Knoll's family, stating that "the evident anti-Semitic character of this murder is denounced and condemned by all the Muslims of France."[46]

The fact that so many perpetrators of antisemitism may themselves be vulnerable to racism might account for the reluctance on the part of many Jews to come forward. Of those Jews the FRA surveyed, 85 percent considered antisemitism to be a "very big" or "fairly big problem" in the country where they lived, and 84 percent identified racism as a problem as well. A majority of these respondents (72 percent) expressed specific concern about "intolerance towards Muslims" in Europe.[47]

In 2018, the FRA's new director observed that antisemitism had become so pervasive that it was "disturbingly normalized."[48] His agency's 2018 report concluded that Jews had faced so much abuse that they sometimes regarded it as trivial.[49] Yet, when one considers the reluctance of the authorities (including the police, public prosecutors, and criminal court judges) to acknowledge the antisemitic character of anti-Jewish harassment and assaults (much less forcefully condemn them), it is understandable that many Jews came to regard their own violations as insignificant.[50]

According to the FRA's 2018 report, "the most common antisemitic statements" that respondents "come across—and on a regular basis" included those that are central to Holocaust inversion.

For example, 51 percent of those surveyed reported encountering the sentiment that "Israelis behave like Nazis toward Palestinians," that "Jews have too much power" (43 percent), and that "Jews exploit Holocaust victimhood for their own purposes" (35 percent).⁵¹ Moreover, the perceptions of these Jewish respondents accorded with CNN's own survey of 7,092 Europeans about their attitudes toward Jews, antisemitism, and memory of the Holocaust. CNN found that one-fifth of those surveyed across seven states believe Jews have too much power, and twice that number agree that Jews are at risk of racist violence within their country.⁵² Released just weeks before the FRA's 2018 survey, CNN also found that although one-third of those surveyed admitted to knowing little or nothing about the Holocaust, 32 percent agreed that Jews use the Holocaust to "advance their position or achieve certain goals."⁵³

Far from countering the troubling sentiments expressed in these data, many of the EU's own statements on the Holocaust might be regarded by the new FRA director as disturbing, if not antisemitic. In detailing several of these statements, the section below explains how the EU's top officials perpetuate the very antisemitism they claim to oppose.

Soft Holocaust Denial

Consider the public statement issued by Catherine Ashton to commemorate International Holocaust Memorial Day in 2014. Representing the EU in her capacity as the polity's first High Representative for Foreign Affairs and Security Policy, she wrote, "On Holocaust Remembrance Day, we must keep alive the memory of this tragedy. It is an occasion to remind us all of the need to continue fighting prejudice and racism in our own time. We must remain vigilant against the dangers of hate speech and redouble our commitment to prevent any form of intolerance. The respect of human rights and diversity lies at the heart of what the European Union stands for."⁵⁴ This statement may sound innocuous, but in substituting platitudinous references to racism, intolerance, and human rights for any mention of antisemitism's centrality to the Holocaust, Ashton managed to withdraw Jewish genocide from a catalogue of Nazi infamy. That she accomplished this in an international Holocaust commemoration statement under the guise of promoting "human rights" offers an ironic victory to the assassins of memory, regardless of her intent.

Tempting though it may be to disregard Ashton's text as politically insignificant, she was no political novice, and her statement on the Holocaust was far from trivial or unrehearsed. As the EU's premier foreign policy chief, Ashton was a privileged political player whose manipulation of "human rights" discourse was seemingly humdrum and in league with other EU statements that downplayed antisemitism, including its centrality to the Holocaust itself.

Consider, for example, the FRA's 2011 brochure on Holocaust education. The brochure was, like Ashton's later statement, averse to recognizing antisemitism. In *Human Rights Education at Holocaust Memorial Sites across the European Union*, the Agency worries that "most of the memorial sites . . . do not systematically include education on human rights in their work."[55] Having excluded lethal antisemitism from the rubric of "human rights," the FRA, like Ashton, employed the Holocaust as a backdrop to foreground the fundamental rights and violations of others.[56]

Islamic Antisemitism

The deflections by EU officials away from antisemitism in statements on or commemorations of the Holocaust were later repeated in responses to recent attacks on Jews. Rather than acknowledging the Jewish character of contemporary targets and resulting casualties, EU officials often focused on providing support to those most closely implicated in harming Jews. Again, Ashton's response proves instructive. In 2012, hours after the targeted killings outside a Jewish day school in Toulouse, Ashton sidestepped the centrality of murderous antisemitism and insisted everyone remember "young people who have been killed in all sorts of terrible crimes."[57] Among these, she mentioned child casualties in Gaza. Israel was swift to condemn her equation of the deliberate massacre of children with the defensive actions of its armed forces against terrorists who utilize children as human shields. Unfortunately, the EU had ample opportunity to alter its response, but it rarely did.

While former commission president Jean Claude Juncker

expressed his swift indignation and "highest solidarity" following the 2015 Islamic massacres at Charlie Hebdo, he issued no similar condemnation after Islamists in France slayed Jews days later at a kosher market.[58] It was only after another Islamist murdered two Danes in Copenhagen the next month, one in a café and the other outside his synagogue, that the commissioner released a curt denunciation of antisemitism. It read: "We stand against anti-Semitism *and all forms of discrimination*."[59] Rarely opposed on its own, antisemitism is often condemned only within contexts that acknowledge discrimination against others, though the converse is rarely true.

In responding to the 2015 murders in France, the European Parliament understandably called for a moment of silence for *all* victims. However, its apparent inability to account for the significant distinctions between them was evidenced in the remarks of its then-president, Martin Schultz. He said, "These 17 cartoonists, journalists, police officers, employees and ordinary Jewish citizens were killed because they represented things that fanatics cannot stand: criticism, humour, satire and free speech."[60] Whether Schultz regarded the murdered Jews as critics, comics, or exemplars of the EU's citizenship is beside the point. His failure to mention antisemitism signals a dangerous reluctance to forcefully confront the reasons why "fanatics" single out Jews.

Like the European Parliament, the FRA conflated all the victims of Islamic terror and refused to name the perpetrators, thus also obscuring the specific threats to European Jews that previous FRA surveys had documented. After expressing its "horror at *the crime* and its sympathy with all those close to the victims," the agency acknowledged the "attacks on the editorial offices of the French magazine ... and the subsequent hostage crisis."[61] As Robert Zaretsky notes, the Jews at the kosher market were "no more hostages than the victims at Charlie Hebdo were insurance adjustors." "The latter were killed," he explains, "because they were cartoonists, while the former were executed because they were Jews."[62]

By contrast, Federica Mogherini, the commission's newly appointed vice president and High Representative for Foreign Affairs, was one of the few EU officials to bring an element of clarity to the horror when she explicitly noted its antisemitic dimensions, but she too refrained from identifying its Islamic perpetrators. Following her meeting with a delegation of the European Jewish Congress after the terror in Paris, she expressed her condolences to all the victims and observed that the subsequent attack on the kosher market exacerbated the horrors that had already transpired. Then, when it came time for the EU to issue its annual statement to commemorate International Holocaust Remembrance Day, she observed that while 2015 marked the seventieth anniversary of the liberation of Auschwitz, the murders at the kosher market served as a sobering and grim reminder of antisemitism's persistence.[63]

Following the carnage weeks later in Copenhagen, EU officials remained diffident about ascribing blame to Islamic terrorists. The FRA's former director Morten Kjaerum, for example, asked *all* religious leaders to unite in a condemnation of the attacks to avoid "polarization." He further advised political leaders "to use the momentum to formulate far-sighted policy that tackles the root causes of radicalization."[64] Sensitive to the implications of this emphasis, Eve Garrard, an authority on antisemitism, warned, "What counts as the root cause may itself be a matter of dispute." In her experience, "prior political commitments and pre-judgments . . . ensure that the blame for the problem lands exactly where the observer has already decided it belongs" (i.e., in the lap of Jews).[65]

Days after the dual murders in Denmark, a Swedish Public Radio reporter, Helena Groll, stepped into the void left by EU leaders in their reluctance to apportion guilt and asked Israel's ambassador whether "Jews themselves have any responsibility in the growing anti-Semitism that we see now."[66] When the ambassador offered to explain why he "reject[ed] the question altogether," an undaunted Groll attributed the attacks in Copenhagen to the conflict in the "Middle East"—code for Israel, the Jewish state. Thus, she had just expressed, however inadvertently, "two of the oldest of anti-Semitic tropes": that Jews are to blame for the hatred against them and that "Jews anywhere are responsible for the actions of Jews everywhere."[67]

Against the background of a public discourse that assumes that prejudice and terror against Jews stem from the Israel-Palestine conflict, the murders by Islamists are at once self-explanatory and contain an element of self-justification. That is, if the terror against Jews is understood as resulting from Israel's treatment of Palestinians, then the treatment of the Jews by Islamists is no different and thus hardly objectionable.

Sadly, much of the antipathy toward Israel now functions as an alibi for acts of terror (against Jews) in several member states. Sweden appears to have led this trend when, in 2006, the former chancellor of justice ruled that the threats of extermination that emanated from a Stockholm mosque were "permissible" because they functioned as a "commonplace feature of the rhetoric surrounding the Middle East conflict."[68] Four years later, hating Israel became a valid criminal defense in Britain when a jury acquitted five vandals after they targeted an arms factory for doing business with the Israeli army. "Incredibly," writes Robert Wistrich, the judge had "instructed the jury that Gaza was hell on earth (for which Israel was held responsible) thereby almost licensing the actions of those accused in breaking the law."[69]

In February 2015 an Austrian prosecutor suspended an investigation into a man's Facebook post of Hitler's photograph beneath which he had written, "I could have killed all Jews, but I left some of them alive to show you, why I killed them."[70] While Austria's prohibition of Holocaust denial extends to "whoever denies, grossly plays down, approves or tries to excuse the National Socialist genocide," the prosecutor's office insisted that no violation had transpired because the statements "were not glorifying Hitler, but expressing displeasure towards Israel."[71] The same month a German court similarly surmised that the 2014 firebombing of a synagogue was motivated not by antisemitism but by a desire to bring "attention to the Gaza conflict," a position in keeping with Ashton's 2012 comments pertaining to the slayings in Toulouse.[72]

If, to many, antisemitism so disguised as social justice promotes Jewish suffering by rendering it righteous, not all Austrian and German authorities have been so gullible. Indeed, Austrian authorities have reopened their investigations into the Facebook case noted above after protests erupted, and the Austrian prosecutor's office was condemned for its position.[73] In a German ruling in January 2015, the county court of Essen sentenced a man for incitement to hatred when he specifically called for the death of Zionists at a protest. His defense was twofold: there is no ethnic minority of Zionists in Germany, and he has no animus against Jews. The Essen court was not persuaded. It responded, "The term 'Zionist' in the current language of antisemitism also is a codeword for Jews."[74] Whether other courts throughout the EU will prove as discerning remains to be seen. Until then, like Holocaust deniers who advanced their "scholarship" by seeking the "truth," their fellow travelers conceal their animus under the auspices of "social justice."

Transnational Remedies?

The conflicting conclusions within and across and these member states will require, among other acts, transnational rulings and leaders willing to regard antisemitism not as a consequence of injustice, but as its leading cause. The Court of Justice of the European Union (CJEU) is unlikely to demonstrate such leadership, because its chief task is to examine the legality of EU measures and not necessarily the merits of domestic rulings and individual grievances. And, unless the member states refer the above rulings to the court for greater clarity, or the European Commission appeals to it for insights about whether the member states are fulfilling their legal obligations under EU law, this transnational venue is ill suited to the task. Moreover, to date, the EU maintains no substantive legal obligations against antisemitism. Recycled declarations that insist the commission "stands firm against any form of Antisemitism" are no substitute for action.[75]

For years the European Commission has implied that the legal expertise needed to address antisemitism lies outside the EU, with the Council of Europe (COE) and its European Convention of Human Rights. The COE's court, the European Court of Human Rights (ECtHR), offers several advantages because all EU member states, as signatories to the convention, must abide by its rulings. Additionally, its precedent and advisory opinions inform those of the EU's Court of Justice. Not least, individuals may file direct grievances with the ECtHR. In this way Europe's Jews can circumvent channels that may be either hostile (e.g., specific member state courts) or unavailable to them as individual claimants.

Yet, for Jews and countless others, the consequences of the ECtHR's rulings are far from clear. Its unanimous ruling in 2003 against the French Holocaust denier Roger Garaudy unambiguously recognized Holocaust denial as "racial defamation" that does not merit the protection of freedom of expression because of its potential to incite hatred against Jews.[76] Fifteen years later, the court was similarly persuaded that Austria's far-right Freedom Party seminars on Islam (run by E.S.) posed a significant threat to Muslims. The court ruled that E.S.'s depictions of the prophet Mohamad as a child molester were an "abusive attack on an object of religious veneration" that would likely "incite religious intolerance."[77] Thus, the seminars were also outside the bounds of acceptable expression guaranteed by the European Convention of Human Rights. In both cases, the court was clearly concerned about the potentially devastating consequences of incendiary speech that targets minorities. Yet critics worry that the court needs to balance those concerns with the need to safeguard freedom of expression.[78] The history of the Weimar Republic reveals how laws against hate speech can backfire to galvanize the forces of bigotry they were designed to suppress.

If, by the 1930s, it seems that Europeans had distanced themselves from the cruelty of their predecessors only to surpass their barbarism, what do we make of Europe's current officials, whose seemingly enlightened rhetoric and culturally sensitive court rulings may serve as a thin veneer of "human rights" beneath which the "age-old swamp" of antisemitism flourishes?[79] Compared with the early 1930s, the data suggest that most European Jews may be no more vulnerable to or menaced by the rabid nationalism of the right than by EU-level actors of the left, who seem impervious to the threats posed by a new transnational protest movement whose adherents and allies hold "extremist Muslim views."

Moreover, with roots in and allies from the 1930s, today's Islamists are unapologetic in their ambition to finish what the Nazis began, a position that EU officials have repeatedly chosen to ignore in ways that are reminiscent of Lord Rothermore, Prime Minister David Lloyd George, and countless gullible others. In 2002 *Al Jazeera* reached millions of its viewers when addressing the question, "Is Zionism Worse than Nazism?" A viewer's response clearly underscores the convergence of Holocaust inversion and Islamic antisemitism that this article was designed to address. His answer was this: "The sons of Zion, whom our God described as the sons of apes and pigs, will not be deterred unless there is a real holocaust, that will destroy all of them at once."[80] This sentiment pervades social media, inspires lethal violence, and cultivates fear throughout Europe in ways not always dissimilar to what occurred in the early twentieth century.

It is in response to this climate that Europe's younger Jews are considering leaving. And it was in watching Europe descend into these depths that Robert Wistrich, one of the world's leading scholars of antisemitism, despaired that the EU would no longer serve as home to the continent's remaining Jews.

Questions for Further Discussion

1. What role does antisemitism play in Europe today?

2. What factors are different today that create a different model for antisemitism in Europe?

3. Are the political complexities of the 1930s similar to the issues around antisemitism in Europe today? How are they the same or different? What lessons can be learned from the Nazi years and applied to antisemitism in today's Europe?

4. What is the European Union?

5. What role, if any, can the EU play in making sure that antisemitism of today does not become the antisemitism of the twentieth century?

6. Is Christian antisemitism still a major issue and threat for Jews in Europe?

8. What is the role of Muslim communities in Europe when it comes to antisemitism?

7. Are there limits on free speech in EU countries when it comes to Nazism and antisemitism? What are they? And how about in the United States?

Notes

1. Jonathan Judaken, "So What's New? Rethinking the 'New Antisemitism' in a Global Age," *Patterns of Prejudice* 42, no. 4–5 (2008): 531–60, here 533.
2. Judaken, "So What's New?," 531.
3. R. Amy Elman, *The European Union, Antisemitism, and the Politics of Denial*, Studies in Antisemitism (Lincoln: University of Nebraska Press, 2014), Introduction.
4. Consider, for instance, the misplaced faith that opponents of antisemitism put in the European Union's Fundamental Rights Agency (FRA) and its forerunner, the European Union's Monitoring Centre (EUMC). Their insufficient grasp of the history and limited powers of these agencies led them to overlook the sustained power of the EU's member states, all of which, without exception, jealously guard their sovereignty. R. Amy Elman, "The EU's Responses to Contemporary Antisemitism: A Shell Game?," in *Deciphering the New Antisemitism*, ed. Alvin Rosenfeld (Bloomington: University of Indiana Press, 2015), 405–29. Additionally, discussions of "Europe" often refer to one or just a few states (usually Britain, France, and Germany), although the EU comprises over two dozen countries within the region. The vast generalizations that result from this limited focus can also prove unhelpful.
5. Deborah E. Lipstadt, *Antisemitism: Here and Now* (New York: Schocken Books, 2019); Robert S. Wistrich, *A Lethal Obsession: Anti-Semitism from Antiquity to the Global Jihad*, 1st ed. (New York: Random House, 2010), 62–63.
6. Lesley Klaff, "Holocaust Inversion," *Fathom*, February 2014, https://fathomjournal.org/holocaust-inversion-and-contemporary-antisemitism/.
7. Wistrich, *A Lethal Obsession*, 934–35.
8. Benjamin Carter Hett, *The Death of Democracy: Hitler's Rise to Power and the Downfall of the Weimar Republic* (New York: Henry Holt and Company, 2018), 106.
9. Von Papen was briefly the German chancellor in 1932. He then served as vice chancellor under Adolph Hitler from 1933 to 1934. Thereafter he was the Third Reich's ambassador in Austria (until 1938) and later Turkey (from 1939 to 1944).
10. Hett, *The Death of Democracy*, 220.
11. Hett, *The Death of Democracy*, 223.
12. In 1932 Salomon received an honorary doctorate from Berlin University and the Silver State Medal from the Prussian State Ministry, both of which the Nazis rescinded after coming to power the following year. Leila Rupp writes that Salomon, "who found that her conversion to Christianity did not distract the minds of the Nazis from her Jewish origins, proclaimed in her autobiography, 'I wanted the whole world to be my country.'" Leila J. Rupp, *Worlds of Women: The Making of an International Women's Movement* (Princeton NJ: Princeton University Press, 1997), 118. Instead, after having been expelled from Germany, Salomon became an American citizen in 1944.
13. James Loeffler, *Rooted Cosmopolitans: Jews and Human Rights in the Twentieth Century* (New Haven CT: Yale University Press, 2018), 22.
14. Flemming Rose, *The Tyranny of Silence: How One Cartoon Ignited a Global Debate on the Future of Free Speech* (New York: Cato Institute, 2014), 61.

15. Rose, *The Tyranny of Silence*, 61.

16. Hett, *The Death of Democracy*, 195.

17. Peter Jelavich, *Berlin Cabaret*, Studies in Cultural History (Cambridge MA.: Harvard University Press, 1996), 226–27.

18. Julia Boyd, *Travelers in the Third Reich: The Rise of Fascism: 1919–1945* (New York: Pegasus Books, 2018), 164.

19. "Prayers and Atrocities," *Time*, April 3, 1933, 17.

20. Boyd, *Travelers in the Third Reich*, 7.

21. Jim Wilson, *Nazi Princess: Hitler, Lord Rothermere, and Princess Stephanie Von Hohenlohe* (Gloucestershire: History Press, 2011), chapter 6.

22. Roland Quinault, *British Prime Ministers and Democracy: From Disraeli to Blair* (London: Continuum, 2011), 92.

23. Boyd, *Travelers in the Third Reich*, 239.

24. Boyd, *Travelers in the Third Reich*, 250.

25. Quoted in Boyd, *Travelers in the Third Reich*, 240.

26. Boyd, *Travelers in the Third Reich*, 240.

27. Boyd, *Travelers in the Third Reich*, 241.

28. Boyd, *Travelers in the Third Reich*, 240.

29. José Manuel Durão Barroso, "From War to Peace: A European Tale" (Brussels: Europa: Press Releases, 2012), https://ec.europa.eu/commission/presscorner/detail/en/SPEECH_12_724.

30. Manfred Gerstenfeld, ed., *Israel and Europe: An Expanding Abyss?* (Jerusalem: Jerusalem Center for Public Affairs, 2005), 95.

31. Gerstenfeld, *Israel and Europe*, 95.

32. The proportion was even higher elsewhere. Forty-eight percent of self-identified Jewish respondents from Hungary, forty-six percent from France, and forty percent from Belgium had considered emigrating. European Union Agency for Fundamental Rights, "Discrimination and Hate Crime against Jews in EU Member States: Experiences and Perceptions of Antisemitism" (FRA, 2013), 37–38.

33. Robert S. Wistrich, "Summer in Paris," *Mosaic Magazine*, October 5, 2014.

34. European Union Agency for Fundamental Rights, "Discrimination and Hate Crime against Jews in EU Member States," 11.

35. European Union Agency for Fundamental Rights, "Experiences and Perceptions of Antisemitism—Second Survey on Discrimination and Hate Crime against Jews in the EU" (FRA, 2018), 11.

36. European Union Agency for Fundamental Rights, "Experiences and Perceptions of Antisemitism," 12–13.

37. European Union Agency for Fundamental Rights, "Experiences and Perceptions of Antisemitism," 12; European Union Agency for Fundamental Rights, "Discrimination and Hate Crime against Jews in EU Member States," 46.

38. European Union Agency for Fundamental Rights, "Young Jewish Europeans: Perceptions and Experiences of Antisemitism" (FRA, 2019), 7, https://fra.europa.eu/sites/default/files/fra_uploads/fra-2019-young-jewish-europeans_en.pdf#page=42&zoom=auto,-317,628.

39. European Union Agency for Fundamental Rights, "Young Jewish Europeans," 34.

40. The Bataclan had been a Jewish-owned theater for four decades. After years of death threats from Islamists and pro-Palestinian activists who objected to the pro-Israel programming, the former owners sold the venue just two months before the November massacre. On the evening of the murders, the American rock band the Eagles of Death Metal was performing at the Bataclan. Months prior, the band played in Israel in defiance of a music industry boycott of the Jewish state.

41. AFP, "Brussels Suspect: Check-in Area for Tel Aviv Flight Was Targeted," *Times of Israel*, April 14, 2016, http://www.timesofisrael.com/brussels-suspect-check-in-area-for-tel-aviv-flight-was-targeted/.

42. European Union Agency for Fundamental Rights, "Discrimination and Hate Crime against Jews in EU Member States," 50; European Union Agency for Fundamental Rights, "Experiences and Perceptions of Antisemitism—Second Survey," 59.

43. European Union Agency for Fundamental Rights, "Discrimination and Hate Crime against Jews in EU Member States," 50; European Union Agency for Fundamental Rights, "Experiences and Perceptions of Antisemitism—Second Survey," 55.

44. European Union Agency for Fundamental Rights, "Young Jewish Europeans," 21.

45. Agencies, "Macron Attends Funeral for Slain Holocaust Survivor, Vows to Fight Anti-Semitism," *Times of Israel*, March 28, 2018, https://www.timesofisrael.com/macron-attends-funeral-for-slain-holocaust-survivor-vows-to-fight-anti-semitism/.

46. Agencies, "Macron Attends Funeral for Slain Holocaust Survivor."

47. European Union Agency for Fundamental Rights, "Experiences and Perceptions of Antisemitism—Second Survey," 15.

48. European Union Agency for Fundamental Rights, "Experiences and Perceptions of Antisemitism," 3.

49. European Union Agency for Fundamental Rights, "Experiences and Perceptions of Antisemitism," 12.

50. European Union Agency for Fundamental Rights, "Experiences and Perceptions of Antisemitism," 32.

51. European Union Agency for Fundamental Rights, "Experiences and Perceptions of Antisemitism," 11.

52. The seven countries were Austria, France, Germany, Great Britain, Hungary, Poland, and Sweden. Data from these countries were weighted to represent each country based on age, gender, and religion.

53. Richard Allen Greene, "A Shadow Over Europe," CNN, November 2018, https://edition.cnn.com/interactive/2018/11/europe/antisemitism-poll-2018-intl/.

54. Catherine Ashton, "Statement by EU High Representative Catherine Ashton on Holocaust Remembrance Day," EU Information Centre, January 27, 2014, https://europa.rs/to-continue-fighting-prejudice-and-racism-in-our-own-time/?lang=en.

55. European Union Agency for Fundamental Rights, "Human Rights Education at Holocaust Memorial Sites across the European Union: An Overview of Practices" (Luxembourg: Publications Office of the European Union, 2011), https://fra.europa.eu/en/publication/2011/human-rights-education-holocaust-memorial-sites-across-european-union-overview.

56. Holocaust education such as this, however ineffective, may be what many Europeans prefer. As noted in the 2018 CNN poll, although one-third of Europeans acknowledge they know little about the Holocaust, the same percentage also believe that Jews advance their own positions and goals through discussing this genocide.

57. Isabel Kershner, "Fury in Israel at Remark Linking Gaza to Toulouse," *New York Times*, March 21, 2012.

58. CEC, "Statement by President Juncker Following the Attacks on Charlie Hebdo Premises," January 7, 2015.

59. CEC, "Statement by the European Commission Following the Attacks in Copenhagen," February 15, 2015, http://europa.eu/rapid/press-release_statement -15–4431_en.htm, emphasis added.

60. European Parliament, "EP Pays Tribute to Victims of Paris Terrorist Attacks," December 1, 2015, http://www.europarl.europa.eu/news/en/press-room /20150109ipr06302/ep-pays-tribute-to-victims-of-paris-terrorist-attacks.

61. European Union Agency for Fundamental Rights, "EU Agencies Express Full Solidarity with Victims of Attacks in Paris," January 8, 2015, https://fra.europa.eu/en /news/2015/eu-agencies-express-full-solidarity-victims-attacks-paris, emphasis added.

62. Robert Zaretsky, "Why 'Jew' Is Rarely Spoken Word in France—Even After Kosher Grocery Terror," *The Forward*, January 13, 2015, https://forward.com/opinion /world/212611/why-jew-is-rarely-spoken-word-in-france-even-aft/#ixzz3poltk2sa.

63. CEC, "Statement by High Representative/Vice-President Federica Mogherini on the International Holocaust Remembrance Day," January 27, 2015.

64. European Union Agency for Fundamental Rights, "FRA Mourns Deaths in Copenhagen, an Attack on the Rights to Life, Dignity and Freedom of Expression," February 16, 2015, http://fra.europa.eu/en/news/2015/fra-mourns-deaths-copenhagen -attack-rights-life-dignity-and-freedom-expression.

65. Eve Garrard, "Anti-Judaism, Anti-Zionism, Antisemitism," *Fathom*, 2014, http://fathomjournal.org/anti-judaism-anti-zionism-antisemitism/.

66. Yair Rosenberg, "Swedish Public Radio Asks: Are Jews Responsible for Anti-Semitism?" *Tablet Magazine*, February 18, 2015, http://tabletmag.com/scroll/189064.

67. As Daniel Goldhagen explains, "looking to Israel and its conduct to explain antisemitism . . . is akin to looking to some of the horrors perpetrated by some African countries to explain racism against African Americans." Daniel Goldhagen, *The Devil That Never Dies: The Rise and Threat of Global Antisemitism* (New York: Little, Brown and Company, 2013), 177.

68. Elman, *The European Union, Antisemitism, and the Politics of Denial*, 92. In 2017 an administrative court ruled that the Young Muslims in Sweden (an alleged affiliate of the Muslim Brotherhood) can receive state support. SVT Nyheter, "Sveriges Unga Muslimer Får Rätt Om Statsstöd," November 15, 2017, https://www.svt.se/nyheter /inrikes/sveriges-unga-muslimer-far-ratt-om-statsstod.

69. Robert S. Wistrich, "From Blood Libel to Boycott: Changing Faces of British Antisemitism," Posen Papers in Contemporary Antisemitism (Jerusalem: The Vidal Sassoon International Center for the Study of Antisemitism, 2017), 3, https://sicsa .huji.ac.il/publications/blood-libel-boycott-changing-faces-british-antisemitism.

70. Erik Famler, "Friseur hetzte gegen Israel. Justiz stellt Verfahren ein," *Nachrichten.at*, February 10, 2015, http://www.nachrichten.at/oberoesterreich/wels/Friseur-hetzte-gegen-Israel-Justiz-stellt-Verfahren-ein;art67,1643504.

71. "The National Socialism Prohibition Law of 1945, Amended in 1992." (n.d.), http://www.genocidepreventionnow.org; Famler, "Friseur hetzte gegen Israel."

72. Jeffrey Goldberg, "Is It Time for the Jews to Leave Europe?" *The Atlantic*, April 2015, http://www.theatlantic.com/magazine/archive/2015/04/is-it-time-for-the-jews-to-leave-europe/386279/.

73. Famler, "Friseur hetzte gegen Israel."

74. Amtsgericht Essen, Urteil Vom 30. Januar 2015, Az. 57 Cs-29 Js 579/14–631/14, https://ra.de/urteil/ag-essen/57-cs-29-js-57914-63114-2015-01-30, p. 4., Az. 57 Cs-29 Js 579/14–631/14 § (n.d.), http://openjur.de/u/762150.html.

75. CEC, "Joint Statement by First Vice-President Timmermans and Commissioner Jourová Welcoming the Council Declaration on the Fight against Antisemitism," 2018, https://europa.eu/rapid/press-release_statement-18-6686_en.htm.

76. Garaudy v. France—65831/01, ECHR (July 7, 2003).

77. See E.S. v. AUSTRIA—38450/12 (Judgment: No Article 10—Freedom of Expression-{general}: Fifth Section) [2018] ECHR 891 (October 25, 2018).

78. Simon Cottee, "A Flawed European Ruling on Free Speech," *The Atlantic*, October 31, 2018, https://www.theatlantic.com/ideas/archive/2018/10/europe-rules-against-free-speech/574369/.

79. Hett, *The Death of Democracy*, 195.

80. Aluma Solnick, "Based on Qur'anic Verses, Interpretations, and Traditions, Muslim Clerics State: The Jews Are the Descendants of Apes, Pigs, and Other Animals," in *The Legacy of Islamic Antisemitism*, ed. Andrew Bostom (Amherst NY: Prometheus Books, 2008), 633–40.

8

BDS, Antisemitism, and Israeli Identity

SHLOMO ABRAMOVICH

Throughout history, antisemitism has had different faces and has appeared in various forms and shapes. There have been times when antisemitism has risen, while in other periods in history it has declined. It is widely accepted that we are currently experiencing a rise in antisemitism throughout the world. An important development of the last decade in dealing with antisemitism is the extensive work done by many scholars and organizations to redefine antisemitism.

One of the main reasons for redefining antisemitism is the rise of anti-Israel and anti-Zionist movements. The continuous Israeli-Palestinian conflict and the criticism of Israel's policies in the West Bank engendered organizations and movements that protest against Israel. The best known among them is the Boycott, Divestment, and Sanctions (BDS) movement, which is the focus of this chapter. These active movements raise concerns of the possible connection between anti-Zionism and antisemitism and have triggered the development of new definitions for the term *antisemitism*.

The discussion in this chapter will be partly theoretical, presenting developments in the definitions of antisemitism and the implications of these definitional changes in attitudes toward the BDS movement. The chapter's core question will be whether the BDS movement should be defined as antisemitic or not, and different approaches will be presented regarding this question. As will be seen, the theoretical discussion is not separate from the political debate, and shaping new definitions for antisemitism is part of the fight against the BDS by those who oppose its goals and tactics.

However, beyond the theoretical debate about the definition of antisemitism and its implications for attitudes toward the BDS movement, this chapter seeks to present the social and political results of this debate in Israel. In short, the chapter will present what Israel "gains" from defining the BDS movement as antisemitic and fighting against it. The discussion about the connection between the BDS movement and antisemitism has unique importance in the Israeli context, as it is part of a wide process of redefining Israeli identity.

This chapter will discuss the BDS movement and its criticism of Israel only briefly. The goal is not to determine whether the BDS should be defined as antisemitic or not, but to present the differing arguments on this question. The discussion about the BDS and antisemitism will serve as a basis for presenting some of the most important social and political processes that are happening in Israel.

What Is the BDS?

The BDS movement is a global campaign launched in 2005 by Palestinian civil organizations. It calls for nonviolent pressure on Israel until it complies with their three main demands, as presented on their official website: "Ending [Israel's] occupation and colonization of all Arab lands and dismantling the Wall; Recognizing the fundamental rights of the Arab-Palestinian citizens of Israel to full equality; Respecting, protecting and promoting the rights of Palestinian refugees to return to their homes and properties as stipulated in UN Resolution 194."[1] The BDS movement claims to be inspired by the South African anti-apartheid movement, and applies multiple types of pressure on Israel, as presented in its name. Among its activities are boycotts of Israeli products and companies, as well as international companies that are "involved in the violation of Palestinian human rights"; an academic boycott of Israeli universities and researchers; and campaigns to pressure governments to end trade agreements with Israel and international fora such as the UN and FIFA to expel Israel.

The actions of the BDS movement catalyzed two types of opponents. Some, such as the Israeli government and its supporters around the world, argue against its goals. There are also those who support the political goals of the BDS, but criticize its tactics. On the other hand, the BDS movement proudly presents several celebrities from different fields who offer their public support of the movement. Among these is Nobel Peace Prize recipient Desmond Tutu, who compared the actions of the BDS to those of his people in their fight against apartheid in South Africa, and also the musician Roger Waters, who is actively involved in pressuring other musicians and artists to boycott Israel and cancel their shows there.

Some of the people who oppose the BDS claim that it is an antisemitic movement. The BDS movement itself explicitly rejects any affinity with antisemitism, and even claims that antisemitism opposes the movement's core values, as presented in their official self-definition: "BDS is an inclusive, anti-racist human rights movement that is opposed on principle to all forms of discrimination, including antisemitism and Islamophobia."[2] In the FAQ area of their website, the BDS addresses this accusation and gives a detailed explanation as to why they should not be defined as antisemitic. First, they explain that they are fighting against the state of Israel and not against the Jewish people. To strengthen this argument, they present the support they have from several Jewish organizations who agree with their criticism of Israel. The BDS also argues that their campaigns target Israel because of its policies and actions, and do not target any individual or group just for being Israeli. They claim that "everyone has the right to criticize the unjust actions of a state."[3]

According to the traditional definition of antisemitism, the BDS's actions do not fall under that category. In the Merriam-Webster dictionary, for example, the definition of antisemitism is "hostility toward or discrimination against Jews as a religious, ethnic, or racial group"—a definition that does not seem to fit the BDS.[4]

And yet, the link between the BDS and antisemitism is heard from many different directions. Not only from the Israeli government, whose response will be discussed later, but also from various groups and organizations around the world who assert that the BDS is an antisemitic movement.

German chancellor Angela Merkel's party passed a resolution in December 2016 against the BDS, describing it as antisemitism dressed in new clothes of the twenty-first century.[5] More recently, in January 2019, Canadian prime minister Justin Trudeau, in a town hall meeting at a Canadian university, insisted on describing the BDS as an antisemitic movement, despite the criticism he had received for similar previous statements.[6] In addition to these political figures, some organizations whose expertise is dealing with antisemitism have made similar statements that the BDS should be defined and treated as an antisemitic movement. Among these are the Anti-Defamation League (ADL) and the Brandeis Center for Human Rights.[7]

The basis for linking the BDS with antisemitism is a process of redefining antisemitism. As noted above, the BDS might not be labeled as antisemitic according to the traditional definition of antisemitism, but new definitions of antisemitism that have expanded its scope to specifically include certain criticisms of Israel have changed attitudes toward the BDS.

Redefining Antisemitism

Over the past decade scholars have presented their views on this topic in articles and books and offered revised definitions of antisemitism, especially regarding the connection between anti-Zionism and antisemitism.[8] These new definitions have been adopted by governments and international organizations, which in turn has changed attitudes toward the BDS and similar movements, as expressed, for example, in new laws that have been passed in different countries against the BDS and its funding.[9]

In 2010, the U.S. Department of State updated its definition of antisemitism. Among other issues, the new definition discusses the question, "What is antisemitism relative to Israel?"[10] To answer this question the State Department adopted the "3D test of antisemitism" developed by Natan Sharansky in 2004.

Sharansky was a dissident in the former Soviet Union, a former Israeli minister, and, at the time of developing this test, the chairman of the Jewish Agency. Sharansky claims that it is harder to expose the new type of antisemitism, in comparison with traditional antisemitism (simple hatred of Jews), which is acknowledged as wrong in most of modern society. The new antisemitism, says Sharansky, is more advanced. It hides behind the veneer of legitimate criticism of Israel, and it acts in the name of unimpeachable values, such as human rights. This is the reason Sharansky developed his test: to distinguish legitimate criticism of Israel from antisemitism.

His test presents three parameters to define when criticism of Israel turns into antisemitism: demonization, double standards, and delegitimization:

> When the Jewish state is being demonized; when Israel's actions are blown out of all sensible proportion—this is antisemitism, not legitimate criticism of Israel.
>
> When criticism of Israel is applied selectively; when Israel is singled out by the United Nations for human rights abuses while the behavior of known and major abusers is ignored . . . this is antisemitism.
>
> When Israel's fundamental right to exist is denied—alone among all peoples in the world—this too is antisemitism.[11]

The general principle behind this test is to reveal the real reasons underlying the criticism of Israel. It is not a matter of the scope of the criticism, as legitimate criticism has no limitations, but the real motives behind it.

Another important attempt to redefine antisemitism came in 2016, when the U.S. State Department adopted a new working definition of antisemitism developed by the International Holocaust Remembrance Alliance (IHRA).[12] This international organization was formed in 1998 "to strengthen, advance and promote Holocaust education, research and remembrance."[13] Thirty-one countries are members of the IHRA, whose founding document is the Stockholm Declaration. This important text was the outcome of an international forum about the Holocaust attended by the representatives of forty-six governments that presented their commitments to the memory and education of the Holocaust.[14]

In addition to promoting Holocaust education and combating Holocaust denial, the IHRA also claims to fight antisemitism. The 2016 working definition of antisemitism was the result of in-depth discussions amomg IHRA members. Their definition discusses the limitations of legitimate criticism of Israel, and presents varied examples of when criticism turns into antisemitism. This definition is a similar and more detailed version of the 2010 definition adopted by the U.S. State Department, and claims that "denying the Jewish people their right to self-determination . . . [and] holding Jews collectively responsible for actions of the state of Israel" are examples of antisemitism. Based on these new definitions, the next section will explain the link between the BDS movement and antisemitism.

BDS and Antisemitism

The reasons for defining the BDS movement as antisemitic can be divided into three main categories: its ideology may be antisemitic, its tactics may be antisemitic, or the people behind the movement may be antisemitic. Most of the arguments focus on its ideology.

One D in the 3D test is *delegitimization*, which was explained by the U.S. State Department in its 2010 definition of antisemitism as "denying the Jewish people their right to self-determination, and denying Israel the right to exist." A common argument against the BDS is that even though their demands officially focus on the West Bank and the end to its occupation, in truth its campaigns target Israel as a whole, and the criticism of Israeli policy in the West Bank is a cover for the denial of Israel's right to exist.[15] For example, the BDS does not call for a boycott only of Israeli companies and institutions in the West Bank but of Israel as whole, and this proves the real goal is the fight against Israel's existence—not only its policies.

The BDS response is that they call for a boycott of "Israel's entire regime of oppression" and that the many companies and organizations outside of the West Bank that are involved in human rights violations against the Palestinians should also be boycotted.[16] As a counterexample they explain that they call for a boycott of all Israeli-produced fruits and vegetables, because "all Israeli agricultural businesses are involved in human rights violations." The call to boycott all Israeli universities is, similarly, because "they are implicated, to various degrees, in the design, implementation, justification, or whitewash of Israel's crimes against Palestinians."

The BDS's demands for the right of return for Palestinian refugees is another example that is often used to accuse the BDS of delegitimizing Israel. First, the fulfilment of this demand, with the return of millions of Palestinian refugees to the state of Israel, would essentially mean the end of Israel in its current form. Israel would not be a Jewish state anymore, due to the dramatic change in demographics. In addition, the demand itself denies the Jewish people's right to self-determination in Israel. Defining all Palestinians as refugees, including those who left of their own volition in 1948, means that the entire country—not only what was taken in the 1967 war—is considered occupied territory. Though the BDS calls for the end of the occupation, the actual meaning of their demands is a denial of Israel's right to exist.

Another common argument regarding the BDS's ideology falls under the category of double standards, described in the 2010 and 2016 definitions of antisemitism as "applying double standards by requiring of it [Israel] a behavior not expected or demanded of any other democratic nation." The BDS is accused of criticizing Israel's actions while ignoring more serious damage to human rights in other countries. This shows that the real motive for the criticism is not a general concern about human rights, but hatred of Israel. The BDS's response to this argument is that they are a Palestinian-led movement and therefore their focus is on the Palestinian-Israeli conflict.

The second type of argument for labeling the BDS as antisemitic addresses their tactics. The last D of the 3D test is demonization, and the BDS is often accused of demonizing Israel in its campaigns. Blaming Israel for genocide and massacres of Palestinians, in a way that is close to the traditional blood libel, and the use of antisemitic cartoons in the BDS campaigns, are among the main reasons for labeling BDS tactics antisemitic.[17]

The main tool used by the BDS, the boycott of Israel, reminds people of the first actions against Jews in Nazi Germany. Angela Merkel's 2016 party statement labeled the BDS as a modern version of the old antisemitism and linked the BDS to the boycott of Jews in 1930s Germany.

The BDS is also charged with creating an atmosphere of fear and terror among Jewish students, as happens on some college campuses in the United States.[18] The ADL reported an increase of 59 percent in the number of antisemitic events on campuses during the first nine months of 2017 in comparison to 2016.[19] Students in Florida received fake eviction notices in their dorm rooms from a pro-Palestinian organization that wanted them to have the feeling of life under occupation.[20] Jewish students and faculty in various universities have described how the Israel Apartheid Week (IAW), an annual event of protest against Israel, has turned into a time of harassment, intimidation, and fear for Jews on campus. A faculty member at Columbia said that, "even as a 35-year-old professional, my heart beats fast and I'm scared to see the shouting and anger that comes with IAW.... I am scared as a Jew—not as a Zionist."[21]

This reality fits the U.S. State Department's 2016 definition of antisemitism, which says that "holding Jews collectively responsible for actions of the state of Israel" is a type of antisemitism. Despite the BDS's claim about not campaigning against Jews but against Israel, Jewish students are being targeted by BDS campaigns in colleges, especially in the United States. If a Jewish student, regardless of his or her opinions about Israel, is targeted by the BDS's aggressive actions on campus, it is a form of antisemitism.

Finally, in addition to labeling the ideology and tactics of the BDS as antisemitic, some claim that the people behind the movement— its founders and supporters—are antisemitic. Among these figures are Omar Barghouti, the cofounder of the BDS movement, and Alison Weir, an American activist, whose criticism of Israel has "crossed the line into distortions customarily found in the literature of anti-Semites," as claims a report about her by the Anti-Defamation League.[22] This argument suggests that even if the actions of the BDS cannot be labeled as antisemitic, the fact that some of the movement's leaders are antisemitic shows that the BDS is just a smart cover for the same old hatred.[23] The BDS rejects the accusation that its founders and supporters are antisemitic.

It seems that the argument about whether the BDS movement is antisemitic cannot be solved, because in the end it is a matter of definition, and each side defines antisemitism differently. In the introduction for his book *The Definition of Antisemitism*, Kenneth

Marcus writes, "Since the term has been deployed for political and other purposes over the generations, its definitions have tended to reflect the political circumstances in which the definitions have been produced."[24] The next section will present the responses to the BDS in Israel. My main argument is that the way Israel chooses to treat the BDS, and Israel's definition of antisemitism, is part of a larger process of change in Israeli policies.

Israel and the BDS

As expected, Israel officially adopted the IHRA's 2016 definition of antisemitism, and many Israeli politicians and leaders labeled the BDS as antisemitic.[25] In some cases, the Israelis convinced other countries to adopt this position, and a close connection to Israel was one of the factors in shaping a country's attitude toward the BDS. In Germany, Angela Merkel's party mentioned Germany's deep friendship with Israel as a consideration in their decision to define BDS as antisemitic.

Israel took the BDS and its campaigns very seriously, and in 2015 the government appointed the Ministry of Strategic Affairs and Public Diplomacy to fight the BDS.[26] One of their main efforts was to create counter-campaigns against the BDS to convince governments and other international organizations to stop cooperating with the BDS and join Israel to fight against it. In February 2019 the ministry published a detailed report under the title "Terrorists in Suits," which claims to present ties between NGOs promoting BDS and terror organizations.[27]

At the 2016 Herzliya conference, two Israeli researchers, Shaul Shai and Alex Minzt, presented a paper titled "The BDS Movement as a Strategic Threat to Israel."[28] In their paper, they presented the damage that the BDS campaigns have caused to Israel, including the cancellations of several international investments, the cancellations of various celebrities' shows in Israel, and the boycotts by a few academic organizations of Israel and Israeli researchers. However, their main argument, as presented in the title of their paper, is that the BDS is a strategic threat to Israel even beyond these specific damages. Shai and Mintz claim that even though the success of BDS campaigns is limited and the direct damage of the BDS is not so severe, the threat it presents to Israel is in the change it causes to the broader attitude toward Israel. As a result of BDS campaigns, some friendly countries have started to adopt the terminology and attitude of the BDS, and in the long term that is a serious threat to Israel. As a small country with hostile neighbors, Israel depends on international support and legitimacy that might be damaged by the BDS. Therefore, claim Shai and Mintz, Israel should take the BDS very seriously and join forces with other countries and Jewish communities around the world to combat this threat.

However, beyond the threat to Israel's image and status in the world, the fight against the BDS has another meaning to Israel. The battle with the BDS, and defining the BDS as antisemitic, are parts of a wider process of shaping Israeli identity and strengthening its Jewish elements. Labeling the BDS as antisemitic creates links between anti-Zionism and antisemitism, and between Israel and Jews. Doing so strengthens Israel's image and self-identification as the representative of the interests of the Jewish people and even of Judaism.

Surprising support for this argument can be found on the official BDS website. In the explanation of why the movement should not be defined as antisemitic, they say, "The world is growing increasingly weary of Israel's attempts to conflate criticism of its violations of international law with antisemitism and to conflate Zionism with Judaism. . . . Israel claims to be acting in the name of all Jewish people but a rapidly increasing number of Jewish people . . . feel compelled to make sure the world knows that many Jews are opposed to Israel's actions."[29] Obviously, this text attacks and criticizes Israel, but it also presents Israel's official policy. Israel is claiming to act on behalf of the Jewish people as a whole and tends to conflate Zionism with Judaism as a strategic and ideological standpoint. Many of Israel's acts and decisions over the past decade have reinforced this approach.

The Jewishness of Israel

David Ben Gurion, Israel's first prime minister, as well as many other founders of Israel, shared the same perspective about the new country: that Israel was established to be the state of all Jewish people. Many of Israel's actions during its first years were based on this belief. For example, the Law of Return, which was passed in 1950, gives citizenship and benefits to every Jew who moves to Israel. In practice, this bill turns all Jews in the world into potential citizens of Israel, whether they like it or not.

The Law of Return created an unusual situation with Israel's national baseball team. Baseball is not a popular sport in Israel, and yet the Israeli team succeeded more than expected in the 2017 World Baseball Classic. The secret behind the success of Team Israel is that the players were professional American baseball players with Jewish ancestry who were therefore eligible for Israeli citizenship. According to the rules of this international competition, the potential citizenship of these players was enough to allow them to represent Israel, a country that some had never even visited.[30]

Over the years this approach became less accepted in Israel. The Law of Return still exists, but the idea of Israel as the country of all Jews has declined in prevalence. The reason for this change might be the spread of universalistic ideals and the decline of nationalism, which weakened the general identification with the country and the perception of it as the only place for Jews. The existence of strong Jewish communities outside of Israel also challenged this perception. The idea of the centrality of Israel as the state of all Jews questions the legitimacy of Jews living outside of Israel. In Israel's early years, similar ideas were common, including *shlilat h'galut*—the negation of the diaspora—and the harsh criticism of Israelis who left the country and chose to live elsewhere. Over the years these approaches became unacceptable, especially as a result of the relationships between Israel and Jewish communities abroad.[31] The reality of strong Jewish communities, especially in the United States, brought a sense of modesty to the perception of Israel as the state of all Jews.

However, during the past decade it seems that this perception came back to life in Israel, as expressed in various fields. It is a result of a wave of Jewishness that spread over Israel, with Jewish elements of Israeli identity being strengthened.[32] This process has implications in internal Israeli issues, as well as in Israel's foreign affairs, and it also affects Israel's attitude toward the BDS movement. A clear example of this process is the controversial Nation-State Bill, which passed in 2018 and edited the Basic Laws (the Israeli equivalent of a constitution) to define Israel officially as the national home of the Jewish people.[33] This bill was harshly criticized mostly because it seemingly limited the rights of non-Jewish minorities in Israel. However, the main reason for its adoption, as explained by Minister of Justice Ayelet Shaked, was not the attitude toward non-Jewish citizens, but the balance between the democratic nature of Israel and the strengthening of Israel's Jewishness.[34] One of the most important Basic Laws in Israel is "Basic Law: Human Dignity and Liberty," which has been the basis for many decisions by the Supreme Court. Shaked and the other supporters of the Nation-State Bill claimed that some Supreme Court decisions ignored the uniqueness of Israel as a Jewish state, and therefore the new bill was needed.

The criticism of this bill focused on the rights of the non-Jewish citizens of Israel, even though the makers of the bill claimed that their rights would not be changed. However, the bill also raised the question of relations between Israel and Jews abroad. If Israel is officially the state of the Jewish nation, as this bill declares, what is the status of Jews in other countries? As is seen from a few recent cases, this bill is an expression of the official policy of Israel and its attitude toward Jews who live abroad.

In 2015, after several terror attacks in Denmark and France, Binyamin Netanyahu, Israel's prime minister, called on the Jews of Europe to immigrate to Israel, saying "Israel is your home."[35] Even though this statement did not sound unusual to most Israelis and is enshrined in the Law of Return, it was considered unacceptable in contemporary international politics. Netanyahu's comment was criticized by European leaders, including French president François Hollande, who rejected Netanyahu's appeal to France's Jewish citizens.[36]

Another example of this policy is Netanyahu's demand for recognition by the Palestinian Authority of Israel as a Jewish state as a condition of renewing negotiations between the nations. This demand is consistently rejected by Palestinians.[37] The first step of the Oslo Accords was the mutual recognition of both sides: Israel recognized the PLO as the representative of the Palestinians and the Palestinians recognized Israel's right to exist.[38] However, in the new phase of the developed Israeli identity, this is not enough, as the Israeli prime minister now also demands a recognition of the Jewish character of Israel.

It should be noted that the change in Israel's Jewish identity does not refer only to the definition of Israel as the state of all Jews, but also is expressed in the strengthening of the role of Judaism in Israel. Many laws in Israel regulate religious issues, which causes frequent tension and conflicts in Israeli society, as some reject the state's intervention in what seems to be a private sphere. These conflicts are often portrayed as a struggle between secular and religious citizens, with the latter accused of forcing their way of life on the rest of society. However, this is not an accurate description of the situation, since religious and secular people can be found on both sides of these conflicts.[39] The heart of these discussions is about the Jewish nature of the country, and the meaning of Israel being a Jewish state.[40] As mentioned, over the past decade there has been a clear tendency to bolster Jewish elements in Israel, as expressed in extensive religious legislation in different fields.[41] These changes, however, are beyond the scope of this chapter, which focuses on the strengthening of the notion of Israel as the state of all Jews and its effect on attitudes toward the BDS.

Several reasons can be offered for these changes in Israeli policies. Some of the internal issues might be caused by the growing power of the country's religious political parties. Their influence is a result of the Israeli political system, which is based on a coalition government that gives disproportionate power to small parties. The demographics of Israel might be another reason, as the population is becoming more traditional and religious.[42]

This process might be also related to political changes in Israel. In the past decade the left has been in severe decline for various reasons.[43] Since the Israeli right represents national and traditional values, its growing power empowers Jewish elements of the Israeli national identity. The strengthening of Jewish elements in Israel's identity might also be part of the wave of nationalism appearing recently in many countries, especially in Europe, as can be seen in the success of several right-wing nationalist parties around the world. In Israel, because its nationality is defined as Jewish, the strengthening of the Israeli national identity might also cause the strengthening of the Jewish identity of Israel.

Conclusion: BDS, Antisemitism, and Israeli Identity

The current battle against the BDS and the fight to label it as antisemitic is part of a wave of increasing Israel's Jewishness. As the BDS itself recognizes, Israel tends to identify itself with Judaism and Jews. Therefore fighting with Israel is presented as attacking all Jews, and anti-Israel campaigns are defined as antisemitism. The BDS is accused of demonizing Israel and using double standards when criticizing Israel, and the identification of Israel with the Jewish people turns unjustified criticism into antisemitism.

For Israel, the contemporary fight against the BDS is more than just a struggle with a hostile NGO. It is an expression of the development of an Israeli identity that has become more Jewish and more aware of its Jewishness. I do not suggest that the fight against the BDS is a manipulation by Israel to strengthen its status because, as mentioned above, the BDS is considered by some to be a strategic threat to Israel. However, underlying Israel's actions is the assumption that Israel is representing the Jewish people, and therefore attacking Israel is an attack against the Jews.

It seems that the battle between Israel and the BDS is revealing the hidden identities of both sides. Israel, which was established on the basis of being the state of all Jews, is returning to its original narrative, correlating Jews and Israel, which the definition of the BDS as an antisemitic movement is creating. On the other hand, new definitions of antisemitism and criticism of the BDS campaigns claim to reveal the antisemitic motivations behind its actions. It is hard to tell how active the BDS will remain in the future, and whether the movement will still be considered by some a strategic threat to Israel.[44] What is clear is that, through its struggle with the BDS, Israel shapes its image and status as a Jewish state and the representative of all Jews.

Questions for Further Discussion

1. The elements of the 3D test of antisemitism are defined in this chapter as demonization, double standards, and delegitimization. Can you extrapolate from the 3D test to explain the persecution of other racial, ethnic, or religious minorities around the world? Why or why not?

2. Can an organization be neutral if those inside the organization are antisemitic? What if only a few are? At what point do the "bad apples" make an organization rotten?

3. Have you ever encountered any aggressive tactics by the BDS while on a college campus or at a Jewish event? What was your reaction?

4. Do you feel that the BDS is a specific threat to Jews? To Israel as a nation? Why or why not? If so, has this threat increased or decreased in the past few years?

5. Has the BDS movement had a bigger impact on Israeli thinking, on the thinking of Jews in the diaspora, or on the thinking of non-Jews? What makes you think so?

6. Has the attention paid to the BDS by the Israeli government done more to hinder or to help the BDS movement?

7. What role has the changing demographics in Israel played in the redefining of antisemitism?

8. Does the IHRA definition of antisemitism make the most sense? Does it include everything that needs to be included in such a definition? Is it missing anything? Does it include too much? Are further redefinitions of antisemitism necessary?

Notes

1. "What is BDS?," BDS Movement, accessed January 6, 2021, https://bdsmovement.net/what-is-bds.

2. BDS Movement, "What is BDS?"

3. "FAQ," BDS Movement, accessed January 6, 2021, https://bdsmovement.net/faqs#collapse16241.

4. *Merriam-Webster*, s.v. "anti-Semitism," accessed January 6, 2021, https://www.merriam-webster.com/dictionary/antisemitism.

5. Benjamin Weinthal, "German Chancellor Merkel's Party Labels the BDS Antisemitic," *Jerusalem Post*, December 7, 2016, https://www.jpost.com/Diaspora/German-Chancellor-Merkels-party-labels-bds-antisemitic-474715.

6. Toi Staff, "Trudeau Blasts BDS Movement as Anti-Semitic," *Times of Israel*, January 17, 2019, https://www.timesofisrael.com/trudeau-blasts-bds-movement-as-antisemitic/.

7. ADL, "What Is . . . Anti-Israel, Anti-Semitic, Anti-Zionist?," accessed January 6, 2021, adl.org/resources/tools-and-strategies/what-is-anti-israel-anti-semitic-anti-zionist; Alyza Lewin, "Why Prohibiting Boycotts of Israel does not violate Freedom of Speech," January 21, 2019, The Louis D. Brandeis Center, https://brandeiscenter.com/why-prohibiting-boycotts-of-israel-does-not-violate-freedom-of-speech/.

8. For example: Kenneth L. Marcus, *The Definition of Antisemitism* (Oxford: Oxford University Press, 2015); Robert Wistrich, "Anti-Zionism and Antisemitism," *Jewish Political Studies Review* 16, no. 3/4 (Fall 2004): 27–31. Naturally, the connection made by many between anti-Zionism and antisemitism was opposed by others, such as Peter Beinart, who argued in an op-ed in *Haaretz* that anti-Zionism should not automatically be equated with antisemitism. Peter Beinart, "No, Anti-Zionism Isn't Anti-Semitism," *Haaretz*, March 30, 2016, https://www.haaretz.com/opinion/.premium-no-anti-zionism-isnt-anti-semitism-1.5424570.

9. For instance, the U.S. House of Representatives overwhelmingly passed a resolution against BDS on July 2019. Cristina Marcos, "House Passes Bill Opposing BDS, Exposing Divide among Democrats," *The Hill*, July 23, 2019, https://thehill.com/homenews/house/454399-house-passes-bill-opposing-bds-exposing-democratic-divides.

10. U.S. Department of State, Office of the Special Envoy to Monitor and Combat Anti-Semitism, "Defining Anti-Semitism," June 8, 2010, https://2009-2017.state.gov/j/drl/rls/fs/2010/122352.htm.

11. Natan Sharansky, "3D Test of Antisemitism: Demonization, Double Standards, Delegitimization," *Jewish Political Studies Review* 16, no. 3–4 (Fall 2004), https://www.jcpa.org/phas/phas-sharansky-f04.htm.

12. U.S. Department of State, Office of the Special Envoy to Monitor and Combat Anti-Semitism, "Defining Anti-Semitism," accessed January 6, 2021, https://www.state.gov/defining-anti-semitism.

13. "About Us," International Holocaust Remembrance Alliance, accessed January 6, 2021, https://holocaustremembrance.com/about-us.

14. "Stockholm Declaration," International Holocaust Remembrance Alliance, accessed January 6, 2021, https://holocaustremembrance.com/stockholm-declaration.

15. ADL, "What Is . . . Anti-Israel, Anti-Semitic, Anti-Zionist?"

16. BDS Movement, "FAQ."

17. "BDS and Antisemitism," NGO Monitor, accessed January 6, 2021, https://www.ngo-monitor.org/key-issues/bds/bds-and-antisemitism.

18. Some members of my own Jewish community shared with me that the power and influence of BDS on campus is a criterion in their decision of which college to attend.

19. Caroline Glick, "The Bill that Protects Jews on Campuses in the US was Rejected by Their Own People." *Maariv*, October 11, 2017, https://www.maariv.co.il/journalists/Article-608168 [Hebrew]. Similar activity also happens in European colleges, especially in the UK. Eldad Beck, "As BDS Runs Rampant on UK Campuses, Jewish Students Are Fighting Back," *Israel Hayom*, February 11, 2020, www.israelhayom.com/2020/02/11/as-bds-runs-rampant-on-uk-campuses-jewish-students-are-fighting-back/.

20. "Florida: Pro-Palestinian Group 'Evicts' Jewish Students," *Ynet News*, September 4, 2012, https://www.ynetnews.com/articles/0,7340,l-4214289,00.html.

21. Carly Pildis, "Enough Is Enough," *Tablet*, April 8, 2019, https://www.tabletmag.com/jewish-news-and-politics/283535/enough-is-enough-2.

22. "Alison Weir," ADL, accessed January 6, 2021, https://www.adl.org/sites/default/files/documents/assets/pdf/israel-international/Alison_Weir_Backgrounder-NW.pdf.

23. Another argument against BDS is that its actions and the atmosphere it creates encourage other declared antisemites to act publicly. Yishai Friedman, "Behind the Masks: The Antisemitism that Hides behind the Boycott Movements," *Makor Rishon*, April 11, 2017, https://www.makorrishon.co.il/nrg/online/1/art2/900/920.html [Hebrew].

24. Marcus, *The Definition of Antisemitism*, 10.

25. Israel's Prime Minister's Office, "Adopting a Working Definition for Anti-Semitism," January 22, 2017, https://www.gov.il/he/departments/policies/2017_des2315 [Hebrew]; Moran Azulay, "Heated Discussion Regarding the BDS' Boycott," *Ynet News*, March 6, 2015, https://www.ynet.co.il/articles/0,7340,L-4664511,00.html [Hebrew].

26. Israel's Prime Minister's Office, "Ministry of Strategic Affairs and Public Diplomacy," accessed January 6, 2021, https://www.gov.il/he/Departments/Units/ministry_of_strategic_affairs_and_public_diplomacy [Hebrew].

27. Israel's Prime Minister's Office, "Special Report," https://www.gov.il/he/Departments/General/terrorists_in_suits [Hebrew].

28. Shaul Shai and Alex Minzt, "The BDS Movement as a Strategic Threat to Israel," 16th Herzliya Conference, June 2016, https://www.idc.ac.il/he/research/ips/Documents/publication/1/bds-ShaulShay2016.pdf [Hebrew].

29. BDS Movement, "FAQ."

30. In 2018 a documentary titled *Heading Home: The Tale of Team Israel* was released. A review of this film in the *New York Times* questioned the ethicality of American Jews representing Israel. Ben Kenigsberg, "'Heading Home: The Tale of Team Israel' Review: When Baseball Is a Religion," *New York Times*, September 5, 2019, https://nyti.ms/2ZvLLdY.

31. An interesting debate between contemporary scholars, an Israeli and an American Jew, about the relevancy of the idea of negating the diaspora and its implications on the relations between Israel and American Jews can be found in Yosef Gorny, "Shlilat Ha-Galut: Past and Present," in *Beyond Survival and Philanthropy: American Jewry and Israel*, ed. Allon Gal and Alfred Gottschalk (Cincinnati: Hebrew Union College Press, 2000), 41–58; Jonathan D. Sarna, "Response: The Question of Shlilat Ha-Galut in Ameri-

can Zionism," in *Beyond Survival and Philanthropy: American Jewry and Israel*, ed. Allon Gal and Alfred Gottschalk (Cincinnati: Hebrew Union College Press, 2000), 59–60.

32. It is a social and a cultural process that has been presented in varied studies. For example, a study of Israeli high school students during the past forty years showed that, over the years, students tend to identify themselves more with Jewish elements rather than Israeli elements. Uri Fargo, "More Jewish, Less Israelis," *Panim* 40 (2007), https://www.itu.org.il/?CategoryID=1215&ArticleID=9639 [Hebrew].

33. Andrew Carey and Oren Liebermann, "Israel Passes Controversial 'Nation-State' Bill With No Mention of Equality or Minority Rights," CNN, July 19, 2018, https://www.cnn.com/2018/07/19/middleeast/israel-nation-state-legislation-intl/index.html.

34. Gilad Morag and Tova Tzimuki, "Shaked Denounces HCJ Illegal Aliens Ruling, Calls for New Constitutional Revolution," *Ynet News*, August 29, 2017, https://www.ynetnews.com/articles/0,7340,L-5009369,00.html.

35. Justin Jalil and Raphael Ahren, "Netanyahu to French Jews: 'Israel Is Your Home,'" *The Times of Israel*, January 10, 2015, https://www.timesofisrael.com/netanyahu-to-french-jews-israel-is-your-home.

36. Peter Beaumont, "Leaders Reject Netanyahu Calls for Jewish Mass Migration to Israel," *The Guardian*, February 16, 2015, https://www.theguardian.com/world/2015/feb/16/leaders-criticise-netanyahu-calls-jewish-mass-migration-israel.

37. Amos Harel et al., "Netanyahu Demands Palestinians Recognize 'Jewish State,'" *Haaretz*, April 16, 2009, https://www.haaretz.com/1.5037954; Jack Khoury and Reuters, "Arab League Backs Abbas' Refusal to Recognize Israel as Jewish State," *Haaretz*, March 3, 2014, https://www.haaretz.com/arab-league-no-jewish-state-1.5331136.

38. Ian J. Bickerton and Carla L. Klausner, *A History of the Arab-Israeli Conflict* (New York: Routledge, 2018), 321–22.

39. For instance, the bill to shutter all shops on Shabbat (Saturday) was spearheaded by a secular MK from the Likud, Miki Zohar. Gad Lior, "Ministers Approve Bill to Shutter All Shops on Saturday," *Ynet News*, December 21, 2015, https://www.ynetnews.com/articles/0,7340,L-4742407,00.html. On the other hand, Moshe Feiglin, a religious former MK who recently tried to be elected again to the Knesset, called to nullify the law that forbids the selling of Chametz (leavened bread) on Passover, as presented in his new party's website: https://www.zehutinternational.com/single-post/2018/03/27/Moshe-Feiglin-on-Israel-Army-Radio-Nullify-Chametz-Law.

40. One example is the continuing argument about religion in the army. A common complaint is that in the past decade the army has become more subordinated to religious laws, for instance regarding the enforcement of *kashrut*, the Jewish dietary laws. In one case a soldier was sent to jail in 2015 because he brought a non-kosher sandwich to his military training. He was immediately released and the army apologized for his imprisonment; however, this case led to heated discussions, and the deputy minister of defense, Eli Ben Dahan, said, "It is a matter of identity: the IDF is the army of the State of Israel, the only Jewish country in the world." Yaki Adamaker, "Minister Regev Opposes Canceling the Soldier's Punishment," *Walla News*, June 5, 2015, https://news.walla.co.il/item/2860689 [Hebrew]; Yagil Levy, *The Divine*

Commander: The Theocratization of the Israeli Military (Tel Aviv: Am Oved, 2015), 12 [Hebrew].

41. For instance, the "Minimarket Law" was passed in January 2018 and bars more stores from opening on Shabbat. Lahav Harkov, "Knesset Passes Contentious Shabbat Law by One Vote After All-Nighter," *The Jerusalem Post*, January 9, 2018, https://www.jpost.com/Israel-News/Knesset-passes-contentious-Shabbat-law-by-one-vote-after-all-nighter-533209.

42. An interesting study about this topic can be found in the Taub Center's study "Is Jewish Society in Israel Becoming more Secular?," http://taubcenter.org.il/he/secular [Hebrew]. The main argument of this study is that the demographic growth of the religious sectors in Israel is not as high as presented in many other studies.

43. In practice, since the 1992 elections, the Israeli left has won election only once. The current situation of the left and its future is discussed in many studies. See, for instance, Uri Izhar, *The Future of the Israeli Left: Decline or Revival?* (Haifa: Pardes, 2014) [Hebrew].

44. There are those who claim that BDS is already in decline and has failed to succeed in their goals, mainly as a result of pro-Israeli organizations fighting back. Eldad Beck, "As BDS Runs Rampant on UK campuses, Jewish Students Are Fighting Back," *Israel Hayom*, February 11, 2020, www.israelhayom.com/2020/02/11/as-bds-runs-rampant-on-uk-campuses-jewish-students-are-fighting-back/.

9

The Role of Antisemitism in Holocaust Education in the Jewish and Secular School Classroom

SCOTT B. LITTKY

"Thou shalt not be a victim, thou shalt not be a perpetrator, but, above all, thou shalt not be a bystander."

—Yehuda Bauer

"God saved me from the Holocaust so I could tell my story. I was cursed with terrible memories . . . so I remember everything in the camps. He saved me again last Shabbos, so I could tell my story."

—Judah Samet, Holocaust Survivor

"Six weeks after Pittsburgh, and almost two years into a presidency that pushed discussion of resurgent bigotry to the front of the political debate, the American Jewish community is grappling with its consequences. The effort suggests that antisemitism in its classic form—a product of white supremacism and conspiracy-mongering—took by surprise a community focused on the threat of radical Islam."[1] This quote, written by Ron Kampeas in a December 2018 article for the *Jewish Telegraphic Agency*, in many ways hit me right in the face. As a Holocaust educator and as a Jew, I found myself again wondering how we as Jews define ourselves as Jews in terms of antisemitism and in terms of the Holocaust.

Do you remember your first reaction to learning of the Holocaust? I am not sure I remember the first time I learned about the experience of the Jews of eastern Europe from 1933 to 1945, but I do remember a number of defining points that began my search for knowledge on the subject. The first was when I was ten or eleven; I was at the Jewish Community Center in Detroit, Michigan, and saw a series of numbers tattooed on the arm of an older man. I am not sure what my reaction was, but I do know that I still often think of seeing the man's arm and somehow knowing what it represented. The second was when the movie *The Man in the Glass Booth* came out. The movie is a fictitious story of an Adolf Eichmann character. I had a conversation with my father and learned then who Eichmann was. The third, and most impactful, time was again when I was young. A survivor was invited to my synagogue around Yom HaShoah to speak to us. We did not receive any notice that this was going to happen or any background information about the visit. It was a very emotional presentation. After it was over, we did not debrief the experience; we just returned to class as though the last hour had not happened. By the time I was about to enter college, I had so many questions about the Holocaust, especially the question of *why the Jews?* As a result, from my first year at Michigan State University through today in my role as the executive director of the Institute of Holocaust Education in Omaha, Nebraska, I have been in search of answers. In this piece I want to share some thoughts on this topic.

Challenges in the Classroom

I believe that, since the early 1980s, much of the approach to teaching the Holocaust and antisemitism has been what I would call "old school." By this I mean that the emphasis was on throwing facts, figures, and outdated materials at students—mostly to shock them, not really to educate them in an organized manner. With no disrespect intended to the textbooks used in supplementary Jewish religious schools, for the most part they were fact-based and provided too many details. As an example, *The Holocaust: The World and the Jews, 1933–1945*, by Seymour Rossel, was first published in 1992 and is still used today in many schools. The text never offers analysis or delves into reasons; instead, Jews are seen as an ethnic group but never as individuals. One need only look to the table of contents to see a deep emphasis on the facts of the Holocaust and not on the personal narratives. There is no coverage of the lessons learned from the Holocaust: the understanding of why antisemitism is wrong and why hatred does not have any place in today's world. With just facts being presented there is no opportunity to learn how one can take the events of the Holocaust and teach empathy, understanding, and skills of intervention. These could have been better taught through the use of personal narrative, which allows students to see the victims of the Holocaust as individual people and not just as an ethnic group. Other textbooks, such as Bea Stadtler's *The Holocaust: A History of Courage and Resistance* and Clara Isaacman's *Pathways through the Holocaust: An Oral History by Eye-Witnesses*, do a much better job of telling the story of the Jewish experience during the Holocaust using firsthand experiences, but still lack an understanding that the study of antisemitism and the Holocaust is more than just the study of the historical facts of the events.

One way to address this issue could be the use of examples of antisemitism happening locally, nationally, and internationally today, and drawing on those examples to help students understand issues of antisemitism as they relate to the Nazi era. Further, these contemporary examples can assist the student in better understanding the complex nature of antisemitism. For example, in Omaha, Nebraska, on or about Halloween 2019, several tombstones were overturned at a local Jewish cemetery. This was a perfect opportunity for classroom teachers to compare and contrast this local example of antisemitism with examples of desecrations of Jewish cemeteries that occurred during the Holocaust. Through this example, teachers could discuss how local communities chose to address instances of antisemitism. Do they ignore the event or do they address the event, and what is the outcome of the event?

In Israel, Yad Vashem has recognized these challenges and their education department has developed a unique approach to the teaching of the Holocaust and antisemitism. Their approach is an attempt to personalize the events of the Holocaust, and their focus is threefold: life before 1933, life during World War II, and life after World War II. As a result, students are much more able to identify with the single-family narrative as opposed to trying to wrap their heads around the number six million. Further, in terms of antisemitism, hearing the individual stories of how people experienced this form of bigotry and hatred allows students to compare and contrast it to their own experiences of prejudice, conspiracy theories, or other events they have seen in the current climate of the United States and in particular here in the Midwest.

In terms of public schools and society at large, antisemitism is a complex issue. In a recent Lunch & Learn event with our local member of Congress, a panelist used the term *Holocaust* when he should have been using the term *antisemitism*. He referred to events such as pogroms against Jews in the Middle Ages as part of a Holocaust and not as antisemitic attacks. The term Holocaust refers only to the genocide against Jews during World War II. Antisemitism is a part of the definition of the Holocaust, but one term cannot simply be exchanged for the other. In the Echoes and Reflections curriculum developed by the Anti-Defamation League, USC Shoah Foundation, and Yad Vashem to be used in secondary schools, the Holocaust is defined as an

> unprecedented genocide, total and systematic, perpetrated by Nazi Germany and its collaborators, with the aim of annihilating the Jewish people. The primary motivation was the Nazis' anti-Semitic racist ideology. Between 1933 and 1941 Nazi Germany pursued a policy that dispossessed the Jews of their rights and their property, followed by the branding and concentration of the Jewish population. This policy gained broad support in Germany and much of occupied Europe. In 1941, following the invasion of the Soviet Union, the Nazis and their collaborators launched the systematic mass murder of the Jews. By 1945 nearly six million Jews had been murdered.[2]

With this definition in mind I met with the community member who had misused the term. The result of the conversation was a positive one: the person recognized that *Holocaust* cannot be used interchangeably with *antisemitism*. He agreed to use the term *antisemitism* in the future when referring to hatred, prejudice, and violence against Jews outside of the time period of the Holocaust (1933–1945). He further recognized that, by confusing the terms, he could give the impression that the Holocaust began with the start of antisemitism and not within Nazi Germany.

Another example of the complexity of antisemitism can be found

in literature classes. In many school districts throughout the United States, *The Diary of Anne Frank* or other books dealing with her story are read between fifth and eighth grades. In material prepared by Scholastic for the book *We Remember Anne Frank*, the learning objectives proclaim that
students will:

> Learn about the historical events through a time line.
>
> Understand how events in Europe during the Nazis' rise to power and the subsequent Holocaust impacted the lives of real people.
>
> Develop empathy for people, Jewish and non-Jewish, who were directly affected by the Holocaust.
>
> Become familiar with the terms and places associated with the Holocaust.
>
> Improve content-area reading skills.
>
> Learn to do online research.[3]

The focus for this unit of study is limited to the period from 1933 to 1945. Further, the unit and material appear to be focused on details and not on building an understanding of the topic. The closest that they come is an attempt to build empathy, encouraging students to understand that the events of the Holocaust impacted real people. The challenge is to see the Jewish experience during the Holocaust as a result of historic antisemitism and not to see Jews solely as victims. Trying to understand the emotional impact of Anne's diary entries might aid the student in understanding the emotional impact that antisemitism had in her life.

Another challenge in public education is the possible confusion of understanding antisemitism only in terms of the Holocaust. The Commonwealth of Virginia lists the following as a standard of learning for world history: "The student will demonstrate knowledge of the worldwide impact of World War II by; (Objective), Examining the Holocaust and other examples of genocide in the twentieth century."[4] The history of antisemitism is listed as essential knowledge. I am not really sure that the teacher has the ability, due to time constraints, to build a true knowledge base on the topic of antisemitism. Further, the Holocaust is a key component only of the Jewish experience from 1933 to 1945; antisemitism has no relationship to other genocides of the twentieth century.

The challenge of understanding the complex nature of antisemitism in a historical context and not as an event of the twentieth century is one that does not seem to be addressed in its reality today. There is a growing desire in many states to legislate mandatory Holocaust education. The challenge lies in determining what this mandate means. The mandates often state that a student will be introduced to the Holocaust and other acts of genocide. For some, this means simply teaching some of the history; for others, it means teaching students to develop empathy. What appears to be missing in some states are commissions to review curricula and materials to determine which will best meet the needs of their state. Further, many states have not developed programs to train teachers to properly approach and teach the subject. Teachers should not approach a mandate with the aim of just checking it off but should use the mandate as a means to teach about the Holocaust in terms of empathy, understanding, and avoiding bystander behavior. It is the role of organizations such as the Institute for Holocaust Education (IHE) to help train teachers to go past the required standard and to teach more than just facts, despite the limited time at hand. As the State of Nebraska, like many other states, moves forward in mandating Holocaust education, it is the role and duty of organizations such as the IHE to be ready to train teachers in approaches to the subject matter. A common issue is that legislation requiring Holocaust education does not contain provisions to fund or or develop materials and systems to make this happen. Currently, the IHE is working with the Nebraska Department of Education to provide teachers the necessary materials for teaching the Holocaust. This is being done in numerous ways, such as holding various workshops for teachers on the latest materials available, and building educational trunks with materials and resources to loan out to classroom teachers.

Exercises for a Better Understanding

The Institute for Holocaust Education holds an annual essay contest for high school students. Students are provided with the following information: "Threatened by their Nazi occupiers, in 1943 the Danish people organized a national effort to send 7,200 of their Jewish co-nationals by fishing boats to neutral Sweden. This effort by the citizens of Denmark resulted in the highest Jewish survival rate of any European country during World War II. The Danish citizens provide a unique example of courage and concern; jeopardizing their own lives to spare those of their fellow countrymen."[5] Of course, Denmark had a very small and thoroughly integrated Jewish population. These features are to be kept in mind when comparing the Danish case with other case studies. In Poland, where millions of Jews lived, rescue operations were hampered by shortages of funds, food stock, and other necessities. Also, there was no obvious safe haven in easy reach.[6] Our objective is for students to build their own personal connections to the Holocaust, their community, and even conflicts a world away based on their study of the Holocaust in the classroom. Through their research into people who aided Jews, as in the Danish case, it is hoped that students develop a greater understanding of moral courage and the importance it can have in their own lives. Our desire is for each student to work to make a positive change in the world. Again, a major goal is to help students learn about and understand empathy, moral courage, and how not to be a bystander, based on the stories of the rescuers. In crafting their essays, they will ideally recognize that they have the ability, even as a single person, to effect change.[7]

Students are given the following definition: "Moral courage is the ability to take a strong stance on a specific issue and to defend it based on one's personal beliefs or convictions regardless of danger or threats to personal safety—physical, emotional or otherwise."[8] The essays must achieve three objectives:

1. Identify and explain the act of moral courage

2. Connect the example to the Holocaust (if a non-Holocaust example is used)

3. Explain how the lessons of their chosen example might be applied to their own life in the future.⁹

I believe that the knowledge gained by students on the topic of moral courage as a result of studying the role of the Righteous Gentiles during the Holocaust has and should have a greater impact on shaping our next generation of students and is much more important than a deep understanding of antisemitism and the role it played in Nazi Germany (and elsewhere). Charles C. Haynes wrote in his article "Schools of Conscience" in 2009 that, after a visit to Yad Vashem and learning about the role of the Righteous,

> I could not help but wonder, why did that nameless German risk his life for a Jew he did not know? More broadly, why did any of the thousands now called the Righteous respond with compassion and courage when so many others were either complicit or indifferent? As I contemplated this question, I could not think of anything that the rescuers during the Holocaust had in common. Some were religious; others were not. Some were wealthy; others were poor. Some were highly educated; others were barely literate. Then it struck me. We may never explain fully what combination of family, faith, education, or grace inspired them to risk everything, and in many cases to lose everything, for people they didn't know. But there's one thing most of them had in common: They did not stop to think about what they did; they simply acted. At the core of story after story we witness spontaneous courage, goodness, and compassion. But people don't acquire these attributes suddenly when faced with suffering and evil. Rather, courage, goodness, and compassion are habits of the heart—shaped over a lifetime—which define individual conscience and determine how a person will respond when fellow human beings are hurt, attacked, or victimized.¹⁰

John Weidner, a rescuer who organized a network in France that helped about eight hundred Jews escape the Nazis, explained:

> During our lives, each of us faces a choice: to think only about yourself, to get as much as you can for yourself, or to think about others, to serve, to be helpful to those who are in need. I believe that

it is very important to develop your . . . heart, to have a heart open to the suffering of others. Developing students' hearts, I believe, is what educators are called to do. Each and every small act of honesty, service, responsibility, and compassion that teachers and administrators encourage daily in their students—and model consistently in their own lives—helps create moral and civic habits of the heart that instill in students the courage to care.[11]

In the supplemental Jewish religious school program, often a year of study in middle school or high school is devoted to the study of the Holocaust. A challenge has been to not focus just on the details of the Holocaust but to spend more time on the role that those such as the Righteous Gentiles played. In listening to Holocaust survivors' stories it is very interesting to hear what they would like students to remember. The IHE hosts an annual Week of Understanding during which more than six thousand students in middle and high schools will hear a survivor's testimony. The program is now in its eleventh year. Each speaker tells their family's story, but all seem to finish their presentations stressing that antisemitism has no place in today's world and that students should focus on learning from the past to improve the future.

When I read Haynes's article in 2009, it occurred to me that in public education in Virginia, where I was living at the time, the state standard of learning was missing an opportunity to turn Holocaust education into an avenue for identifying and explaining acts of moral courage, as we now require for the IHE's annual essay contest. One cannot and should not take the element of antisemitism out of the study of the Holocaust, but one should not miss the opportunity to use the topic of the Holocaust to teach empathy and the avoidance of bystander behavior to our students. I believe that this can and should be the focus of Holocaust education with our high school students today, even with the limited time that can be devoted to teaching the subject.

Guidelines for Teaching

As states begin to mandate the study of the Holocaust, another ready source of good materials for teachers to use are those provided by the United States Holocaust Memorial Museum (USHMM) in Washington, DC. Their *Guidelines for Teaching about the Holocaust* provides a fabulous framework for teaching.

First, in defining the term *Holocaust* there is the challenge of realizing that Jews were not the only minority to be persecuted by the Nazi government. The term Holocaust refers only to the genocide perpetrated against the Jews of Europe and Northern Africa but should not and does not diminish that others fell victims to the Nazis. This area is a challenge to some.

Second, "do not teach or imply that the Holocaust was inevitable."[12] In this statement, the USHMM recognizes that governments and people in Europe and throughout the world could and should have acted to make sure that Nazi Germany could never have become such a powerful military force or enacted the Final Solution. Further, this statement helps us to understand how important the role of the Righteous Among the Nations really was. Though it is very hard to teach the concept of *what if?*, one can imagine what the result might have been if more than twenty-five thousand people had risen up and helped the Jews of Europe. When we guide students through our exhibit at the Strategic Air Command & Aerospace Museum in Ashland, Nebraska, we finish with a discussion of the Righteous Among the Nations. Although we do mention that it would have been amazing if more had helped, our emphasis is on having empathy and not being a bystander in the hope of teaching students to act rather than be passive.

Third, "avoid simple answers to complex questions."[13] When teaching the Holocaust, teachers should "be wary of simplification. Seek instead to convey the nuances of this history. Allow students to think about the many factors and events that contributed to the Holocaust and that often made decision making difficult and uncertain."[14] In taking this approach, students will begin to understand that each and every component of the Holocaust was complex and multileveled. In the Jewish religious school setting this has often been a major challenge. Often in the past the answers were simple. For example, when looking at the question of *why the Jews?*, the answer would have been in terms of a basic antisemitic response: *because they hated the Jews*. This answer is much too simple, of course, and really does not help the middle or high school student in developing a deeper understanding of the topic or an understanding of the complex nature of antisemitism and how the Nazis used it to advance their goals.

Next is "strive for precision of language." A teacher must avoid teaching in general terms or in ambiguous language. This may be a difficult challenge but is of great importance in Holocaust education. As the USHMM states in their guidelines for teaching about the Holocaust,

> Any study of the Holocaust touches upon nuances of human behavior. Because of the complexity of the history, there is a temptation to generalize and, thus, to distort the facts (e.g., "all concentration camps were killing centers" or "all Germans were collaborators"). Avoid this by helping your students clarify the information presented and encourage them to distinguish, for example, the differences between prejudice and discrimination, collaborators and bystanders, armed and spiritual resistance, direct and assumed orders, concentration camps and killing centers, and guilt and responsibility.[15]

We are currently living in a situation where stereotypes and name-calling have become the standard. This is all the more reason that teachers must strive for precise language in the classroom.

The next area is one that has been of concern to me over the years, both as a student in my teens and later as a classroom teacher. The USHMM suggests that the teacher should "strive for balance in establishing whose perspective informs your study of the Holocaust."[16] As stated earlier in this chapter, in Jewish religious schools there was often little or no effort to see Jews as anything but victims—not also, for example, as a group who attempted to live during the Nazi era, not just die. One need only look to life in the Warsaw ghetto to see examples of how Jews attempted to deal with their situation. On another level there is a need to make sure that Jews are not shown as bringing the Nazis' treatment onto themselves. The USHMM suggests that a "helpful technique for engaging students in a discussion of the Holocaust is to think of the participants as belonging to one of four categories: victims, perpetrators, rescuers, or bystanders. Examine the actions, motives, and decisions of each group. Portray all individuals, including victims and perpetrators, as human beings who are capable of moral judgment and independent decision making."[17] Further, the teacher should be very careful to allow students to

> make careful distinctions about sources of information. Students should be encouraged to consider why a particular text was written, who wrote it, who the intended audience was, whether any biases were inherent in the information, whether any gaps occurred in discussion, whether omissions in certain passages were inadvertent or not, and how the information has been used to interpret various events. Because scholars often base their research on different bodies of information, varying interpretations of history can emerge. Consequently, all interpretations are subject to analytical evaluation. Strongly encourage your students to investigate carefully the origin and authorship of all material, particularly anything found on the Internet.[18]

By doing this, students should be able then to find truthful and accurate material.

Teachers must also make sure to "avoid comparisons of pain."[19] The USHMM suggests that it is important to avoid generalizations in this area. Each person's horror was individually their own, and, by avoiding terms such as "the Jews" or "Jewish people," we allow students to see the person and not just an ethnic or religious group. In terms of approaching this in the classroom, teaching individual stories allows the student to avoid this concern. They learn about individual challenges facing families and avoid seeing generalizations and comparisons. The more a student can see a victim as an individual person and not as part of a group, the easier it is to assist in developing an understanding of the personal experience and not a ranking of who suffered more.

The topic of the Holocaust must always be taught in the context of nonfiction. Under the USHMM guidelines it is taught that the subject should not be romanticized. In using fiction, a teacher runs a great risk of students internalizing the fictionalized account as truth: "in exposing students to the worst aspects of human nature as revealed in the history of the Holocaust, you run the risk of fostering cynicism in your students. Accuracy of fact, together with a balanced perspective on the history, must be a priority."[20] Too often today in books and in movies we are seeing the use of fiction in Holocaust education. For example, the story of the film *The Boy in the Striped Pajamas* did not happen, and it could not have happened. The problem lies in the area of truth. It is one thing to use fiction to help the audience connect to the story if it could have happened, but it is another to use fictional accounts that never could have happened, such as the friendship between children inside and outside of a concentration camp depicted in *The Boy in the Striped Pajamas*. Teachers have a moral obligation to teach the truth, and they have the ability to do so with the many amazing nonfiction sources that exist. In the IHE's teacher workshops we always provide lists of appropriate materials to use that are both age appropriate and factually accurate.

The Holocaust was not an isolated event, and it did not take place outside of other historical events. That is to say, as the USHMM guidelines suggest, it is important to contextualize the history. Holocaust topics and history must be taught in the context of European and world history. By doing so, students will gain a broader and greater understanding of all elements that played into Nazi Germany becoming what it became. "Encourage your students not to categorize groups of people only on the basis of their experiences during the Holocaust; contextualization is critical so that victims are not perceived only as victims. By exposing students to some of the cultural contributions and achievements of 2,000 years of European Jewish life, for example, you help them to balance their perception of Jews as victims and to appreciate more fully the traumatic disruption in Jewish history caused by the Holocaust."[21] This is particularly true in terms of how Jewish life in central and eastern Europe is portrayed in the period of time leading up to the Holocaust. In Jewish religious school classrooms, the Jews of the time are often shown as all being like the characters in *Fiddler on the Roof*. Again, more emphasis should be given to individual stories and less to grouping people together as "the Jews." The result would be a better understanding of the individual contributions and achievements of various Jewish people, and a greater understanding of what was truly lost as a result of the Holocaust.

The Jewish victims of the Holocaust were not and should not be taught only as statistics. The victims were not a number; they were six million individual lives and stories. They must be seen as unique individuals, as members of families, communities, countries, and nations. The USHMM's display of pictures of one town that was destroyed is a perfect example of doing this right. By seeing these pictures, you see individual lives and experiences, rather than just a group or a series of numbers. Students are better able to learn empathy and understanding when they have an opportunity to get to know the person and not just the number.

Finally, the USHMM recommends "making responsible methodological choices." Put very simply, know your students. Understand where they come from and their level of maturity. Teachers have an obligation to be sure that the material they are using is age appropriate. The use of horrific pictures and films should be carefully monitored. Our goal should never be to shock our students but to help our students gain an understanding of why the Nazis chose the Jews. The use of extremely troubling material runs a risk of the student not being able to process what to do with this material. Our goal, as stated by the USHMM, is to allow for critical analysis of the materials presented.

Conclusion

As we move forward into a period when our survivor population is greatly decreasing and firsthand testimony is becoming limited, we must continue to incorporate the topics of antisemitism and Holocaust education into our materials. "Educators across the country are grappling with how to make the lessons of the Holocaust relevant to children at a time when it is vanishing from the collective memory. Sixty-six percent of millennials could not identify what Auschwitz was, and twenty-two percent had not heard of or were unfamiliar with the Holocaust, according to a 2018 survey by Claims Conference, a group that negotiates restitution for Holocaust survivors. Additionally, sixty-eight percent of millennials wrongly think Hitler came to power by force."[22] The Anti-

Defamation League, which collects information on antisemitic incidents around the world, has published reports showing that antisemitic attacks are on the rise. In 2019, in parts of New York, it seemed that attacks on Orthodox Jews happened weekly. According to Peter Nelson, formerly the ADL's director of Holocaust education, the rise of antisemitism in K-12 schools is "impossible to ignore at this point. It's not clear that these [students] are neo-Nazis necessarily," he said; "it may not even be directed at Jews in particular. But it is woefully ignorant."[23]

So, what is the answer in terms of Holocaust education? There are some in both the government and teaching realms who feel that mandatory Holocaust education should be legislated, and there are twelve states that have done so.[24] There are others who feel that mandating Holocaust education will have the opposite effect, and that less will be taught because teachers will teach only to fulfill the obligation to meet the mandated standard. What we do know is that we must do something. When one in four adults does not know what Auschwitz was, we know we have a problem. I was recently part of a discussion on a Holocaust educator listserv. The discussion centered on the use of the term *concentration camp*. Some in the group were upset that the term was being used in the context of the immigration debate in the United States. They failed to see that the term does not belong exclusively to the Holocaust and that it has a history that predates Nazi Germany. In my view they were missing the point: taking the lessons learned from the Holocaust to teach empathy, an understanding of how we can make the world a better place, and how to not be a bystander.

Questions for Further Discussion

1. Why is antisemitism an essential topic of study when trying to understand the Holocaust?

2. Scott Littky identifies three challenges in teaching antisemitism in the context of Holocaust education. Summarize these challenges.

3. Explore the significance of "moral courage," first concerning antisemitism and the Holocaust, then concerning your life today.

4. The author references recent comparisons between current events and the Holocaust. Discuss the pros and cons of drawing these comparisons.

5. In Holocaust education it is helpful to study the topic from at least four points of view: those of victims, perpetrators, rescuers, and bystanders. Connect each point of view with antisemitism and its effects on this point of view.

6. Evaluate how the study of antisemitism is valuable beyond the confines of Holocaust education.

Notes

1. Ron Kampeas, "The Pittsburgh Shooting Caught the US Jewish Community Off Guard. Can They Catch Up?" *Jewish Telegraphic Agency*, December 20, 2018, https://www.jta.org/2018/12/20/united-states/the-pittsburgh-shooting-caught-the-us-jewish-community-off-guard-can-they-catch-up.

2. "What Was the Holocaust?" Yad Vashem, accessed May 12, 2020, https://www.yadvashem.org/holocaust/about.html.

3. "Teacher's Guide: We Remember Anne Frank," Scholastic, accessed May 12, 2020, http://teacher.scholastic.com/frank/tguide.htm.

4. "World History & Geography 1500–Present," Virginia Department of Education, History & Social Science, accessed May 12, 2020, http://doe.virginia.gov/testing/sol/standards_docs/history_socialscience/.

5. "The Germans captured only 468 of 7,800 Jews, 112 remained hiding in Denmark, and the rest found sanctuary in Sweden"; quoted in Lawrence Baron, "From Saints to Sinners: Teaching about the Motivations of Rescuers of Jews through Documentary and Feature Films" in *Unlikely Heroes: The Place of Holocaust Rescuers in Research and Teaching*, ed. Ari Kohen and Gerald J. Steinacher (Lincoln: University of Nebraska Press, 2019), 169–97, 180.

6. Compare Baron, "From Saints to Sinners," 169–97.

7. See also Liz Feldstern and Amanda Ryan, "Teaching the Lesson of Moral Courage through Writing" in *Unlikely Heroes: The Place of Holocaust Rescuers in Research and Teaching*, ed. Ari Kohen and Gerald J. Steinacher (Lincoln: University of Nebraska Press, 2019), 222–32.

8. "The Tribute to the Rescuers Essay Contest," Institute for Holocaust Education, http://ihene.org.

9. Virginia Department of Education, "World History & Geography 1500–Present."

10. Charles C. Haynes, "Schools of Conscience," *Educational Leadership* 66, no. 8 (May 2009): 6–13.

11. Carol Rittner and Sondra Myers, eds., *The Courage to Care: Rescuers of Jews During the Holocaust* (New York: New York University Press, 1986), 65.

12. "Guidelines for Teaching about the Holocaust," United States Holocaust Memorial Museum, accessed May 12, 2020, https://www.ushmm.org/educators/teaching-about-the-holocaust/general-teaching-guidelines.

13. USHMM, "Guidelines for Teaching about the Holocaust."
14. USHMM, "Guidelines for Teaching about the Holocaust."
15. USHMM, "Guidelines for Teaching about the Holocaust."
16. USHMM, "Guidelines for Teaching about the Holocaust."
17. USHMM, "Guidelines for Teaching about the Holocaust."
18. USHMM, "Guidelines for Teaching about the Holocaust."
19. USHMM, "Guidelines for Teaching about the Holocaust."
20. USHMM, "Guidelines for Teaching about the Holocaust."
21. USHMM, "Guidelines for Teaching about the Holocaust."
22. Marcia Robiou, "With Anti-Semitic Incidents in Schools on the Rise, Teachers Grapple with Holocaust Education." *PBS Frontline*, April 30, 2019, https://www.pbs.org/wgbh/frontline/article/with-anti-semitic-incidents-in-schools-on-the-rise-teachers-grapple-with-holocaust-education/.

23. Robiou, "With Anti-Semitic Incidents in Schools on the Rise."
24. "Where Holocaust Education is Required in the US," United States Holocaust Memorial Museum, https://www.ushmm.org/teach/fundamentals/where-holocaust-education-is-required-in-the-us.

Contributors

Shlomo Abramovich is a lecturer in the Department of Education at Shaanan College and a researcher in the Department of Middle Eastern Studies and Political Science at Ariel University. He completed his PhD in Jewish History at Bar Ilan University and was a research fellow with the Harris Center for Judaic Studies at the University of Nebraska–Lincoln. His research areas include changes and developments in Israeli orthodoxy, society and politics in religious Zionism, and the military and society in Israel.

Joseph W. Bendersky is a professor of history at Virginia Commonwealth University. As an expert on German history, antisemitism, and the Holocaust, he has authored numerous books and articles. His book *The "Jewish Threat": Anti-Semitic Politics of the U.S. Army* (Basic, 2002) was a finalist for the National Jewish Book Award and has been translated into Japanese. Most of his work focuses on Carl Schmitt, the most controversial political and legal thinker in twentieth-century Germany.

Jean Cahan is a senior lecturer in philosophy and was the longtime director of the Norman and Bernice Harris Center for Judaic Studies at the University of Nebraska–Lincoln. Her research interests include philosophy of religion and philosophy of history. She has published on Spinoza, modern Jewish philosophy, and Marx. Her paper "Can Antisemitism Have a Sacral Quality?: A Reply to Wistrich and Others" was published in *Antisemitism Studies* 3, no. 1 (April 2019).

R. Amy Elman is the Weber Professor in Social Science at Kalamazoo College. She is the author of *The European Union, Antisemitism, and the Politics of Denial* (University of Nebraska Press, 2014) and *Sexual Equality in an Integrated Europe* (Palgrave Macmillan, 2007), among other works.

Leonard Greenspoon is the Philip M. and Ethel Klutznick Chair in Jewish Civilization and a professor of Classical and Near Eastern Studies at Creighton University. He has authored or edited almost three dozen books, among them *Rites of Passage: How Today's Jews Celebrate, Commemorate, and Commiserate* (Purdue University Press, 2010).

Ari Kohen is a professor of political science, the Schlesinger Professor of Social Justice, and director of the Norman and Bernice Harris Center for Judaic Studies at the University of Nebraska–Lincoln. He has written two books, *Untangling Heroism: Classical Philosophy and the Concept of the Hero* (2014) and *In Defense of Human Rights: A Non-Religious Grounding in a Pluralistic World* (2007), both published by Routledge.

Scott B. Littky is the director of the Institute for Holocaust Education in Omaha, Nebraska. Littky holds a BA in history from Wayne State University and did his graduate work in education and Judaic studies. He served as a Jewish educator and education director for over thirty-four years in Detroit and Ann Arbor, Michigan; Alexandria, Virginia; and Omaha, Nebraska.

Jürgen Matthäus is a historian and research director at the Jack, Joseph and Morton Mandel Center for Advanced Holocaust Studies of the United States Holocaust Memorial Museum in Washington DC. He is an author and editor of multiple works on the history of World War II and the Holocaust. His recent book publications include *Beyond "Ordinary Men": Christopher Browning and Holocaust Historiography* (Schöningh, 2019), edited with Th. Pegelow Kaplan, and *Predicting the Holocaust: Jewish Organizations Report from Geneva on the Emergence of the "Final Solution," 1939–1942* (Rowman & Littlefield, 2018).

Łukasz W. Niparko is a PhD student in the Department of Political Science at the University of Nebraska–Lincoln and a human rights advocate. He holds an LLM in international human rights law from the European University, Viadrina. Niparko was the Pat

Cox Fellow in the European Parliament and worked with the delegation chair to the Korean Peninsula and EU-China Group. His interests include international affairs and the legal prevention of discrimination.

Gerald J. Steinacher is the James A. Rawley Professor of History at the University of Nebraska–Lincoln. He is the author of numerous publications on twentieth-century German, Austrian, and Italian history, most recently *Humanitarians at War: The Red Cross in the Shadow of the Holocaust* (2017) and *Nazis on the Run: How Hitler's Henchmen Fled Justice* (2011), both published by Oxford University Press.

Timothy Turnquist is a PhD student in the History Department of the University of Nebraska–Lincoln. His research interests include Holocaust studies, transatlantic antisemitism, Christian-Jewish relations, and immigration. His dissertation investigates the relationship between American antisemitism in the 1930s, immigration, and the Catholic Church.

Index

abolitionism, 144–45. *See also* slavery
Abramovich, Shlomo, 16–17
Adler, Cyrus, 107
Adorno, Theodor, 24, 30
Africa, 53–55; racism in, 54, 143–46; slave trade in, 188
Afrikaners. *See* Boers
Algeria, 53
Al-Jazeera, 199–200
alt-right, 1
Anglo-Saxon civilization, 99
Anti-Defamation League (ADL), 3, 5, 11, 209, 213, 238–39
antisemitic Polish publications: *National Self-Defense*, 165; *Poznań Courier*, 165; *Spider*, 165; *Under the Pillory*, 165; *The Voice of Homeland*, 165. *See also* Poland
antisemitic propaganda, 8, 69, 76, 81, 86; and German Christian pastors, 138. *See also* antisemitism; conspiracy theories; ideology
antisemitism: American, 8, 106, 111; Austrian, 49; Boycott, Divestment, and Sanctions movement and, 211–14; cartoons of, 19n11; concept of, 17; contemporary, 10–12; definition of, 211, 214; fantasies of, 5–6, 58; fears of transatlantic, 104; fictional allegations of, 6; French, 189; German, 13, 15, 23–26, 30, 60, 76, 186; German Christian, 124–47; in Holocaust education, 225–39; Islamic, 10, 184, 194–200; modern, 14, 47, 50–51, 65; nationalism and, 14; Nazi, 75–94, 186; new definitions for, 206; nineteenth-century political currents of, 25; and the pan-movements, 58–67; political, 38, 51–52; racism and, 25, 76;
redefining, 209–11; religious, 5–7; rise of, 11–12, 20n25, 47, 50; secular, 7; socioeconomic, 51; and totalitarian movements, 46–71; traditional, 51; traditional definition of, 208; and transnational inhibitions, 183–200; violent, 13; Western European, 47. *See also* antisemitic propaganda; anti-Zionism; delegitimization; racism; Völkisch movement
anti-Zionism, 16–17, 184, 206, 209, 215, 221n8. *See also* antisemitism; Zionism
Arab nationalism, 9. *See also* nationalism
Archaeological Institute of America (AIA), 107
archaeology: American biblical, 104; of ancient Israel, 99; science of, 119
Arendt, Hannah, 13–14, 46–71; *Eichmann in Jerusalem*, 64, 67; *The Origins of Totalitarianism*, 46–47, 50, 52, 59–60, 63–66; political philosophy of, 57, 70; scholarship according to, 71; "Truth and Politics," 70–71
Arnold, William Rosenzweig, 117
Ashton, Catherine, 193–94, 197
Association of National Socialist German Jurists, 36
Assyriology, 99–101, 108
Augustine, 6, 136, 139
Augustus III, King, 159
Auschwitz-Birkenau, 93, 168, 196, 238–39. *See also* Final Solution; genocide; Holocaust
Australia, 53
Austria, 48–50; Freedom Party of, 199; legislation against the Jews of, 63; prohibition of Holocaust denial in, 197. *See also* Austrian Republic

Austrian Republic, 52. *See also* Austria
Austro-Hungarian railway, 14. *See also* Austria

Bahr, Ehrhard, 26
Baltic States, 80–85. *See also* Estonia; Latvia; Lithuania
Barghouti, Omar, 213
Barlow, Biddy, 186–87
Batory, King Stefan, 157–58, 175n19
Bauer, Yehuda, 225
Bauman, Zygmunt, 151
Bayles, William, 77–78
Beecher, Henry Ward, 145
Belgium, 189
Bendersky, Joseph W., 13, 71
Ben Gurion, David, 215–16
Benhabib, Seyla, 47
Benjamin, Walter, 66
Bergen, Doris, 6
Bergman, Bronisław, 164
Bernstein, Richard, 46, 65
Betlejewski, Rafał, 172
Bible, 15–16, 124–47; abuses of the, 16; Christian, 16; and the demonizing of Jews, 131–38; German criticism of the, 102–3, 137–38; Hebrew, 15, 55, 101–3, 145; nationalistic translations of the, 55; Old Testament and New Testament of the, 125–26; and the opposition to the Nazis, 139–42. *See also* Christianity; interpretation, biblical; Judaism; religion
Biden, Joe, 1
Bildung, 30
Bloch, Phillipp, 161
Bluecher, Heinrich, 57
Boers, 54–58, 143–46. *See also* South Africa
Bolshevism, 52, 58, 67, 111, 187. *See also* communism
Bonhoeffer, Dietrich, 139, 141
Boston, 109–10, 114
Boston Evening Transcript, 107–8
Boston Post, 115
Bowers, Robert, 3–4
Boycott, Divestment, and Sanctions movement (BDS), 9–10, 16–17, 206–19, 221n9, 221n18, 222n23, 224n44
Boyd, Julia, 187
Brandeis, Louis B., 110

Brazil, 162
Britain, 9, 185, 197, 201n4
Buchanan, James, 144

Cabral, Pedro Álvares, 162
Cahan, Jean, 13–14
Camp of Great Poland, 164. *See also* Poland
Camus, Renaud: *Le Grand Remplacement*, 3
Canada, 53
Canovan, Margaret, 57, 64–65, 70
capitalism: corporate monopoly, 24, 40; critique of, 23; hostility to, 51. *See also* financial system; imperialism
Carlson, Tucker, 4
Catholic Center Party, 34
Černý, David, 160
Christianity, 6, 54; the Bible and, 125–26; Calvinist, 143; and the Confessing Church, 137–41, 150n16; conversion of Jews to, 135–37, 139, 161, 201n12; criticism of Jews in, 132, 135; German, 102, 126–31, 137–39, 147; Hebrew civilization and, 99; Polish, 155. *See also* Bible; Crusades; Jesus of Nazareth; Protestants; religion; Roman Catholics
Churchill, Winston, 144
Claims Conference, 238
communism, 186; Soviet, 14, 81, 187. *See also* Bolshevism; Soviet Union
Confederate monuments, 1–2
Congress of Vienna (1815), 162
conservatism, 23. *See also* Republican Party
conspiracy theories, 4–6, 8, 225; Jewish world, 8, 67–69. *See also* antisemitic propaganda; *Protocols of the Elders of Zion*
Coulter, Ann, 5
Court of Justice of the European Union (CJEU), 198. *See also* European Union (EU)
critical theory, 23–24. *See also* Frankfurt School
Crusades, 136. *See also* Christianity; religion; Roman Catholics
culture: Christian, 27; German, 27–28, 33, 40; modernist trends of Weimar, 27, 33

da Gama, Gaspar, 151, 161–62
da Gama, Vasco, 161–62
Darwin, Charles, 186
Dearborn Independent, 8, 111. *See also* Ford, Henry

delegitimization, 211–12. *See also* antisemitism
Delitzsch, Friedrich, 101–2
democracy: in Germany, 186; hostility to, 51; liberal, 37; militant, 29; parliamentary, 63; transgression of the standards of, 10
Denmark, 217, 231, 240n5
Diaspora, 6, 9, 62, 67, 222n31. *See also* Jews
Dieckmann, Christoph, 87
Disraeli, Benjamin, 48
Dmowski, Roman, 164–65
Dreyfus Affair, 48, 60
Drummond, Elizabeth A.: "On the Borders of the Nation," 163
Drumont, Édouard: *La France Juive*, 3
Du Bois, William, 187–88
Duke, David, 1

eastern Europe, 25, 61, 78, 80; Jewish immigrants from, 110; Judaism in, 71, 225
Eger, Akiva, 151, 160
Egypt, 9, 53, 160
Eichmann, Adolf, 61, 92, 226
Einhorn, David, 146
Einsatzgruppen: commanders of, 86, 89–90; Himmler and his, 93; and police units, 84–85; units of, 86–87. *See also* National Socialism (Nazis)
Einsatzstab Reichsleiter Rosenberg (ERR), 78. *See also* National Socialism (Nazis)
Eisler, Fritz, 33
Eisler, Georg, 33
Eliot, Charles T., 100–104, 107, 111–12, 117
Elman, R. Amy, 16
Emerson, Ralph Waldo, 102
Enlightenment, 7; German, 103; inclusion of Jews in the nation-building of the, 163
Estonia, 87. *See also* Baltic States
European Convention of Human Rights, 198–99
European Court of Human Rights, 198–99
European Union (EU), 183–85, 188–98; human rights discourse of the, 193–94; origins of the, 188–93. *See also* Court of Justice of the European Union (CJEU); Fundamental Rights Agency (FRA)

Facebook, 5, 197
fascism, 67. *See also* National Socialism (Nazis)

Federal Republic of Germany, 24. *See also* Germany
Feiglin, Moshe, 223n39
Feilchenfeld, Wolf, 161
Feuchtwanger, Ludwig, 34
Final Solution, 25, 64, 75, 86–93, 168, 234. *See also* Holocaust; the Jewish question; Wannsee conference
financial system: the media and the, 8; the role of Jews in the, 8, 56–57. *See also* capitalism
Ford, Henry, 8, 111
Fraenkel, Ernst, 23
France, 52, 54, 142, 185, 201n4, 217; Jews of, 190, 217, 232; Vichy collaborators of, 142
Frank, Hans, 36
Frank, Leo, 8
Frankfurt, 159. *See also* Germany
Frankfurt School, 13, 23–27, 36–37, 40; Marxist orientation of the, 30; study of antisemitism of the, 26, 29. *See also* critical theory
Freimann, Ajkob, 161
French Revolution, 47–48
Friedländer, Saul, 94
Friesenhahn, Ernst, 37
Fundamental Rights Agency (FRA), 189–92, 194–95, 201n4. *See also* European Union (EU)

Gaetz, Matt, 5
Garaudy, Roger, 199
Garrard, Eve, 196
Gaza Strip, 9. *See also* Israel; Palestine
Gazeta Wyborcza, 164
Generalgouvernement, 83, 90, 167–68
genocide, 15–16, 75, 80–93, 204n56, 228, 234; gravitational center of, 93; Jewish, 184, 193; nationalism and, 188; public discussions by top Nazis of, 168. *See also* Holocaust; pogroms
Gentile, Emilio, 59
Germany: antisemitism in, 71, 184–85, 228; "collective guilt" of, 26; denazification of, 27, 29; foreign policy of, 184; German-Jewish relations in, 39; Jewish identity in, 27, 164; postwar, 30, 32, 75; race-thinking in, 54; response to antisemitism in, 201n4; totalitarianism in, 53. *See also* Federal Republic of Germany; Munich Beer Hall Putsch; National Socialism (Nazis); Third Reich; Weimar Republic

Gilman, Sander, 71
globalization, 183–84
Goebbels, Joseph, 78, 92, 185–86
Golan Heights, 9. *See also* Israel
Goldhagen, Daniel, 204n67
golem, 160, 172
Göring, Hermann, 36
Great Depression, 31
Greenspoon, Leonard, 15–16
Groll, Helena, 196
Gurian, Waldemar, 59
Gurland, Arkadij, 37

Halimi, Ilan, 191
Halimi, Sarah, 191–92
Hannity, Sean, 4
Harvard University, 15, 99–119; the "Jewish question" at, 112–18. *See also* Semitic Museum
Haupt, Paul, 102
Hayes, Peter, 30
Haynes, Charles C.: "Schools of Conscience," 232
Hebrew Immigrant Aid Society, 3
Heidegger, Martin, 60, 71
Heine, Heinrich, 27
Hensel, Albert, 34
Herz, John, 26–30, 36
Herzl, Theodor: *Der Judenstaat*, 9
Hett, Benjamin Carter: *The Death of Democracy*, 184–85
Heydrich, Reinhard, 83, 86, 88, 92
Heyer, Heather, 1
Himmler, Heinrich, 80, 84–86, 88–90, 93, 168
history: American, 2; antisemitic "interpretations" of modern, 50; burdens of European, 184; German, 51, 95n3; of the Holocaust, 236–37; Jewish, 51, 65, 70, 106; Jews as the final victors in world, 62; modern European, 14; philosemitic interpretations of Jewish, 104; Polish, 152–57; religious, 55; social, 55; writing, 66
Hitler, Adolf, 8, 14, 23, 52, 60, 69, 76–84, 82, 88, 94, 96n17, 186–87, 238; biblical characters as precursors to, 129; dictatorship of, 31; *Mein Kampf*, 15; regime of, 65, 84–85. *See also* National Socialism (Nazis)
Hobson, J. A., 66
Hollande, François, 217

Holocaust, 12, 65, 75, 81–93, 135, 140–41, 147, 184, 188–89, 204n56; antisemitism and, 228–30; in Belorussia, 87; definition of the, 234; education about the, 225–39; in Estonia, 87; inversion of the, 184, 192–93, 200; in Latvia, 87; in Lithuania, 87; methods of teaching about the, 46; Nazi genocide and the, 81; in Poland, 161, 167–70; soft denial of the, 193–94; in Ukraine, 87. *See also* Auschwitz-Birkenau; Final Solution; genocide; Judaism; pogroms; Righteous Gentiles
Holy Roman Empire, 59
Horkheimer, Max, 29–30, 34
Hull, Cordell, 187
humanism, 27–28
human rights, 46, 193–99; homelessness and, 70; rudimentary, 81; violations of, 10, 207, 210–11

identity: American Jewish, 110, 118–19; Aryan, 68, 118; crisis of, 51; German, 71; German Jewish, 27–28; Israeli, 206–19; Jewish, 62, 136–37; "the Jewish question" and, 68, 118; Polonism as a national, 163
Identity Dixie, 2
Identity Evropa, 2, 18n4
ideology: antisemitism as the mainstay of a national, 60, 163; differences of, 23; Marxist, 26; Nazi, 26, 32, 55, 60, 69, 76, 81–82, 228; racist, 54, 228; totalitarian, 60–70. *See also* antisemitic propaganda
Illowy, Bernard, 145
immigration: from eastern and southern Europe, 110–12; Jewish, 119; in mainstream right-wing rhetoric, 3; as a menace, 4
imperialism: Arendt's analysis of, 66; continental, 58–59; Marxist-Leninist analysis of, 53; nineteenth-century, 52; and racism, 53–58; socioeconomic analysis of, 57. *See also* capitalism
India, 100, 162
indigenous peoples, 53
inequality, 64
Ingraham, Laura, 4
Institute for Holocaust Education (Omaha), 17, 226, 230–33, 237
International Holocaust Remembrance Alliance (IHRA), 210, 214

interpretation, biblical, 127–29, 140, 149n7. *See also* Bible
Intifadah, 9. *See also* Palestine
Iran, 10
Iraq, 99
Isaacman, Clara: *Pathways through the Holocaust*, 227
Islamic State of Iraq and Syria (ISIS), 189
Israel, 105, 183, 206–19; Basic Laws of, 217; and the Boycott, Divestment, and Sanctions movement, 214–15; criticism of, 9, 206, 210, 213, 215; foundation of the state of, 8–9, 217; Jewish right to self-determination in, 212; Jewish society in, 224n42; Law of Return in, 216; music industry boycott of, 203n40; and Palestinian refugees, 212; rights of the non-Jewish citizens of, 217; role of Judaism in, 218; universities of, 211. *See also* Gaza Strip; Golan Heights; Israeli-Palestinian conflict; Jerusalem; Jews; Palestine; West Bank
Israel Apartheid Week (IAW), 213
Israeli-Palestinian conflict, 17, 196–97, 206, 212. *See also* Israel; Palestine
Italy, 185

Jacobi, Erwin, 34
Jaffé, Philipp, 162
Jägerstätter, Franz, 148n3
Jefferson, Thomas, 2
Jerusalem, 6, 105. *See also* Israel; Palestine
Jesus of Nazareth, 6, 102, 131–35, 138; as Jewish, 105, 124–27. *See also* Christianity
Jewish Elysium Club (Boston), 109–10
Jewish Enlightenment (*Haskalah*), 162
Jewish gminas, 155–62, 165, 170. *See also* Poland
the Jewish question, 7, 14, 34, 64–65, 75, 83–93, 100, 104, 118. *See also* Final Solution; National Socialism (Nazis)
Jewish Telegraphic Agency, 225
Jews: American, 103, 146; central European, 237; character of modern, 65–66; in Christian society, 6–7; civil rights for, 162; critique of the historical and socioeconomic role of, 71; demonizing the, 131–38; divine wrath on the, 130; eastern European, 71, 78, 80, 237; exterminations of, 12, 25–26, 64–65, 75, 81–93; as financiers, 7, 56–57, 67, 70; German, 40, 42n25, 71, 103, 186; on the Iberian Peninsula, 136–37; illusion of the acceptance of German, 26, 39–40; liberal, 160; Marxist-Leninist suspicion of, 57; massacres of, 19n15, 136; the mentality of, 29; murder of Soviet, 87; pan-movements and the hatred of the, 60–62; Poznań, 16, 151–73; prominent Bostonian, 110; Reform, 109; secularized, 62–63, 68, 70; as socially progressive moderate democrats, 28; stereotypical images of, 28–29, 56–57; Western European, 47. *See also* Diaspora; Israel; the Jewish question; Judaism; religion; Zionism
John Hopkins University, 102
John Paul II, Pope, 172
Jordan, 9
Judaism, 60, 136, 215; ancient civilization of, 103–4; history of, 70; indifference of Arendt to, 71; "Jewishness" as opposed to, 62; religious idea of chosenness of, 63. *See also* Bible; Holocaust; Jews; religion
Judaken, Jonathan, 183
Judeo-Christian tradition, 61
Juncker, Jean Claude, 194–95
Jung, Edgar Julius, 184–85, 188

Kampeas, Ron, 225
Kateb, George, 46, 65, 70
Kelsen, Han, 26
Kershaw, Ian, 169–70
Kirchheimer, Otto, 13, 24, 26–27, 30, 33–40; *Political Justice*, 37; "Weimar—and What Then?," 35
Kjaerum, Morten, 196
Klaff, Lesley, 184
Knoll, Mireille, 192
Kollenscher, Max, 167
Korczak, Janusz, 173
Kruger, Paul, 144
Ku Klux Klan, 1–2, 111

Langmuir, Gavin, 60
language: abuse of religious, 60; antisemitic, 51; Germanic, 120n1
Latvia, 87, 92. *See also* Baltic States
League of Nations, 185–86
Lehmans, 7, 19n14
Leibholz, Gerhard, 34

Lelewel, Joachim, 161–62
Ley, Michael, 59
liberalism: abstract Jewish Other defined by, 111, 116; American, 102; blind spots of, 119; critique of, 31; hostility to, 51; nationalist, 118; tribalistic challenges to, 112
Life Magazine, 114–15
Limbaugh, Rush, 4
Lipstadt, Deborah, 10–11, 184
Lithuania, 87, 158, 163. *See also* Baltic States
Littky, Scott, 17
Lloyd George, David, 187, 199
Loewenstein, Karl, 29, 34, 37
Lohse, Hinrich, 88
Longfellow, Alexander and Henry Wadsworth, 106
Löw ben Bezalel, Judah, 151, 160
Lowell, Abbot Lawrence, 100, 110–17
Lublin, 158–59. *See also* Poland
Ludendorff, Martha, 63
Luther, Martin: *The Jews and Their Lies*, 135
Luxemburg, Rosa, 57
Lyon, David Gordon, 15, 99–119

Mack, Julian W., 115, 117
Macron, Emmanuel, 192
Madagascar, 83
Maier, Hans, 59
Marciniak, Janusz, 152, 172
Marcus, Kenneth: *The Definition of Antisemitism*, 213–14
Marr, Wilhelm, 7; "Victory of Judaism over Germandom" of, 101
Marx, Karl: "On the Jewish Question," 70
Marxism, 13, 25–26, 28, 35; suspicion of Jews and Judaism of, 57; Western, 23. *See also* neo-Marxism
mass shootings, 4–5
Matthäus, Jürgen, 14
McMaster, H. R., 5
media: newspapers in the Weimar Republic as antisemitic, 186; popular television news programming of the, 4; social, 3; surveys of antisemitic views as reported in the, 193
Mehring, Reinhard, 31
Mendelssohn, Moses, 48
Merkel, Angela, 208, 212, 214
Merrill, Selah, 108–9

Mesopotamia, 100–101, 108; ancient, 105
Mieszko I, Prince, 155. *See also* Poland
Mieszko III the Old, Prince, 155. *See also* Poland
Mintz, Alex: "The BDS Movement as a Strategic Threat to Israel," 214–15
modernity: critique of, 23; as fundamentally Semitic, 107
Mogherini, Federica, 195
monotheism, 105
Mościcki, Ignacy, 164, 167
Munich Beer Hall Putsch, 77. *See also* Germany
Muslims: immigrants as, 3; radical, 225. *See also* religion

nationalism, 12, 55, 185, 189; age of resurgent, 63; and antisemitism, 164; Christian, 101; fanatical, 14, 51, 199; German, 28, 76, 101, 163, 184; of Polish publications, 165; tribal, 59–60; Western, 59. *See also* Arab nationalism; white nationalism
National Policy Institute, 2
National Refugee Shabbat, 3
National Socialism (Nazis), 2, 25–26, 32–35, 39–40, 58, 75–94, 186; administration of the concentration and death camps by, 58; antisemitism of, 51; Christian churches under, 54; Europe under, 78; faithfulness to, 34; ideology of, 26, 32, 76–77, 82; leadership of, 82; party program of, 77; propaganda of, 67–68, 187; supporters of, 124. *See also* Einsatzgruppen; Einsatzstab Reichsleiter Rosenberg; fascism; Final Solution; Germany; Hitler, Adolf; the Jewish question; pan-Germanism; Rosenberg, Alfred; Third Reich; *Völkischer Beobachter*
nativism, 12
Nazi party. *See* National Socialism (Nazis)
Near Eastern civilizations, 100
Nelson, Peter, 239
neo-Marxism, 24, 40. *See also* Marxism
Netanyahu, Binyamin, 217
Neumann, Franz, 13, 23–26, 30, 33, 36–40; *Behemoth: The Structure and Practice of National Socialism* of, 25, 37
New Era Illustrated Magazine, 108
New Republic, 115
New York, 109, 239

New York Times, 4, 112, 145, 222n30
Niparko, Łukasz W., 16
Norton, Charles Eliot, 107
Noskowicz, Mieczysław, 165
novel, nineteenth-century German, 29
Nuremberg War Crimes Trials, 24, 27, 29, 81, 185

Office of Strategic Services (OSS), 27
Oslo Peace Process, 9, 218
Ottoman Empire, 9

Pakuła, Zbigniew: *The Jews of Poznań*, 159
Palestine: American biblical archaeology in, 104, 108; Biblical, 62; civil organizations in, 207; human rights violations in, 211; Jewish settlements in, 9; question of, 65; recognition of the PLO as the representative of, 218. *See also* Gaza Strip; Intifadah; Israel; Israeli-Palestinian conflict; Jerusalem; West Bank
pan-Europeanism, 185
pan-Germanism, 58–59, 62. *See also* National Socialism (Nazis)
pan-Slavism, 58–59, 61
Paris, 156
Parliament of World Religions (1893), 99, 104
Perles, Joseph, 160–61
Persia, 100
Petraeus, David, 5
philosophy: Christian, 71; German, 71
physiognomy, 104, 137
Piłsudski, Marshall Józef, 164–65
Plessner, Salomon, 160
pogroms, 7, 86, 141, 228; in Poland, 158–59. *See also* genocide; Holocaust
Poland, 16, 83, 88, 91, 172, 231; Chmielnicki uprising in, 158; German occupation of, 88, 93, 167, 171; history of Jews in, 151–73, 174n3; Nazi concentration camps in, 168; Partition of, 162, 167; Second Partition of, 157; Statute of Casimir III the Great (1356) of, 155; Statut Kaliski (1264) of, 155; Swedish Deluge in, 158. *See also* antisemitic Polish publications; Jewish gminas
Poniatowski, King Stanisław August, 159
Poznań (Posen), 151–73; antisemitic fresco in the Church of the Most Precious Blood of Jesus in, *156*; artistic performance and installation titled "Atlantis" in the former building of the New Synagogue in, *153*, *154*; Lamdej Posna (Talmudic school) in, 159–60; lost synagogues of, 170–71; New Synagogue in, *169*, 171; petite bourgeoisie of, 166. *See also* Poland
Prague, 159–60
Preuss, Hugo, 38
Price, Arnold, 36
Princeton University, 112
propaganda. *See* antisemitic propaganda
Protestants: abolitionist, 144–45; Anglo-Saxon, 119; education of elite white, 112; German, 124, 131, 139, 147, 148n4; Huguenot, 142; white, 111. *See also* Christianity; religion
Protocols of the Elders of Zion, 8, 67–70, 76. *See also* conspiracy theories
Proust, Marcel, 48
psychology: extension of the critique of modernity and capitalism into the sphere of, 23; Freudian theories of mass, 26

race: antisemitism and, 25, 111, 183; ideal types of, 77; Judaism conceived as a, 136–37; pseudoscientific theories of, 7, 77, 136; and "race defilement," 82; theories of, 33. *See also* racism
racism, 3, 7, 13; Afrikaner (Boer), 55; and antisemitism, 25, 111, 183; and bureaucracy, 53; imperialism and, 53–58, 64; Jews as exemplars of, 184; Nazi, 55; and pan-movements, 61–64. *See also* antisemitism; race; white supremacy
Raphall, Morris Jacob, 145–46
Rathenau, Walter, 30
Reddit, 5
refugees: Arabs as, 64; Jews as, 70
religion: antisemitic, 5–7; in the Israeli army, 223n40; of nationalism, 60–61; of pan-movements, 60–61; political, 14, 59–60. *See also* Bible; Christianity; Crusades; Judaism; Muslims; Protestants; Roman Catholics
replacement theory, 3–4
Republican Party, 4. *See also* conservatism
Righteous Gentiles, 232–33. *See also* Holocaust

Roman Catholics, 148n4; in Poland, 157–61, 164–65. *See also* Christianity; Crusades; religion
Roman Empire, 6
Romania, 87
Ropes, James Hardy, 113
Rose, Flemming, 186
Rosenberg, Alfred, 14–15, 75–94, 79, 82, 95n7; *Immorality in the Talmud*, 76; *The Myth of the Twentieth Century*, 14–15, 77–78; *The Tracks of the Jew throughout the Ages*, 76, 81; *Zionism as an Enemy of the State*, 76. *See also* National Socialism (Nazis)
Rosenfeld, Alvin, 10
Rossel, Seymour: *The Holocaust*, 226
Rothschilds, 5, 14, 48–50, 52, 59; French, 50
Rupp, Leila, 201n12
Russia, 25, 75, 91; the digging of mass graves in, 92; totalitarianism in, 53. *See also* Russian revolution
Russian revolution, 76. *See also* Russia

Sachs, Paul, 115
Salomon, Alice, 185, 201n12
Samet, Judah, 225
Sartre, Jean-Paul: "Anti-Semite and Jew," 58
Sayoc, Cesar, 4
Scheuner, Ulrich, 39
Schiff, Jacob, 15, 99–100, 103–7, 110–12, 116–17
Schmitt, Carl, 23–24, 26, 29, 31–39; *Constitutional Theory*, 33; "The Führer Protects the Law," 36; *Glossarium*, 32–33; *Legality and Legitimacy*, 35–36; political and legal theory of, 43n40; struggles with Nazi rivals of, 44n63
Schudrich, Michael, 161
Schultz, Martin, 195
Semitic languages, 99–101
Semitic Museum, 105–13, 106, 117–19. *See also* Harvard University
Sender, Dawid Szyje, 161, 171
Serbia, 91
Shabbtai Zvi movement, 66
Shai, Shaul: "The BDS Movement as a Strategic Threat to Israel," 214–15
Shaked, Ayelet, 217
Shakespeare: *The Merchant of Venice*, 7

Sharansky, Natan, 209–10
Sigismund II Augustus, King, 156–57
Sigismund III Vasa, King, 170
Sinas, Georgios, 50
slavery, 145–46. *See also* abolitionism
Smend, Rudolf, 39
Sochaczew, 156. *See also* Poland
social Darwinism, 55
Social Democrats, 34
socialism, 8, 23, 35; hostility to, 51
Soros, George, 4–5
South Africa, 53–58; anti-apartheid movement of, 207–8; early Dutch settlers in, 143; gold and diamond industries of, 56; the role of Jews in the development of, 55–57. *See also* Boers
Soviet Union: dissidents in the former, 209; German invasion of the, 15, 78, 80–87, 228; German occupation of the, 86–93; totalitarianism of the, 67, 187. *See also* communism; Stalin, Josef
Spanish Inquisition, 136–37, 188
Spencer, Herbert, 55
Spencer, Richard, 1
Spengler, Oswald: *The Decline of the West*, 28
Spinoza, Baruch: *Theologico-Political Treatise*, 70
Stadtler, Bea: *The Holocaust*, 227
Stalin, Josef, 69. *See also* Soviet Union
state: German Christian, 101; Jews living as a religious minority, 6; Nazi organization of the, 82
Stoddard, Theodore Lothrop, 77
Straus, Isidor, 110
Strauss, Leo, 34
Streicher, Julius, 186
Students for Justice in Palestine, 10
Sweden, 231, 240n5
Syria, 9, 99

terrorism: Islamic, 190–91, 195–96, 203n40; white supremacist, 4
Thessaloniki, 160
Third Reich, 30–31, 34, 37, 39; genocidal turn of the, 93; totalitarianism of the, 187–88. *See also* Germany; National Socialism (Nazis)
totalitarianism, 13–14, 60–70, 152; antisemitic element of, 52; in eastern Europe, 61;

in Germany, 59; imperialism and, 57; Nazi form of, 60; propaganda of, 69; in Russia, 59; Soviet, 67
Toy, Crawford Howell, 107
Traditionalist Workers Party, 2
Triepel, Heinrich, 39
Trochmé, André, 142, 150n17
Trudeau, Justin, 209
Trump, Donald, 1–4, 225
Trump, Donald, Jr., 5
truth: of fact, 70; of interpretation, 70
Turkey, 10
Turnquist, Timothy, 15
Tutu, Desmond, 208
Twitter, 4–5

Ukraine, 85–87
United Nations, 9, 187, 210
United States, 11, 30, 118–19; Jewish place in the, 100, 212–13
United States Holocaust Memorial Museum (USHMM), 95n1, 234–38
Unite the Right rally, 1–3, 18n4
universalism, 117

Vanguard America, 2
Varnhagen, Rahel, 48
Venice, 160
Vienna, 8, 13, 49, 83, 159, 162
Voegelin, Eric, 59
Völkischer Beobachter, 76. See also National Socialism (Nazis)
Völkisch movement, 76. See also antisemitism
Volkov, Shulamit, 50–51
von Hindenburg, Paul, 31, 35
von Papen, Franz, 35, 184–85, 201n9
von Schönerer, Georg, 14, 49, 52, 60, 63; biography of, 50; pan-Germanism of, 59
von Schönerer, Matthias, 50

Wahl, Saul, 175n19
Wannsee conference, 92–93. See also Final Solution
war: of German unification, 51; of Germany with Russia, 80–87, 92
Warsaw ghetto, 235
Waters, Roger, 208
Wechsler, Harold, 103, 119
Weidner, John, 232–33
Weimar Republic, 2, 13, 31, 52, 184–86, 199; antisemitism of the, 51; denunciation by Rosenberg of the, 76; Jewish elites of the, 23; parliamentary democracy in, 31; racial nationalism of late, 28. See also Germany
Weir, Alison, 213
Weiss, Bari, 11
Weiss, Szewach, 173
Weizmann, Chaim, 68
West Bank, 9; settlement expansion in the, 10. See also Israel; Palestine
white nationalism, 1, 11. See also nationalism
white supremacy, 1–5, 11, 111, 225. See also racism
Wielkopolska, 155, 157–58, 160, 164, 168. See also Poland
Wistrich, Robert, 189, 197, 200
Wolfson, Harry, 116
women: genocide for Jewish, 90; universal suffrage in Europe for, 185
World War I, 33, 63–64, 100, 163
World War II, 23, 27, 118–19, 131, 142, 151, 166, 172, 227–31
Wynot, Edward D., 164

xenophobia, 12

Yad Vashem, 227
Yale University, 112
Young-Bruehl, Elisabeth, 50

Żabotyński, Ze'ew, 167
Zaretsky, Robert, 195
Zionism, 28, 68, 185, 197; near-genocidal, 66; political, 8–9, 105; political responsibility and, 64; Poznań, 167; Rosenberg's early support for, 81. See also anti-Zionism
Zionist Congress, 8
Zohar, Miki, 223n39

In the Contemporary Holocaust Studies series

Unlikely Heroes: The Role of Holocaust Rescuers in Research and Teaching
Edited by Ari Kohen and Gerald J. Steinacher

Antisemitism on the Rise: The 1930s and Today
Edited by Ari Kohen and Gerald J. Steinacher

To order or obtain more information on these or other University of Nebraska Press titles, visit nebraskapress.unl.edu.

www.ingramcontent.com/pod-product-compliance
Lightning Source LLC
Chambersburg PA
CBHW030616230426
43661CB00053B/2010